LORDS of the EARTH

An Incredible but True Story from the Stone-Age Hell of Papua's Jungle

DON RICHARDSON

Regal

From Gospel Light
Ventura, California, U.S.A.

PUBLISHED BY REGAL BOOKS
FROM GOSPEL LIGHT
VENTURA, CALIFORNIA, U.S.A.
PRINTED IN THE U.S.A.

Regal Books is a ministry of Gospel Light, a Christian publisher dedicated to serving the local church. We believe God's vision for Gospel Light is to provide church leaders with biblical, user-friendly materials that will help them evangelize, disciple and minister to children, youth and families.

It is our prayer that this Regal book will help you discover biblical truth for your own life and help you meet the needs of others. May God richly bless you.

For a free catalog of resources from Regal Books/Gospel Light, please call your Christian supplier or contact us at 1-800-4-GOSPEL or www.regalbooks.com.

All Scripture quotations in this book are the author's own paraphrase.

Photos by Frank Clarke, Stan Dale, Bruno de Leeuw, Phil Masters, Phyliss Masters and John Wilson.

First Edition, 1977
Second Edition, 2008

Library of Congress Cataloging-in-Publication Data
The Library of Congress has catalogued the first edition as follows:
Richardson, Don, 1935–
    Lords of the earth / Don Richardson.
        p. cm.
    Includes bibliographical references.
    ISBN 978-08307-4663-7
    1. Jalâe (New Guinea people)—Missions. 2. Dale, Stanley Albert, 1916-1968. 3. Dale, Patricia McCormack. 4. Missions—Indonesia—Papua. 5. Jalâe (Papuan people)—Indonesia—Papua. I. Title. II. Series.

1   2   3   4   5   6   7   8   9   10   /   12   11   10   09   08

Rights for publishing this book outside the U.S.A. or in non-English languages are administered by Gospel Light Worldwide, an international not-for-profit ministry. For additional information, please visit www.glww.org, email info@glww.org, or write to Gospel Light Worldwide, 1957 Eastman Avenue, Ventura, CA 93003, U.S.A.

*To these my very human—
yet charmingly unique—
colleagues who lived,
loved and labored for the
eastern highland people
of Irian Jaya.*

*To those who allowed me to
tell their story frankly.*

To those who continue their work.

CONTENTS

Natives of the Swart Valley, "Lords of the Earth," in their finery

Yali wearing yards of rattan coiled around their bodies

PREFACE

THE NAMES of some of the Yali characters in this book have been shortened or altered to make them easier to pronounce and remember.

The events in Part One, "The Three-Rimmed World," are of course undated as narrated to me by Yali informants, since the Yali possessed no dating system. I have therefore taken some liberties in arranging these events in a chronological order, which enables readers to understand cultural significance more readily. In a few cases, gaps in the memory of my informants concerning certain persons or events have been filled with culturally typical material from other Yali persons or events.

My heartfelt thanks:

To my Yali friends—Foliek, Sar, Dongla, Luliap, Yemu, Erariek, Latowen, Aralek, Suwi, Emeroho, Engehap, Kusaho, Nalimo, and others—for spellbinding data on Yali culture and history.

To my longtime friend and coworker, Tuanangen, one of the five courageous Dani who stayed with Stan and Bruno until the Ninia airstrip was completed, for historical detail on that dangerous first advance into the Heluk Valley.

To my Scottish colleague, John Wilson, whose expert knowledge of the Yali tongue was my main bridge of communication with the Yali people, and who guided me to the site of many of the events here narrated.

To John's wife, Gloria, and to Art and Carol Clarke, for kind hospitality during research at Ninia.

To Stan Dale's sisters, Sadie Murley and Elaine Cook, and to Alex Gilchrist, Ted Hoel, and Lindsey and Claire Slade for sharing their memories of Stan Dale's youth and early ministry.

To Pat Dale for lending me her own and her husband's diaries and notes.

To Phyliss Masters for sharing her memories of Phil and of the early days at Korupoon.

To Bruno and Marlys De Leeuw and Costas and Alky Macris for their recollections of early days of struggle in the Heluk. To Don and Alice Gibbons, Gordon and Peggy Larson, and John and Helen Ellenburger for background on the spiritual movement among the Damal and Dani tribesmen. To my wife, Carol, and to Barbara Willis for many hours spent typing this manuscript.

Don Richardson

RBMU, Sentani, Irian Jaya
Indonesia

INTRODUCTION

THE YALI. Cannibals with a difference. Masters of jungle warfare who keep shooting until arrows stand in their victims' bodies "as thick as reeds in a swamp." Black demons glistening with lard-and-soot cosmetic, wearing hundreds of yards of rattan coiled about their bodies like wire around magnetos, sporting penis gourds that jut before them like jib booms flaunting their maleness.

They called themselves "men of power . . . lords of the earth," for in their remote mountain-walled valleys, no one challenged their sway. In league with the *kembu* spirits, Yali males bowed to no one and needed nothing.

Or did they?

Rawhide-tough missionary-commando Stan Dale and gentle Dutch-Canadian Bruno de Leeuw believed that the Yali needed the gospel of Jesus of Nazareth. Buoyant with faith, Stan and Bruno entered the Heluk Valley and were joined later by Stan's wife, Pat, and their four children. Little did Stan or Bruno dream how complex their mission really was.

Or how chilling were the hazards awaiting them.

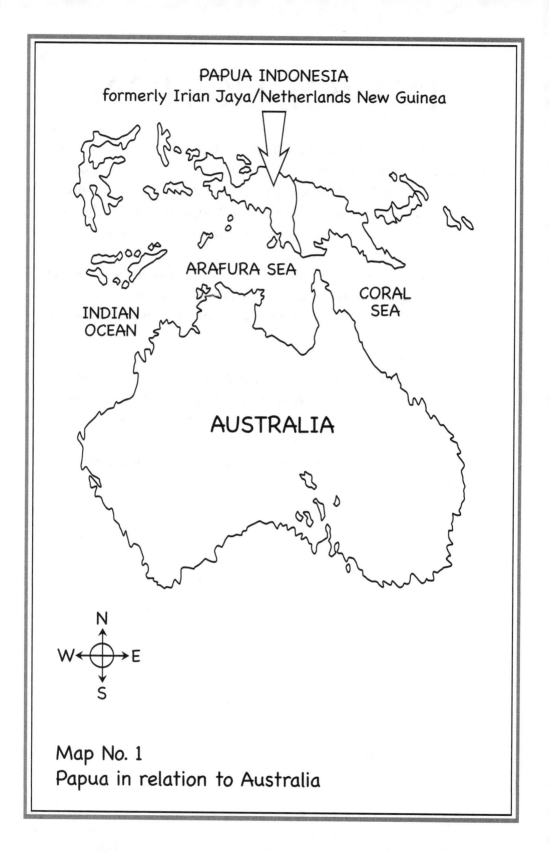

PAPUA INDONESIA
formerly Irian Jaya/Netherlands New Guinea

ARAFURA SEA

CORAL SEA

INDIAN OCEAN

AUSTRALIA

N
W — E
S

Map No. 1
Papua in relation to Australia

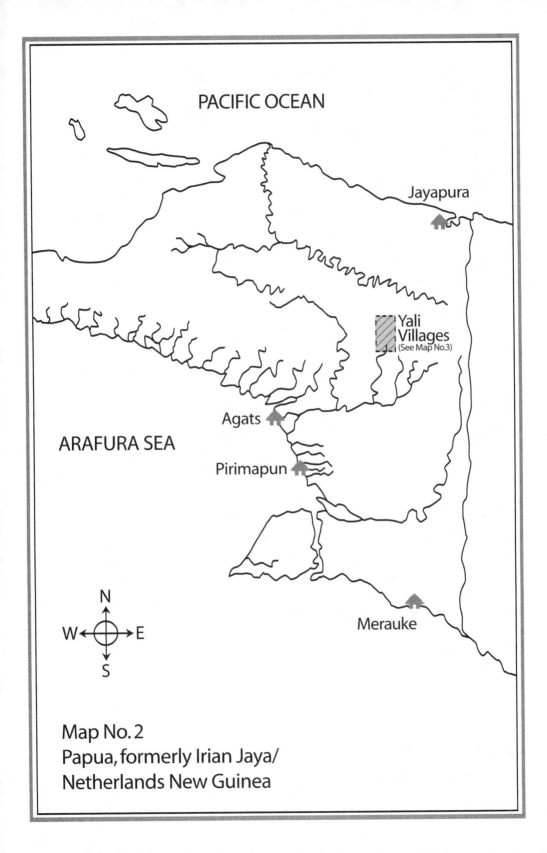

PACIFIC OCEAN

Jayapura

Yali
Villages
(See Map No.3)

Agats

Pirimapun

ARAFURA SEA

N
W ←⊕→ E
S

Merauke

Map No. 2
Papua, formerly Irian Jaya/
Netherlands New Guinea

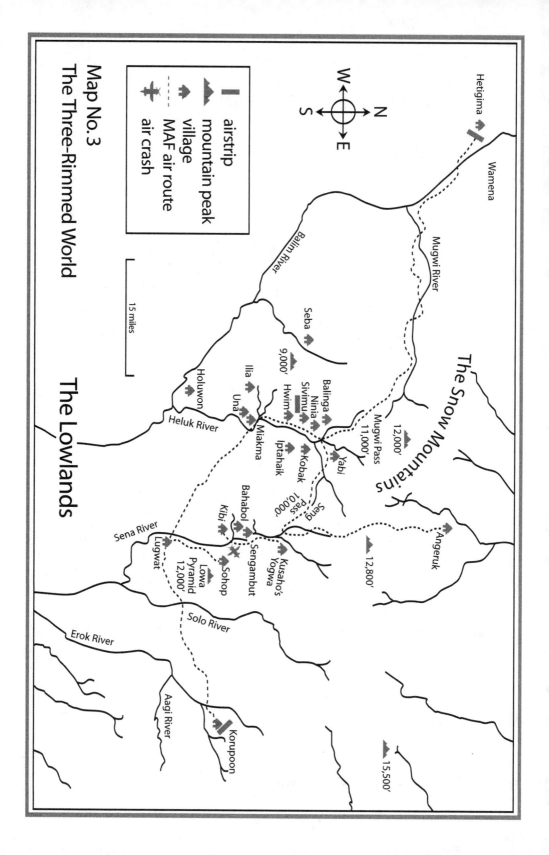

Map No. 3
The Three-Rimmed World

The Lowlands

The Snow Mountains

airstrip
mountain peak
village
MAF air route
air crash

W N S E

15 miles

Hetigima
Wamena
Mugwi River
Balim River
Seba
9,000'
Mugwi Pass
12,000'
11,000'
Holuwon
Ila
Una
Hwim
Sivimu
Ninia
Balinga
Miakma
Heluk River
Iptahaik
Kobak
Yabi
Seng Pass 10,000'
Bahabol
Kibi
Sengambut
Kusaho's Yogwa
12,800'
Angeruk
Sena River
Lugwat
Lowa Pyramid 12,000'
Sohop
Solo River
Erok River
Aagi River
Korupoon
15,500'

Part I

THE THREE–RIMMED WORLD

THE DAY THE SKY FELL

Chapter 1

KUGWARAK peered into the gray abyss like some sinister gargoyle. Hoary brows, hoarier now with condensed mist, beetled over the black hollows of his eyes. Flaps of skin, no longer filled with the muscle of youth, hung down on his sunken chest like an old woman's paps. Yet despite his age, he huddled in an oddly fetal position, sitting back on his heels, arms folded on knees, chin resting on bony wrist.

Kugwarak shivered.

High above him, black ramparts of Dutch New Guinea's Snow Mountains loomed in three sweeping rims against the dawn glow, dwarfing Kugwarak's world. Far below, dimly visible through a thousand feet of mist, the Heluk River bled white through a chaotic gash. Its thunder rose and fell on the wind, like a pulse of time itself.

Kugwarak shivered again and looked for the sun.

Instead, a vivacious brown cherub materialized out of the mist and ran to his side—Nindik, his granddaughter. She wore only a skimpy reed skirt. In her hands she bore two freshly cooked yams. The larger one she gave to her grandfather. She herself ate the smaller yam, ash-encrusted skin and all. Kugwarak would have scolded her if she had thrown the skin away.

Then, leaning warm against Kugwarak's trembling side, she began plucking lice from his balding pate, popping them between her teeth for dessert. Like a stream against a stone, her laughter rippled around him. Then fell the first ray of sun, suffusing elder and child in gauzy golden light.

Soon full sunlight burst upon them, burning back the mist.

Askew on a knoll behind them leaned the old man's dwelling, a badly dilapidated *yogwa,* or man's hut, of the Yali tribe. It was circular in structure, walled with stone-hewn boards and capped with a conical roof of nine-foot-long *pandanus* fronds. From the summit of its roof, a single wooden spike fingered the sky. Smoke from the last embers of Kugwarak's night fire seeped out through a thousand cracks.

Nindik heard footsteps and looked up. From beyond the *yogwa,* a formidable figure loomed through the mist. Nindik turned and fled, her tiny reed skirt flouncing behind her.

The figure approached her grandfather.

Still munching the last of his yam, Kugwarak cricked his neck and looked up at the man towering behind him. Now he knew why the little girl fled. Not only little girls but even many a seasoned warrior would not hesitate to give place to the man who grinned down at him.

Selambo!

Gleaming black in lard-and-soot cosmetic, Selambo was the living essence of a Yali storyteller's ideal—"a man whose liver is dry." Coolly self-possessed, Selambo could harbor a steely purpose and not betray it until an opportune moment. He could kill or spare life with the dispassionate aloofness of a god.

Selambo's eyes were bloodshot, glowing like coals. His hair, heavy with pig fat, hung in shaggy masses around and almost over his countenance. Bands studded with white cowrie shells glistened, incongruously halo-like, across his temples. Curved ends of an ivory boar-tusk jutted menacingly from the severed septum of his nose.

He stepped past Kugwarak, thigh muscles flowing, naked buttocks swollen yet hard. He turned to face the old man, barrel-chested torso arched vainly forward, achieving the swayback stance admired by Yalis. Like all mature Yali males, Selambo wore a penis sheath cut from a long, dried yellow gourd. Anchored to his waist by a length of string, the sheath craned at an upright angle, ostentatiously emphasizing his sexuality.

"*Halabok!*" Selambo exclaimed, stooping to scratch the old man under his chin. *Halabok,* a typical Yali scatological greeting, means simply, "I prize even your feces!"—a way of saying, "If that which is most unpleasant about you appeals to me, imagine how much I appreciate your good points!"

Kugwarak responded even more endearingly, "*Hal bisoksok!*" the translation of which would sicken visitors from tribes whose languages do not feature scatological greetings. Most strangers never learn the meaning of Yali greetings but simply repeat them by rote—a method much easier on their stomachs.

Cracking one of his grotesquely disarming smiles, Kugwarak gripped Selambo's forearms as the latter squatted down before him. The two men conversed amiably, while the mist lifted around them, unveiling a sweep of hillside potted with dozens of other *yogwas,* most of them in better repair than Kugwarak's. Ranged around the *yogwas* were an equal number of smaller dwellings called *homia*—women's huts.

"Tell me about the recent pig feast at Ombok." Flies ferreted Kugwarak's grizzled beard as he spoke.

"It was a strange feast," Selambo said with a sly smile. "We had just finished dedicating a new vengeance fetish in the house of the *dokwi* spirits when—" Selambo looked around to make sure no one was eavesdropping. "When my friend Buli from Ombok gave me a chunk of raw pork and said, 'Cut it up for these men to cook.'

"I took a bamboo cutting edge and began cutting, but the blade struck something in the center. I said to myself, 'There's no bone in this meat; why can't I cut through it?' I looked inside, and guess what I found buried in the meat?"

"A bamboo arrowhead!" cackled Kugwarak with a knowing leer.

"I looked up at Buli and saw him watching me out of the corner of his eye."

"Of course!" The old man interjected

"Then I noticed that Buli had distributed similar pieces of pork for men of other villages to slice. I sat watching as one by one they made the same discovery I had made. Buli had hidden an arrowhead in every piece!"

"So you were all committed to join him in a raid!"

"Yes! We all grew quiet as the knowledge spread among us. Then Buli divulged his plan."

Spired *yogwas* and *homias* oozed smoke around Nindik as she scurried homeward. On all sides the village known as Hwim stirred to life. Women bearing children on their backs and digging sticks in their hands trundled to work in yam gardens below the hamlet. Young boys practiced throwing miniature spears through loops of rattan tossed in the air. Men sat hunched outside their *yogwas,* ominously binding bamboo arrowheads to lengths of white cane.

Festooning lower ridges to the north, Hwim's sister village, Sivimu, caught the morning's golden light on a hundred conical roofs. Between the twin villages, on a separate knoll called Yarino, towered two grim structures nearly twice the height and circumference of the usual Yali dwelling. These were very special *yogwas,* each dedicated to one of two kinds of spirits recognized by the Yali people.

The one on somewhat lower ground was a museum of sacred objects dedicated to the *dokwi*—spirits of ancestors who had perished in war, and who constantly goaded the living to avenge their deaths. It was known therefore, in the Yali language, as *dokwi-vam*—house of the *dokwi.*

The second structure, towering on the highest point of the knoll, was a temple of the *Kembu*—nonhuman spirits who controlled the Yali cosmos. Behind the temple stood a grove of sacred *pandanus* and pine, and a hallowed garden, the produce of which could be eaten only by "men of knowledge," a select group of elders who alone knew all the dreaded secrets of life and death.

Surrounding temple, grove and garden, and emphasizing their importance, ranged a rambling wall of jagged white stones. Both this wall and all that it enclosed were known to the Yali as an *osuwa*—"a sacred place." And so, for longer than any living Yali could remember, the Yarino knoll and the *kembu-vam* that crowned it had been the center of the religious life of Hwim and Sivimu and surrounding related hamlets.

Only once in every generation had the *kembu-vam* been rebuilt and the stone wall surrounding it restored. Kugwarak, Nindik's now-aging

grandfather, and his protégé Marik, had been the last elders to rebuild
the *kembu-vam* and restore its stone wall. They had done this just a few
years earlier, when Kugwarak was still in his prime. Since that time the
men of Hwim and Sivimu had referred respectfully to the Yarino knoll
as "Kugwarak and Marik's place."

But for Yali women, including little Nindik, "Kugwarak and Marik's
place" was a source of terror. How often Nindik had heard the stern
warning repeated: *Any female who trespasses that stone wall, or even touches it,
must be cast into the rapids of the Heluk River! Even males not yet consecrated to
the* kembu *spirits must die if they set foot upon the sacred ground!*

Nindik shuddered and carefully avoided a path leading close to the
osuwa. Her cousin Foliek, she recalled with a further tremor, had nearly
been executed when someone saw him eat a mushroom thought to have
been plucked from inside that dreaded stone wall.

Rounding a bend in the trail, little Nindik saw her uncle Kiloho
climb up onto the roof of his new *yogwa*, now nearly ready for thatching.
Deko, another of Nindik's uncles, sat on a stone near the new dwelling,
holding a wooden stake while his brother, Bukni, adzed it into a sharp
spike for Kiloho's roof. Nindik merged shyly with a group of children
who stood watching them.

"Father Bukni," one of the children ventured (any elder could be called
"father" in Yali), "why must a wooden spike stick up from the roof?"

The speaker was little Yekwara. He had already asked his mother the
same question, but she replied, "Don't ask me such questions. I'm a
woman. Ask the men."

Friendly-faced "Father" Bukni held his adze poised and looked whim-
sically at Yekwara. Then he squinted at the brightening sky and said, "In
case the sky fell, you wouldn't want it to hit the roof directly, would you?
The spike will pierce it first and slow it down."

Bukni, serious-faced, continued his work, while every child peered
up at the sky and wondered, *Can the sky really fall?*

Then Bukni laid down his adze while Deko rose to his feet and handed
the long sharp spike up to Kiloho. The children watched intently as Kiloho climbed to the summit of the roof and thrust one end of the spike
down into a small opening where all the rafters converged.

The children decided it must be true that the sky might fall.

Yekwara whispered a secret. "If this had been a house for our village's *kembu* spirit, they would have put pig fat in the hole first, then anchored the spike down into it. I watched them do it when they rebuilt the *kembu-vam* at Balinga."

Oldest among the children was beautiful Alisu, Kiloho's own daughter. At Yekwara's words she gasped and put her hand over his mouth.

"You should not have watched such a thing, Yekwara. You have not yet been dedicated to the *kembu*. If a priest had noticed you, he would have rubbed a pig's blood in your eyes to make everything right again." Alisu glanced nervously at her father and uncles in case they were listening. They were absorbed in their work. "And you should never tell such things to Nindik and me, for we are female."

The sun was now hot, and gazing up at the sky made sweat stand out on Alisu's brow.

"Let's go bathe under the waterfall!" she exclaimed, stifling for the moment all their half-formed questions about falling skies and pig fat on the roof. Alisu dashed toward the leafy mountain crevice where the waterfall tumbled. Nindik, Yekwara, and Alisu's little brother, Toli, ran after her, squealing with excitement.

Naked, the boys leaped immediately under the wispy cascade. Alisu and Nindik took a moment to untie their skirts. As she laid her simple garment across a rock, Nindik looked back across the smoke-brushed hamlet of Hwim, her home. Beyond it, she saw her grandfather Kugwarak and Selambo still squatting on a ledge above the gorge, locked into one of those mysterious conversations that only men could share.

"Where will you strike?" The flies in Kugwarak's beard buzzed with annoyance each time he spoke.

"At Kobak."

"When?"

"Tomorrow before dawn."

"It's about time someone took the initiative," gruffed Kugwarak. "The enemy has gone too long unpunished."

The two men sat squinting across the Heluk gorge. Smudges of smoke marked the locale of some seven villages of the eastern alliance—the enemy.

"I ask one favor of you, my father," Selambo continued. "When I return from this raid, I want to consecrate my nephew to *Kembu*. For that I will need a choice pig."

"You want to buy my last pig? I'm not about to sell it!" Kugwarak said flatly.

"Please, my father. Reconsider," Selambo pleaded, scratching Kugwarak again under the chin.

Suddenly a cruel, unholy light shone in Kugwarak's sunken eyes. His wizened hand reached out and gripped Selambo's wrist.

"You may have my pig if—" he croaked.

Selambo's face glowed under its layer of soot, anticipating an easy deal.

"If you bring me a human body in return."

Nindik and Alisu emerged giggling from the falls. Together they perched back-to-back on a sun-warmed rock, brushing drops of water from their spongy hair. When they were nearly dry, fat little Toli, his brown skin tight from the coldness of the stream, splashed more water on them.

Alisu chided him. "Look at you, Toli. Your funny nose sticks out straight, like a caterpillar reaching for another branch! Whatever happened to make it so big?"

All eyes turned to Toli, who looked sheepishly from face to face, covered his nose with his chubby hands, and blushed a dusky blush.

"A bee must have stung it!" he said in a husky whisper.

The children exploded with laughter and thronged around Toli, splashing water on him.

"O Toli, you're so funny!"

Reassured, Toli squealed for sheer pleasure and joined the melee, until Alisu turned and led the troop down a forest trail and out onto a wide rock overlooking the valley. They settled down quietly in the sun to dry, looking out over a blue-green panorama of mountains, hamlets, and awesomely deep gorges.

Then Yekwara laid back on the rock and looked up at the sky. Tiny puffs of cloud were forming in rows across the zenith.

"Look!" he called, pointing upward. "The *domil-mil* must be making their gardens!"

The children all laid back and studied the gardens in the sky, and wondered what it was like to be a *domil-mil*, the little white people who played and worked together in peace so high above the earth, and whose tinkling voices could sometimes be heard falling on the wind, if one listened very hard.

Nindik's tiny, birdlike voice broke their reverie. "If the sky should fall, what would happen to the *domil-mil*?"

There was a long silence.

Nindik sighed wistfully. "I hope the sky doesn't fall on *me*!"

Selambo's face betrayed shock. The skin of his stomach trembled slightly. Kugwarak grinned. It was no small accomplishment for an old troll like him to unnerve such a strong young warrior.

A sudden gust of wind whipped the ledge where they crouched. Soon the Heluk gorge would fill with cloud and rain, perhaps even before noon. Already the first hints of a new storm's cloudy masses schooled around the high blue peaks.

Selambo squatted speechless, while the specter before him continued musing, half to himself, "Long ago, when I was young, we were not content simply to *kill* an enemy. Whenever possible, we brought back their corpses as *food*! But you younger men—"

Kugwarak cleared his throat and spat on the ground, while Selambo's insides churned. He was thinking how quickly the enemy would counterattack down that steep slope from Kobak. And how nearly impossible it would be to drag or carry a corpse to the river in time, ahead of the inevitable rain of arrows and spears. Unless—unless it was a very *small* victim: a woman—or a child.

"You younger men," Kugwarak rambled eerily, "once you have killed, have no heart for anything more—you run for home!" He cocked a taunting eye at Selambo. "I guess pork is such an *easy* substitute!"

Selambo's stomach tightened into a hard knot. He grimaced. Then he sucked in air through gritted teeth and grimaced again. Finally he rose to his feet and clicked a finger against the base of his gourd, a sign of admiration for the old man's temerity.

"I'll bring you a victim or die in the attempt, you dried-up old root!"

Kugwarak cackled. The cackle triggered a hacking cough that wracked the old man's wizened body into tortured spasms. Selambo turned and strode down a steep trail toward his *yogwa*.

He had more arrows to make before dark.

As he ducked under the low doorway of his *yogwa*, he could still hear the old apparition on the knoll hacking out its hideous cacophony of cackling and coughing.

Sternly they strode toward the little *homia*. Children scurried out of their path like leaves before the first dark breath of a storm. They halted before the door of the lowly dwelling, their long yellow penis sheaths jutting like jib booms before them.

"Wilipa! Where is my son Yekwara?"

A woman's voice, thin and fearful, quavered within the *homia*, "He went to watch Kiloho finish his roof."

"He's not here now, my brother," Kiloho called from the summit of his *yogwa*, now partially thatched. "He's bathing under the waterfall."

Kebel, powerful and deep-chested, growled low in his throat. He had warned his son to wait by his mother in the *homia*. It was a fearful day for the boy, a day to prepare him for the cutting-through-of-knowledge, but he was treating it like any other day.

Yekwara looked down from the rock. He saw six priests—one of them his own father, Kebel—halt in front of the little *homia* he had shared with his mother, aunts, and sisters since birth. Suddenly he recalled his father's strange command to wait at the *homia* and knew now that the men were looking for *him*.

Yekwara shuddered.

The sight of even one of the spirits' advocates was fearful enough. Six of them in one place was terrifying. Wherever they gathered, all authority and power in the universe seemed to crackle around them. Dreadful enough to watch them drag *other* boys away for their mysterious purposes! But now his own turn had come.

As he watched his father wheel about and advance down along the path toward the waterfall, he felt it coming, the ominous power that brooded in the presence of those six priests, stalking him through his own father.

Yekwara whimpered. Nindik and the others looked at him, confused. Then he lept to his feet and ran down from the rock. Nindik's delicate voice called behind him, "Yekwara! Where are you going?"

He made no answer but fled back to the village by a different trail. From behind the bushes, he watched until the five other priests drifted away from his mother's *homia*. Seeing his chance, Yekwara darted out of the bushes, jumped over the small, stone village wall, and ran through the low doorway of the tiny dwelling.

Kiloho, still working on his roof, saw him and called, "Kebel! Your son has returned to your wife's *homia*."

Yekwara sensed dreadful footsteps turning and converging toward him. He groped for his mother and found her huddled in semi-darkness against the far wall of the windowless dwelling. Gradually Yekwara's eyes focused on his mother's strained countenance.

"They are taking you away from me, Yekwara," she said, trying to sound resigned. But when she uttered his name, her voice quavered.

"I want to stay with you."

"You cannot. They are taking you away. As they have taken all my sons away—" The footsteps interrupted her.

"Yekwara! Come!" His father called in a low voice, edged with anger.

Impulsively Yekwara snuggled into his mother's lap and suckled, for he was not yet weaned. In this way he had resolved every fear in the past, and now again—

"Yekwara! Come to me!" Kebel commanded. Yekwara ignored him. The sweetness of Wilipa's milk possessed for the moment a magic stronger than his father's spirits. But Wilipa suddenly pushed him away.

"Go to them!" she hissed. He tried to return to her breast, but she pushed him away more violently. "Go to them! My time to hold you has ended. Go! Go and become a man!"

Yekwara recoiled, shocked by her unprecedented rejection. Tears welled. A strong hand caught his wrist and pulled him out of the *homia*.

Nindik and Alisu followed Yekwara down from the rock and perched along the village wall to watch. They saw Kebel drag Yekwara out of the *homia*. When she saw the tears on Yekwara's cheeks, fear stabbed Nindik's tiny heart. She recalled again her cousin's close brush with death when someone accused him of eating a sacred mushroom. Perhaps Yekwara had intruded upon forbidden things and was now to be executed!

Forgetting for the moment her fear of the priests, Nindik darted in among them and threw her arms around Yekwara's slim waist. He turned and looked at her, his chin trembling. Roughly they pulled him from her and led him briskly away. Alisu laid a comforting hand on Nindik's shoulder.

"It is not an execution," she explained. "They are going to prepare him for the cutting-through-of-knowledge. From now on he will be one of *them*."

"He won't play with us anymore?" Nindik asked.

Alisu shook her head.

Nindik watched as the priests dragged little Yekwara up a steep slope beyond the hamlet. For a moment they stood, etched in bold outline on a ridge, and then disappeared beyond it.

Nindik sighed. Strange emptiness gnawed at her heart. She ran to her own *homia,* wanting to cuddle in the reassuring arms of Ongolek, her mother.

The *homia* was empty.

Then she mounted a village wall and scanned a slope of mounded yam plots adjacent to the sacred knoll of Yarino, where Ongolek usually gardened.

There was still no sign of her mother.

"Where is Ongolek?" she whimpered to a passing relative.

"She is planting a new garden today."

"Tell me where."

"It is far away. You better not try to find it."

"Just tell me where it is."

"See the ridge where our fathers dance after they kill an enemy? The new garden is just below it. Have you ever been down there?"

"No."

"Then don't try to find your mother today. Wait and go with her tomorrow. You might get into trouble."

Nindik waited until her informant disappeared among the *homias*. Then she scuttled down from the wall and, giving wide berth to the sacred knoll with its two forbidding structures, followed a trail toward "war dance ridge."

"Do not be frightened, young one."

Slowly Yekwara raised moist brown eyes in response. Through his tears he saw Mena, one of his maternal uncles. Mena's wide mouth, turned down at the corners, framed guttural words, while his eyes alternately narrowed with mystery and then bulged with emphasis. "In a little while we will eat pig together, but there are certain things we must do first."

"Until now—" Yekwara shifted his gaze quickly to Kebel, his father, who continued, "—you have been powerless, a nonentity, living with the women, knowing nothing."

"But *now*—" this time the voice echoed out of the august graybeard of Helevai, the great high priest, Yekwara's oldest maternal uncle, "—you must experience the 'cutting-through-of-knowledge.' "

Yekwara gazed past Helevai's gray-bush beard into his eyes. Eyes cold with disregard for anything but the will of the spirits. Eyes that warned, *Even though you are my nephew, I would execute you in a moment if the* kembu *spirits so required!*

Yekwara trembled and wanted to flee to his mother, but he was surrounded.

Helevai continued, raising gaunt arms toward a darkening sky, "The knowledge of the *kembu* spirits that will make you like one of us—*a lord of the earth!*"

In spite of his foreboding, Yekwara felt awe burst within him at Helevai's words. Wide-eyed, he scanned the circle of powerful men and wondered, *Do I really belong with them?* The bracing spirit that united them began to invade his young heart.

The priests discerned the change of expression on his face, and for the first time, they smiled at him.

"First we must cleanse you with water," said Mena matter-of-factly. Then, looking around to make sure no women were watching, he raised a heavy bamboo cruse and from it poured water into a hollowed-out gourd.

Next he dipped a clump of moss into the water, soaked it, and raised its dripping mass over Yekwara.

Nindik panted as she mounted the grassy crest of war dance ridge. Patches of blue sky dwindled and vanished as heavy clouds burgeoned up the gorge. Gusts of wind whipped sharp grass against her legs. She hesitated when she saw how close the enemy side of the valley appeared from this vantage point. But her mother had come this way; it must be safe. She advanced to the very point where warriors returning from raids rendezvoused to celebrate their successes in full view of enraged enemies.

The trail divided.

Confused, Nindik peered over opposite sides of the ridge for some sign of her mother. The slopes visible to her were deserted. "There are more gardens on the north side of the ridge," she said to herself.

She scampered lightly down the north side. Her home village was now lost to view, and the roar of the Heluk boomed unnervingly louder.

"With this water, Yekwara, we have cleansed ordinary dirt from your skin." Mung, his mother's younger brother, whispered the words directly into Yekwara's ear.

Now Mung's brow dipped sternly. "But there is still something else on your skin that water cannot wash away."

Yekwara gazed inquisitively into Mung's wide-boned face. He saw Mung's narrowed eyes bulge suddenly with awesome intensity. "The stain of your mother's blood!" he rasped. "Since your birth it has remained upon you! Until it is cleansed, the *kembu* cannot accept you!"

A feeling of uncleanness swept through Yekwara. He had been about to ask their permission to go and nurse from his mother, but now he thought better of it.

Kebel, his father, stepped forward out of the enclosing circle of crouching figures. He held up a small net bag full of leaves.

"The *kembu* spirits have revealed only one substance that can fully cleanse the contamination of female blood—juice from the *musan* leaf."

Squatting beside Yekwara, Kebel opened the net bag. Both Mena and Mung now gathered up handfuls of *musan* leaves and crushed them in their fists until oil glistened on their fingers and palms. Then they rubbed their palms over Yekwara's skin until his entire body shone with *musan* juice.

"Now, for the first time, *Kembu* looks upon you with favor, my son," Kebel said, using the generic term *kembu* as a name, in much the same way that our generic term *god* may become a name—God. "Only now is it fitting for the high priest to anoint you with the fat of a pig long ago sacrificed to *Kembu*."

As Kebel finished speaking, gray-bearded Helevai arose, his claw-shaped hands dripping with two partially melted lumps of pig fat. Silhouetted against glowering clouds, the old man swayed closer, reaching toward Yekwara. Cold blasts of wind struck the glade. Dust-devils scurried like pages through the council of crouching men.

Lightning flashed behind Helevai as he loomed above Yekwara. Thunder pealed, as if the sky were already failing.

Nindik cast anxious glances from side to side as thunder echoed around her. She had come such a long way down and still had not found her mother. The thought of returning home alone in such a storm frightened her.

"Ongolek!" she called and heard her own tiny echo ring from ledge to looming ledge. She stumbled farther down a narrowing trail.

"*Ongolek!*" Now the wind whisked her mother's name away and brought no answer.

"*Ongolek!*" Panic edged her voice. She looked up at the ridge she had descended. It now seemed so fearfully high. Mist curled over its crest. If the mist grew thick, she would not be able to see her way home.

I must find Ongolek, she said within her heart and plunged still farther down the slope.

Once again the trail branched. She veered to the left. Ahead on the crest of a knoll stood a grove of casuarina pine trees surrounded by a stone wall. Perhaps just beyond it she would find her mother. She climbed over the wall and ran in among the pines. Thunder pealed ominously, like a threat from *Kembu* himself. Towering pine trees whispered as if discussing her presence. Within the wall she stumbled over rotting remains of an old building long since collapsed. *Who would have dared build a yogwa or a homia this close to the enemy?* she queried to herself.

"Ongolek!" she screamed. For an answer, the wind slapped her teary face with a pine bough.

Overwhelmed with loneliness, Nindik wept, mingling her mother's name with sobs.

She had not wept more than a few minutes when a black figure attracted by her final scream struggled up from the far side of the knoll and lurched toward her.

Nindik saw him looming among the pine trees and froze.

Andeng, high priest of Sivimu, Hwim's sister village.

Andeng wiped sweat from his eyes and focused grimly upon the tiny figure standing on the holy ground. He hoped against hope it was some young boy already consecrated to *Kembu,* and not a girl.

His heart sank as he saw the reed skirt wrapped about her.

It was darker now. Cold drops of rain splattered through the pine needles. Andeng sighed. Doubtless the little one before him knew only the prohibition against entering the holy place surrounding the actual sanctuary of *Kembu* in her own village. She could not have guessed that the rotting boards around her feet were the remains of an even holier temple, a temple rebuilt for special ceremonies only once in every generation. It was the temple for *kwalu,* third in rank among the four sacred ceremonies of the Yali people.

Andeng rushed forward, his chest heaving with emotion. A solemn duty had been thrust upon him. To prevent such tragedies, the ancestors chose this remote knoll in an obscure gorge far from inhabited areas, and yet somehow this wandering waif happened upon *kwalu*'s holy place.

Nindik drew in her breath, backing away from Andeng. He caught her and wrenched her quickly outside the stone wall.

"Why did you come here?" he growled indignantly.

"My heart is swollen because I cannot find my mother," Nindik sobbed.

"Tell me your father's name," he demanded.

"Sar."

Andeng set her on his shoulder and bore her quickly back up the trail.

Yekwara felt strangely warm as Helevai's melted pig fat spread over his entire body, insulating him against the chill wind. Now Mung and two other of his maternal uncles approached him, each bearing an empty *sum*, or net bag. Gently they eased the straps of the three bags over Yekwara's head and let them drape down, one over his back, the others over his left and right shoulders.

Then Mung proudly crowned his nephew with a headband of gleaming white cowrie shells, fixing the straps of the three net bags in place. Other uncles adorned him with a priceless necklace of tiny cowrie shells called *walimu*, long braids of larger shells, looping from his neck almost to the ground, and a wide section of bailer shell shielding his chest.

"Now you are a splendid young man!" the council chortled.

"But still there is fear in your eyes," said Mung grimly. "A *lord of the earth* must not show fear." Mung strode to a nearby tree and drew a ten-foot-long black spear from its branches. Suddenly he fixed tiny Yekwara with a cruel glare, crouched low, and slunk toward him, gaining speed.

"This is what it is like to face an enemy," whispered Kebel. "Do not show fear!"

Shrieking, Mung lunged, and the speartip missed Yekwara's shoulder by inches. Shaking with terror, Yekwara cowered behind his father. The council rocked with laughter and shouted, "Try it again! He'll learn."

This time Mena charged through the windswept clearing, an arrow drawn in his long palmwood bow.

"Face him. Yekwara! Face him! Don't turn away!"

Yekwara's blood ran cold. He closed his eyes and shielded himself with his hands until he heard the bowstring twang against the side of the arrow, and knew it was only a bluff. The men laughed again, and Yekwara laughed with them, weakly. So it was only a game, a lesson.

"Again! Again!" they bellowed. "He's learning."

Yekwara kept his eyes open this time and squealed with excitement as Mung's speartip jog led rapidly closer. He managed to limit his reaction to a mere flinch as the weapon barreled past his left shoulder.

The council erupted with praise this time, not laughter, and Yekwara steeled himself for Mena's second charge with the bow, determined not to show fear.

Through drizzling mist, Andeng bore Nindik solemnly into the center of Sivimu village and set her in front of his wife's *homia*.

"Who is this child?" a lesser priest asked.

Andeng stepped aside and whispered, "Sar's daughter. I found her inside the *osuwa* called Ninia."

The inquirer sighed grimly. "The river was close by; why didn't you just throw her in?"

"Her father could accuse me of killing her for some other reason. There were no witnesses. It is better they do it themselves. But it must be done before nightfall, or the wrath of *Kembu* will be kindled. Take word quickly to her father. Tell him to come and get her."

The lesser priest hurried away toward Hwim.

Owu, Andeng's wife, overhearing her husband's conversation, turned sadly toward Nindik.

"You belong to Ongolek, don't you?"

Nindik nodded, shivering.

"Poor little girl," she sighed and led her to the warm *homia*.

Next the council of elders escorted Yekwara to his father's *yogwa* and, with elaborate ceremony, carried him across its threshold. It was his first entrance into a man's dwelling, and its strangeness at first repelled him. Roasted pork lay spread on banana leaves around a flickering central fireplace. Its tantalizing scent quickly dispelled the repulsive strangeness. Proudly Yekwara sat erect on the dry hard floor among the six priests and partook with them, reveling in being accepted into their world. Moment by moment, he absorbed more and more of their indomitable male pride.

After the feast, his uncles handed him a bow and arrows and led him out to the same rock where earlier he dried himself in the sun with Alisu, Nindik, and little Toli.

"Stand here holding these weapons until it is dark," Mung commanded. "Do not sit down or crouch when you get tired. A lord of the earth must learn to endure."

The thunder and lightning now receded into the distance, leaving only cold, oppressive mist and drizzling rain. Yekwara faced it bravely, stretching to full height, a stripling sentinel above the smoke of Hwim village. Soon mingled rain and mist began to drip from his hair, his eyebrows, his nose, the cowrie bands, and the bailer shell on his chest. He shivered.

Mung, Mena, and Kebel, his father, crouched around him. Mung was saying, "Today you have learned only the first of the four sacred experiences of manhood—the ceremony called 'putting-you-into-the-yogwa.' Soon you will learn also the second, which is much more sacred. It is called 'putting-you-into-Kembu-himself.'"

Mena leaned close to Yekwara in a confidential manner. "After many moons we will teach you *kwalu*—a celebration so holy that it cannot be performed close to a village where women are. We will go down to the sacred knoll hidden in the gorge, to the *osuwa* called Ninia. There we will rebuild the rotted house *of Kembu* especially for your generation. We will 'put-you-into-*kwalu*,' and you will learn the secret of the health that flows from *Kembu*."

As Yekwara listened in amazement, he heard a sound of wailing. From the north, from Sivimu village, he saw three men approaching in procession, one of them bearing a child on his shoulder. Soon he recognized them. The one bearing a child was Sar. The child on his shoulder was Nindik. The other two men were her uncles, Deko and "friendly face" Bukni.

Why were they wailing? he wondered.

Now Kebel continued the discourse. "But *kwalu* is still not the deepest secret of our ancestors. To impart that deepest secret, after many more moons, we will prepare a feast so sacred that it cannot be held even near paths where women walk or near gardens where they work."

Kebel swiveled around and pointed toward the high peaks, now shrouded in dark cloud. His voice filled with intense awe. "Up there, my son, high up in the moss-hung forests where the eyes of women never see, where *Kembu* dwells in silence and sacred marsupials hide, there we will impart to your generation the same sacred experience our father imparted to us—*morowal!*"

"What is *morowal?*" asked Yekwara, still watching little Nindik and her wailing escort.

"It is the secret of the origin of mankind! Have you ever wondered how we came into being?"

"No."

"It is a great mystery! The highest experience of manhood is to know the secret of our own—"

A woman's call interrupted Kebel. Yekwara saw Nindik's mother, Ongolek, climbing the trail from the low gardens where she had been working.

"Husband! What has happened?" she queried.

Sar made no answer but climbed doggedly over the stone wall into Hwim village. It was Bukni who turned aside to answer her question in a low voice that neither Nindik nor Yekwara and his teachers could hear.

Ongolek dropped her digging stick and net bag and threw herself, screeching, into the mud beside the path. Other relatives now emerged from *yogwas* and *homias,* keening with low cries as Sar and Nindik passed through the village.

Anxiety stabbed Yekwara. "Nindik!" he shouted. From her father's shoulder, she turned and tried to see Yekwara in the dimness. He started toward her, but all three men gripped his arms.

"You must stand firm until dark!" warned Mena.

"Why are they crying for Nindik?" he asked, remembering how she had sympathized with him in his fear that morning, wanting now to go to her in return.

"I will ask them, but you must stay here," Kebel warned and strode down into the village. Soon he returned and said grimly, "Nindik violated the holy place at Ninia."

Mung and Mena sucked in air and grimaced.

"What will they do to her?" Yekwara asked under his breath.

"She will be hurled into the Heluk!"

Yekwara's eyes started with alarm. Then the full meaning of his father's words bore down upon him. His lips trembled, and his eyes welled with tears.

"No, my fathers! They must not destroy my friend!"

The three men looked at each other sagely. Mung's eyes bulged again as he spoke. "Her own father will see to it that she is killed!"

"How can he do such a thing?" Yekwara wept. "And how can you let him do such a terrible thing?"

"Don't you understand, Yekwara? Her father's heart has long been planted into *Kembu*. We have experienced the wonder of both *kwalu* by the river and *morowal* upon the mountain. We could not possibly reject the ancient commandment that any female who violates a holy place must die."

Yekwara struggled between rejection and acceptance of their sage-sounding words. Then a desperate thought surfaced. "Could they not simply rub pig's blood in her eyes?" he pleaded. "Wouldn't that make everything right?"

Yekwara could not know that he had been born into one of history's most fanatically religious cultures and that all his protests on Nindik's behalf would avail nothing.

"My son, my son!" Kebel chided. "If there was a way to save her, we ourselves would have thought of it. Do you presume to teach the ways of *Kembu* to *us*?"

Despair mingled with embarrassment in Yekwara's heart.

Kebel continued, "The commandments of *Kembu* are contained in *wene melalek*, 'the ancient words.' From the origin of mankind, each generation has recited the *wene melalek* to its children at the time of putting-them-into-*Kembu*. If mankind ever forsakes the *wene melalek*, *Kembu* will forsake mankind. Do you know what that would mean?"

Yekwara shook his head, and his whole body shuddered from cold and sorrow. Kebel stretched his hand out over the misty panorama of rain-drenched yam plots surrounding Hwim.

"It would mean that these gardens must yield less and less produce. Pigs will sicken and die. Children like you will grow up too weak and stunted to defend our villages!" Kebel's voice rose in pitch. "Heavy clouds and rain will blot out the sun, moon, and stars until men begin to wonder if sources of light still exist. Earthquakes will make everyone afraid. Landslides will wipe out villages and sweep entire gardens into the river! It has happened before, and it could happen again! Our people have learned not to forsake the *wene melalek*!"

Kebel crouched down in front of Yekwara and looked straight into his son's tear-filled eyes. "According to the *wene melalek*, if a female observes a sacred ceremony, a pig may be killed in her place and its blood rubbed into her eyes. But if she actually steps upon *Kembu*'s ground, she herself must die! Do you understand?"

Yekwara gazed in agony into his father's eyes. After a long silence, he replied, "Yes."

Nindik felt Sar's and Ongolek's tears scalding her shoulders. She heard their low keening, the suppressed sobbing of her other relatives.

Finally she asked the question that had been gradually forming in her child's mind. "Father, why is everyone sad?"

The question brought no answer but only louder keening. She spoke again, "Father, why are you crying?"

"Because someone we love is in danger," he managed between convulsive sobs.

Nindik was about to ask who when someone else with a tear-streamed face thrust a cooked yam into her hand and said, "Don't ask questions, little one. Eat this."

Nindik had not eaten since she shared yams with Kugwarak at dawn. She grabbed the hot yam and bit hungrily into it.

Her uncle Deko sat beside the small rectangular door of the *homia*. He looked out at the brooding sky.

"It will soon be dark," he commented.

"It is only midafternoon!" Bukni protested. His normally mild face was now distraught. His fists were clenched, as if he were on the verge of anger.

"The people are beginning to mutter against us," Deko ventured again. "They say we are taking too long."

"Let them wait!" snapped Bukni.

Kiloho laid a comforting hand on Bukni's shoulder. "My brother, no matter how great our sorrow, you know we must not forsake the *wene melalek*."

Bukni turned slowly toward Kiloho. His mouth opened, but he could not speak. His culture contained no utterances to convey what he wanted to say. Nor did he know how to invent new utterances. He bowed his head again and wept.

Kiloho spoke gently to Sar. "My brother, have you decided which of us should—?"

Sar shuddered and clutched Nindik in desperation to his chest. Ongolek shielded her daughter with her body.

Long moments passed before Sar raised his grizzled head. In the *homia*'s dim light, his visage transfixed the assembled relatives. Never had they seen grief more deeply etched in human flesh. To Kiloho he said, "Will you?"—and felt something die within him.

Kiloho dropped his gaze and mourned, "No, my brother, I am too close."

Sar turned to Deko. "Will you?"

Deko, too, looked down, pondering the dreaded responsibility. At last he nodded assent.

Sar turned to Selan, another of Nindik's uncles, and repeated the question. Selan covered his tears with his forearm. At length they heard him say, "Yes."

A menacing voice growled outside the *homia*, "Why are you taking so long? If the condemned one excretes or waters on the ground, this entire hillside will be under a curse!"

It was the voice of the big warrior Selambo. Nindik did not understand the word "condemned."

With an anguished cry, Sar released Nindik from his embrace. Ongolek caressed Nindik's forehead one last time as Deko lifted her from Sar's arms and bore her quickly out of the *homia*. Selan followed.

The two men started down the ridge toward the Heluk with Nindik sitting on Deko's shoulder. Relatives crowded around them, reaching out to touch Nindik.

Lastly Alisu raced after the two men.

"Alisu! Don't tell her!" cautioned an older woman.

Alisu reached up and gripped Nindik's ankle. Nindik reached down and touched Alisu's fingers.

Nindik was about to ask Alisu why everyone was acting so strangely, but Alisu turned her back and fled weeping into the crowd before Nindik's question could reach her ears. Alisu saw Bukni and fled into his arms, but he was too distraught to comfort her.

And above the village, still standing erect upon the great stone, Yekwara shuddered so violently that his father embraced him, lest he fall.

The crowd was now only a small black mass watching from a crest of the ridge high above. Nindik saw how far down Deko had carried her and anxiously asked, "My fathers, where are you taking me?"

Deko cleared his throat. "Down by the Heluk there are plenty of ripe *werema* nuts. We are taking you to help us gather them."

At a branch of the trail, Selan bore to the right. "No, my brother," Deko cautioned. "We must stay away from the gardens, even though that trail is shorter." They bore left.

The rain had stopped now, and most of the mist had lifted from the tree-rimmed valley, leveling into a dark overcast tinted with the ruddy glow of some higher sunset. They passed a clump of *werema* trees, and the savage roar of the Heluk struck their eardrums. Nindik stiffened with fear.

"Have you never seen the river up close?" asked Deko.

"No," she said.

"We will show you what it is like up close."

"I'm afraid."

The air reverberated now with the river's thunder.

"My fathers, are there no enemies here?" she asked, looking anxiously from side to side.

"They live high above us on the other side," Selan offered, struggling to control his voice.

"Can they cross the river?"

"Not here, little sister. It is too wild," said Deko. "See how wild it is! Stand here on this high rock, and look out over the water."

They set Nindik carefully on the point of a rocky ledge leaning over the channel. She threw an arm around Deko's leg to steady herself above the dizzying slipstream. "If you were not here with me," she confided, "I would feel very afraid." She gazed up with soulful eyes at her anguished uncles. Deko and Selan looked at each other and horror flooded their hearts as they realized *it was time to do it!* Almost uncontrollable impulses surged within Selan—wild, irrational impulses to snatch up his niece and flee with her to some far corner of the world where her crime would not be known. But of course cannibals would eat them both. And even if they eluded the cannibals, the *kembu* spirits themselves would find and destroy them. There was no escape.

Selan glanced up at the mountainside they had descended. Every bush and rock seemed full of eyes watching sternly lest he fail. He looked again in desperation at Deko, who said evenly, "Set your will, my brother." Then Deko's eyes flared with purpose and he hissed, "Now!"

Simultaneously they bent and lifted Nindik by her wrists and ankles.

They heard her gasp as they swung her back. As the forward motion began she screamed, "*Oh, my fathers!*"

They hurled her with all the force their trembling limbs could summon. She cartwheeled, a tiny spread-eagled figure, and vanished with a little splash scarcely noticeable in the churning rapids.

The sky had fallen.

On a high bluff Selambo turned and relayed to the crowd above that the dreadful deed was accomplished. He smiled to himself. If the child had been spared, *Kembu*'s blessing would be withdrawn from all activities of the western people, including the planned raid on Kobak. And no Yali warrior would dare risk his life on a venture that could not possibly have *Kembu*'s blessing.

Now the raid was *on!*

Atop a still higher bluff at the edge of Hwim, lonely Kugwarak sighed. He would have to cook his own yam next morning. The little girl who cared for him was gone. But then, perhaps by noon Selambo would return with a special delicacy to comfort him.

THE RAID

Chapter 2

YEKWARA sobbed in the flickering shadows of his father's *yogwa*.

"Go to sleep, my son," Kebel yawned.

How could he sleep when in one day they had removed him from his mother's breast, subjected him to a dozen frightening rituals, and killed Nindik? Yekwara dried his tears and closed his burning eyes. Soon the steady patter of light rain on the grass roof and the fire's warm glow lulled him, and Yekwara slept.

He did not hear Kebel and his uncles get up about midnight. They stirred up the flames in the central fireplace and by their light quietly painted each other for war with red berry juice, ocher earth, and white limestone powder. Next, they rubbed on fresh pig fat for insulation against the cold of the Heluk. Finally, gathering their bows and bundles of cane-shafted arrows, they slipped out into the pattering rain and joined the dozens of shadowy figures gathering just outside the high stone wall of the *osuwa* on Yarino knoll.

Selambo towered above them, calling the names of clan leaders.

"We are all here except the relatives of the little girl," someone said. "Their hearts are too swollen."

Selambo first checked his weapons and then slipped a small bamboo shaft into his pierced earlobe. It contained something he would need to help him fulfill his pledge to Kugwarak.

Adrenaline surged within him, and he began to leap up and down, working it through his muscles. A low cry of exultation broke from his lips, triggering similar outcries among his fellow warriors. Then they broke into a wild dance called *siruruk*, rattling their bow vines. They shouted, but not at full force, lest layers of mist focus the sound across the gorge, warning the enemy.

By now the women and children knew.

Selambo turned away from the dance and felt his way past a swamp cupped just below Yarino. The armed horde followed. Down the trail Nindik had taken they moved like wraiths, quieter now. Soon Andeng and the warriors of Sivimu village joined them. On the war dance ridge, the men of Ombok village chided them, "What took you so long?"

Buli was leader now, with Selambo close behind. Descending past the pine grove of Ninia *osuwa*, they soon reached deeper chambers of the Heluk gorge. There, where foaming water created its own light in otherwise Stygian darkness, they threaded a precarious trail upstream.

An hour later they reached a place where the Heluk widened and shallowed enough to allow fording at low water. Here their allies from the villages of Balinga and Yehera were waiting. Several days had passed since the last heavy rain. They *hoped* the Heluk was by now dwindled enough to permit fording, but not until the first man waded into the current would they know for sure. Often a heavy rain on the high mountains could swell the river even when the valley was dry.

Buli and Selambo plunged first into the icy whiteness, bearing with them a length of rattan anchored to a tree. As those on shore meted out the knotted vine, Buli and Selambo pressed slowly out into the channel, leaning hard against the current's increasing pressure. Soon they were lost to view. Only the direction of the rattan lifeline assured the nearly breathless watchers on shore that their two companions had not been swept down.

Tense moments later, the rattan lifted slightly above the slipstream. The watchers relaxed. Buli and Selambo had reached the other side and were fastening the far end of the vine to a tree.

In small groups the raiders waded into the river, letting the current sweep them nearly horizontal while they moved hand over numbed hand along the vine.

Assembled on the enemy shore, they quickly strung their bows and loosened sheaves of arrows for action. Selambo allowed himself but a moment for self-congratulation. The most difficult part of his herculean task was still before him. He cursed old Kugwarak's temerity, but at the same time he grinned, anticipating the adulation his proposed feat would bring him before day's end, hopefully.

"I really ought to thank the wizened one for putting me up to it," he told himself.

Of the many risks they were taking, only one came close to unnerving the other raiders. If at daybreak they took too long to ambush and kill a victim, enemies might discover the safety vine, cut it, and then prepare a counterambush before they returned. Heavy men like Buli and Selambo still stood a good chance of wading home. But lighter men, without the vine as an anchor, would lose their footing. Once lost, it could not be regained, and none of them could swim. Worse yet, deeper, more violent channels were waiting below the next bend.

With Buli leading, they filed upward into the chill blackness of alien forest.

Diminutive Heruluk of Kobak village ducked shyly out of her *homia* and stood shivering, arms folded across her chest against the morning chill. Her nose was pert and tiny, her eyes soft and pensive, reflecting the amber glow of dawn. Her hair was cropped close in the style favored by Yali women, leaving only a circular bob at the back of her head. Two tufts of shredded fibers were her only clothing. One was tucked under her abdomen and the other under her buttocks. Both were held in place by a string belt around her supple hips.

Heruluk frowned at the dawn's spreading glory. In the cloudy Snow Mountains, brilliant displays of color in the sky were rare and were regarded as an omen of death.

"How sad, Maho," she said aloud. "Someone will die today. The sky is red."

Maho, an older woman, also emerged from the *homia* and stood blinking sleepily at the dawn.

"At least we can start work early on our garden," she responded.

Maho wore a long net bag draped down her back. Within it, her youngest child lay cradled against the small of her back, cushioned in soft leaves. In one hand she held her well-worn digging stick, and in the other, a cape of interfolded *pandanus* leaves, lest afternoon rains overtake her.

Similarly equipped, Heruluk followed Maho out of the village. Su, Maho's oldest daughter, joined their procession. Several hundred feet below, yet within sight of the village, their garden waited beside a bank of trees.

No Yali woman enjoyed gardening downhill in the direction of the Heluk, because of the danger of ambush. But eons of heavy rain had washed most of the fertile soil to lower elevations. Someone had to take chances if hungry mouths were to be fed.

Maho started down the trail. Heruluk followed her, humming a sad Yali air.

Selambo saw them coming, trundling slowly down from the hut-festooned ridge. He grinned. Women were the easiest victims. Their constant gardening duties saw to that. And the laziness of their husbands in declining to give them armed escort further suited an enemy's purpose.

The little girl, he noted, was small enough for his secondary and still secret purpose.

Kobak men were stirring now. Smoke from cooking fires drifted up from huddled *yogwas*. But no one was looking down the slope toward the ambush. Perhaps they thought an enemy would not risk an attack under the very brow of Kobak's fortress-like position.

As the raiders slunk lower in the undergrowth, the older of the two women stopped and removed the net bag from her back. She placed it tenderly under the shade of a bush and left the little girl to mind the baby it contained. It was close enough for the mother to return and suckle the child if it cried but far enough uphill for the little girl to bear him swiftly away at any sign of danger.

Selambo grimaced with disappointment. The little girl was too far away. So it would have to be the smaller woman.

Slowly Selambo removed the bamboo ornament from his ear. *Now is the time,* he thought, as he saw the two women resume their descent, closer—closer. He removed a stopper from the end of the small bamboo shaft and shook its contents onto the palm of his hand. It was a single lump of dried fat from a pig long ago sacrificed to *Kembu*. For years he carried it hidden in his ear ornament, waiting for its magical power to ripen with age, that it might come to his aid at a moment like this.

If now it slipped from his fingers, that would be a sign that *Kembu* was not with him. Carefully he took it between his lips and worked it back into the corner of his mouth. At the right moment, he would place the pig fat between his lips and suck on it to receive special strength from *Kembu*.

Strange things were said to happen when brave warriors in crisis called upon their *kembu* spirits in this time-honored manner. Perhaps Selambo would even find himself able to take flight and soar across the gorge to safety (with his intended victim), as Yali heroes Bupu, Mali, and Wehendek were said to have done long ago.

Maho eyed the forest suspiciously but saw no danger. With Heruluk behind her, she moved down to the garden clearing and thrust her sharpened digging stick into the fresh sod. Then she noticed a man's berry-red face grinning at her through parted bushes. At the same instant, Heruluk saw a hundred painted warriors burst out of the forest behind Maho. Heruluk bolted uphill, screaming. Maho turned and caught a fleeting glimpse of Su fleeing uphill with the baby flopping over her shoulder. Then the first two arrows slammed through Maho's waist and knocked her face down in the grass. While she writhed on the ground, a dozen more arrows pierced her. She tried to rise but cane shafts protruded from her flesh the way the Yali liked to see them—"as thick as reeds in a swamp."

Selambo overtook Heruluk and choked her scream with an arrow through the throat. Before he could fit a second shaft to his bow, a swarm of younger men surged past him, shrieking with blood lust, shooting arrows into her as she sank to earth. Even after both women fell, the shooting continued, each man striving to pierce the flesh while it was still alive. It was a Yali ideal for *every* member of a raid to draw living human blood.

Selambo waited impatiently. Those dozens of arrows would have to be removed before he could carry off Heruluk's body.

In the quiet of Kobak village, there was a momentary scuffling as men scrabbled for their weapons in semi-dark *yogwas*. Then, like angry hornets diving from their nests, they ejected in rapid succession from the low doorways and swarmed down the hillside. Some, whose bows were unstrung, paused briefly to string them.

Maho's husband, Mulip, remained by his fireplace. He was nursing a lame leg. When a boy shouted to him that two women had just been killed, Mulip sneered caustically. "It serves them right. These women who are always sneaking away from the village! What were they looking for—lovers?"

The boy ducked his head into the *yogwa* again and said, "Father Mulip, they say one was your wife!"

Mulip stared quietly into the fire. Then he began to cry.

Frenzied with blood lust, the younger raiders seemed momentarily to forget about the enemy village looming like the outline of doom itself on the ridge above them. But Selambo and Buli were watching. They saw armed warriors sweeping like ants down the slope below Kobak. Within moments enraged men would attack with almost superhuman fury, raining arrows down from the higher elevation—an advantage the Yali feared.

Buli and Selambo shouted an alarm. The younger men looked up and saw the enemy coming. Still, they paused for a few seconds to raise an exultant shout of defiance against their swooping foes. Dignity would not permit them to bolt precipitously like a woman or a child. Then they turned and, with apparent casualness, melted downhill among the trees, as if to prepare an ambush. But as soon as they were hidden from enemy view, they surged at breakneck speed toward the river. Their blood lust purged, they were now consumed by an overwhelming instinct merely to survive the journey home. If an enemy had cut that vine across the river—

Only Selambo remained, bending intently over the corpse of Heruluk, frantically extracting handful after handful of arrows from her. When he removed them all, he looked up. The Kobak horde already covered one quarter of the distance from their village to the killing site! For a moment he considered abandoning his secret purpose, but then the memory of old Kugwarak's leering face taunted him. He looked down between his feet at the tantalizing vision of the woman's flesh, passive in death, waiting to be eaten. An obsession to renew his people's fading heritage of cannibalism gripped him. If his forefathers ate human flesh, so would he! He would not leave this corpse for Kobak's cremation fires. It belonged to him!

He heaved the corpse up onto his shoulders.

The enemy saw and knew what he intended. Their great cry of outrage seemed to shake the mountainside, and he imagined they quickened their descent toward him. Sclambo turned and began running with his burden. She was heavier than he expected. He felt her warm blood soaking into his matted hair and streaming down over his chest and back. This was something he had not foreseen! Blood made her so slippery! With every jolting step, the victim shifted on his shoulders, nearly throwing him off balance. Stringers of thorns clawed him as he barged through undergrowth. Vines tried to trip him. Rampant shrieking resounded now from the direction of still other clumps of enemy *yogwas,* but Selambo could barely hear them. The rush of his own blood past his eardrums drowned almost every sound except the thunder of his own heartbeat. Desperate, a wild-eyed demon, half black with pig grease and soot, half red with the blood of his victim, he saw the last of his companions vanish beyond a clearing ahead of him.

Doggedly he lurched across the clearing, crashed through bushes and nearly fell over a cliff. But with a burst of inspiration, he dropped his victim down the face of the cliff, skirted quickly to where she sprawled in the bushes, and shouldered her again.

The sacred lump of pig fat was still lodged behind his teeth, and he could see the white water of the Heluk through the trees below! There was hope!

An ancient stone wall barred his way. He tottered up through a breach where it had crumbled and, in his haste, dared to jump down into the grass beyond it. The jolt of landing and the sudden pressure of his victim's weight thrusting against the back of his head knocked the sacred pig fat from his mouth. At the same instant, his right foot wedged between grass-covered rocks. Selambo sprawled forward with full force and felt his lower leg snap.

His victim forgotten, he sprang in utter terror to his feet but floundered again into the grass, nearly fainting with pain. He looked down and saw his lower leg hanging limp at a ludicrous angle below his knee, useless.

A great hoarse cry of despair burst from his throat, "Buli!" And again, "Buli! Help me!"

Surely, he thought, *they are now too close to the thunder of the river. They cannot possibly hear me!*

Miraculously Buli and another man emerged from a bank of trees and saw him. For a moment they stood undecided, and Selambo feared they might forsake him and flee for their own lives. Then they rushed forward and lifted him by the arms.

Almost immediately an arrow skittered off the stone wall and flexed past them. Already some of the enemy were within range!

"Hurry!" Buli shouted to his helper. They lunged forward while Selambo hopped desperately on one leg between them.

A second long cane arrow struck ground beside them.

Another ancient wall barred their way, and they dragged Selambo over it. Three strides beyond the wall, Buli heard a loud thump and felt Selambo shudder and lose his grip upon Buli's shoulder. Looking down, Buli saw the long arrow shaft protruding from Selambo's back. Kobak men were closing in, their faces beaming in anticipation of three easy kills.

"There's no point! He'll die anyway! Come!" Buli's helper hissed. Instantly he was gone. Still Buli hesitated. Selambo gripped Buli's hand and pleaded, "Buli! Don't leave me! You realize what this means! They won't just kill me. They'll—"

Buli shuddered under the ultimate humiliation which was about to crown the raid he so carefully planned. Then an enemy voice rang out, cruel with caustic wit, "Thank you very much, friend! Just leave our meal right there!"

Buli wrenched himself free from Selambo's grip and fled with arrows sniping at his heels.

Nearly insane with pain and terror, Selambo bellowed after him, "Buli! Buli! *They'll devour me!*"

Half-forgotten nightmares of Selambo's childhood returned with chill reality as the enemy surrounded him.

A leading Kobak warrior, Nemek, motioned to his fellow-pursuers to lower their weapons. Then he crouched down and beamed a smile into Selambo's face. "Hello, my friend; I see you decided to stay for dinner!"

The clearing rocked with laughter. Selambo glared defiantly at the armed host as they hooted and danced to express their enjoyment of Nemek's joke. Then they fell silent, straining to hear Nemek's every word, for he was a renowned wit.

"It was very kind of your two fellow murderers to try to help you, but actually they did you a grave disservice."

Selambo was totally unprepared for the cruel revelation Nemek now sprang upon him.

"That stone wall—" Nemek pointed to the heap of stones three paces away over which Selambo was dragged "—is the wall of one of our holy places, an *osuwa* we have not used since our generation was put into *kwalu*. When you first fell and broke your leg—"

A cry of anguish rose from Selambo's pallid lips. Nemek pressed home every word of the awful truth. "You were lying on holy ground! If you had stayed there, we could not have killed you! To show my reverence for *Kembu* and the *wene melalek,* I myself would have carried you on my back to the river and stood guard over you until your friends came to get you! Your friends, however—" Nemek clicked his tongue as if expressing sincere regret "—carried you out of the *osuwa,* and now—"

Selambo lunged in utter desperation toward the stone wall, but one of his tormentors grabbed the arrow shaft protruding from Selambo's body and yanked backward on it. Selambo gasped with pain as the bamboo head razored its way out of the wound. Then, lunging on hands and knees, squirming on his stomach, he pressed again toward the nearest sacred stone.

This time a dozen laughing men caught him and lifted him from the ground. While he writhed and kicked and cursed, they held him *almost* within reach of the stone that could save his life, then brutally hurled him onto the meaningless ground of the surrounding forest.

Selambo crumpled and lay still.

"Too late, my friend," Nemek continued. "But surely you can understand our position. You have murdered two of our women. You have desecrated our holy place with female blood! It will cost us many pigs to cleanse it. Surely you understand why we cannot let you touch that stone."

Some of the warriors lifted their victim and placed him face up across Nemek's back and helped Nemek carry him back up the slope to the village.

"You are going to do something very unusual today, my friend," said Nemek, when the young men tied the barely-conscious Selambo upright against a tree. The entire population of Kobak and several other villages of the eastern alliance gathered on a bluff below the village to hear Nemek torment his victim.

"Today you will journey to several places at the same time!"

Puzzled expressions knitted the brows of the onlookers. Nemek picked up a twig and traced an imaginary line down the center of Selambo's chest.

"This rib cage and your left arm will pay a short visit to Heruluk's relatives." Laughter erupted and continued for several minutes. Then Nemek continued, "And this rib cage and your right arm will go to Mulip's *yogwa*!"

Again, hilarity broke loose.

"Your right leg—"

Selambo stared, misty-eyed, at the rooftops of Hwim, Sivimu, Ombok, and Balinga, barely visible across the gorge. No smoke rose from those rooftops. The people were in mourning already. Hundreds of Selambo's friends from all six western villages were descending to the point of a ridge facing the scene of the impending act of cannibalism.

The people of the eastern alliance faced their enemy across the gorge, their voices swelling into an uproar of defiance. Some shouted, "Rescue him if you dare!" Others gathered hundreds of banana leaves their womenfolk brought to cook Selambo in. Waving them like huge green feathers, they taunted the distant mourners. "See these leaves! See these leaves! We're going to cook your hero in them!"

Then they raced in a great milling dance around the tree, drawing the mourners' attention to Selambo's pathetic figure.

Older Yali women, relatives of Maho and Heruluk, rushed up to Selambo, spat on him, and thrashed him with their digging sticks, screaming vile abuse.

Soon the dancing ceased, and Nemek approached Selambo again. "You leave us with a difficult decision, friend—how best to kill you! We don't often have opportunity to choose." Nemek turned to the crowd.

"Do I hear any suggestions?"

"Choke him!" screamed an old woman.

"Dissect him alive!" roared a relative of the slain women.

"Spear and stir!" snarled a younger warrior.

"You are much too rash, all of you," Nemek replied casually. He picked up a boulder and approached Selambo. "If I were in your place," he whispered up close, "I would want it done this way."

With a mighty heave, he crushed Selambo's skull with the rock. Selambo shuddered and sagged against the tree trunk. Then the young men broke into a throaty chant celebrating Selambo's death. Older men closed in with their bamboo knives, the women with their banana leaves.

Always, they were careful not to block the view of the watchers across the gorge.

Thus did Selambo achieve his purpose—he revived the Heluk Valley's fading heritage of cannibalism.

Loathe to provide an audience for Kobak's pleasure, yet unable to tear themselves away, the western people stared in huddles. For some, the spectacle of the waving banana leaves was enough to make tears gush. Others restrained their tears until the horrible death chant echoed across the gorge. Warriors paced back and forth in front of the crowd, fiercely vowing to avenge Selambo.

Later, the mourners gradually drifted homeward under a darkening sky, until only Bukni remained. He squatted alone, gaping into space like a man beginning to see a new world—though as yet very dimly. Soon, cold rain began to beat upon him, increasing in intensity until finally he stirred, covered himself with a *pandanus* leaf cape, and trudged slowly across the mountainside toward Hwim.

It rained unabated all night and through the dawn. Men, women, and children huddled in the shelter of their *yogwas* and *homias*, hoping the weather would break by afternoon. But after easing to a drizzle at midday, it regained full force and battered their dwellings through a second night.

By the third day of rain, men and women were compelled to venture outdoors for firewood and food in spite of the downpour. Those related to Nindik and Selambo, however, remained indoors. Their in-laws, according to tribal custom, would provide food and firewood for them during their mourning.

By the sixth day of rain, depression began to darken the spirits of the people. On the eighth day, quarrels erupted, especially in the more crowded *yogwas* and *homias*. In the village of Hwim, "friendly face" Bukni could usually be counted on to talk people out of fighting by his disarming diplomacy, but with the worsening weather, even jovial Bukni withdrew more and more into himself. The deaths of his beloved niece and of his friend Selambo had wounded his optimism, and it was not yet certain that he could nurse it to recovery.

But something else happened to deepen even further Bukni's intense sorrow. Because firewood was so scarce in the hamlet, Kugwarak's relatives, still mourning for Nindik, neglected to bring him fuel for his fire. To keep warm, Kugwarak tore boards from the walls of his *yogwa* and burned them. Cold drafts of the *o-sanim* blew through the widened cracks. The old man suffered a fatal siege of pneumonia.

One gray, drizzly morning, Bukni found the neglected patriarch dead beside the ashes of his fire. Bukni wept over Kugwarak, then asked men of the village to help him gather firewood for Kugwarak's cremation. No one would help, so Bukni had to further dismantle Kugwarak's ill-fated dwelling, leaving an empty half-shell barely able to support its roof. Beside it, Bukni built a pyre, laid Kugwarak upon it, and during a brief lull in the rain, set it aflame.

Kugwarak vanished in fire and smoke.

Around the tenth day of the *o-sanim*, someone's pig sickened. Two nights later it died and three other pigs lay ill. By this time yam plots were languishing for sunshine much as desert plants languish for water. Some of the women gradually neglected their weeding duties because of the cold and the rain, and their husbands beat them to compel them to work.

"Stop saying, 'The sun will shine tomorrow; I'll weed then!' " Kebel shouted at Wilipa and beat her until she trudged gloomily down a muddy path to her garden, dragging a crooked digging stick behind her and crying.

A few men were too selfish to care for their small children while their wives labored out in the howling wind, so mothers tried to keep the children on their backs while they worked, protected under sometimes inadequate *pandanus* leaf capes. Some of the children took pneumonia, and two died.

One day a man who was depressed flew into a fit of rage and thrashed his wife. She fled from her *homia* screaming. As her husband returned to his *yogwa,* someone ran to him calling, "You had better go after your wife; she is running down toward the Heluk!"

The man started with alarm. "No! No!" he cried, and pursued his wife down the slippery slopes. But he was too late. She reached the swollen Heluk a few paces ahead of him and, with a final scream of despair, hurled herself in. The sharp rocks and rushing water quickly dismembered her body. The Yali mourned her death but not for long. Female suicide was a common event in their valley.

From the village of Yalisili, one day's journey to the south, came word of a further tragedy. A pig became partially covered by a mudslide, and the woman responsible for the pig, fearing her husband's wrath if the pig were lost, floundered through the mud to rescue it. When she almost reached it, more mud dislodged from the embankment above her. Both she and the pig were buried beyond rescue.

After a month of nearly incessant rain, a mudslide blocked a tributary of the Heluk below Hwim village, wiping out several gardens. The people crouched along a ridge and watched in horror as a mass of churning water built up behind the mud dam. When the dam collapsed under the pressure, a wall of mud, water, and debris thundered down into the Heluk, wiping out some of Hwim's most fertile gardens on its way.

"Everything is going bad," rumbled Andeng, high priest of Sivimu.

"What could be causing this?" asked the other priests.

Soon everyone was saying, "Everything is going bad. What could be causing this?"

"Someone has secretly disobeyed the *wene melalek!*" decided Helevai. "We must find out who it is and punish him, or we will all perish!"

Word went out, and everyone began to watch. Each man feared lest he himself should inadvertently arouse suspicion and find himself unjustly accused of a heinous crime against the *wene melalek*. Just being accused could mean death.

Before many days, an informer came to Andeng by night and whispered in his ear, "I know who has incurred the wrath of *Kembu*."

Andeng gripped the informer's wrist and hissed, "Who?"

IN FEAR OF THE KULAMONG

"ONCE mankind lived happily—like animals—without the *wene melalek*." Kebel was continuing the instruction of his son, Yekwara. "But when the *kulamong* came upon them, they had no protection, and they died like animals too."

"What is the *kulamong*, father?" Yekwara queried.

"A plague of darkness, my son—darkness that came at midday. People who were caught in their gardens could not find their way home! As they groped in fear, a terrible water came and swept them all away. Later their bones were found lodged under rocks and trees *uphill* from their villages and gardens!"

Yekwara's eyes grew round with awe. Kebel continued, "Even many who were sheltered in their homes died suddenly, without symptoms of illness. They just died from *darkness!*"

Yekwara winced at the vision of horror his father conjured.

"But then the *kembu* spirits gave mankind the *wene melalek*—the ancient words—and taught us that if we obeyed them, the *kulamong* would not return. But still sometimes wicked men among us forsake the ancient words, causing us all to suffer under an *o-sanim* like this present one."

"*O-sanim?*"

"Yes. When heavy rain continues for a long time, that is an *o-sanim*. If the cause of it is not discovered and removed, it may turn into a *ku-*

lamong, and mankind will have to start all over again from a handful of survivors."

Yekwara leaned back against the *yogwa* wall, firelight reflecting from his soulful eyes, and listened as the rain continued its steady drumming.

"What are the commandments contained in the *wene melalek?*" he asked.

"I will recite them for you, Yekwara," Kebel responded. "Count them on your fingers, and try to remember them. First is, *Thou shalt not commit incest, on pain of death—*"

The informer pressed closer to Andeng and whispered, "Today I saw Kiloho emerge from the forest above the waterfall. He did not see me, because I was standing behind bushes. He looked from side to side, as if afraid someone might be watching. Then I saw—"

The informer hesitated and shuddered, knowing that the next words he uttered would cause a man's death.

"You must tell me!" growled Andeng. "Do not hide what you saw!"

"I saw his daughter!" blurted the informer. "The beautiful one called Alisu. She descended from the same area where her father had been. Later I traced her footprints and her father's back to a place where they had been together. I saw the signs in the grass where they—"

"*Incest!*" snarled Andeng, his eyes widening with horror. "No wonder the fury of the *kembu* spirits has beset us!"

The old man's eyes narrowed grimly. "Kiloho is a popular healer in Hwim village. If he denies his guilt, there may be many who will take his side," he mused. "Say nothing of this to anyone until I call you tomorrow!" he commanded the informer and dismissed him.

When the informer left, Andeng pulled a *pandanus* cape over his head and moved through the inky downpour to the *yogwa* of his brother, Wanla the seer.

"The second commandment," Kebel continued, looking down into Yekwara's rapt face, "is, *Thou shalt not steal thy neighbor's wife, land, pigs, or produce!*

"Violating this part of the *wene melalek* does not call for a public execution. Nevertheless, breaking it may cost a man his life when those he has thus offended rise up against him. And the *kembu* spirits themselves will bring woe into the life of the man who breaks this commandment, even apart from the action of those whom he offends.

"The third commandment is for young men like you, Yekwara. *Thou shalt not marry before thy beard appears!*"

Kebel chuckled at the startled look on his son's face.

"No fear, father!" he piped. "I will never marry at all!"

"We all said so once. Next come the commandments governing war, such as the fourth: *When thou art on a ridge and thine enemy is in the valley, kill two or three men!*"

Yekwara had often heard warriors use this expression as a proverb. Now he realized that it was no mere proverb but an esteemed part of the *wene melalek.* He knew also that the converse of its wording was as strongly implied: "When the enemy is on the ridge and you are in the valley, *don't be foolhardy!*" This commandment, even more than common sense, gave basis to the Yali aversion against fighting uphill.

Forgetting its converse side had cost Selambo his life.

Yekwara's interest was now fully engaged. "What are the other commandments about war?" he asked breathlessly.

"The fifth," said Kebel solemnly, "is unique to our people. *Thou shalt not wage war on holy ground!*

"Learn it well, my son, for someday the knowledge of this commandment may save your life! You already know about the holy ground, the *osuwa,* surrounding the *kembu-vam* and *dokwi-vam* in each of our villages. There are also the *kwalu-osuwa* below our villages and the *morowal-osuwa* above, upon the mountains. By the time you become a warrior fully dedicated to *Kembu,* you must learn well the location of all such holy places, lest someday you accidentally release an arrow in the direction of one of them! For it is a great evil ever to pierce holy ground with arrow or spear or to shed human blood upon it. It means also that, if ever you are standing upon holy ground, you may not release an arrow at an enemy, even though he may be standing outside its border. You must yourself leave the holy ground first.

"And know also that your enemy may not harm you while you stand on holy ground, nor may you harm him if he enters holy ground. If ever you break this commandment and kill an enemy on holy ground, then we your own people must take your life, otherwise all things will become bad.

"Know also that if you stand on holy ground, surrounded by your enemies so that you cannot leave, you may command them to give you safe escort back to your own people, and they will obey you.

"The savage people who live in the hot lowlands do not know this discipline. They kill indiscriminately, like senseless animals. And even our Yali brothers on the north side of the high mountains regard their *osuwa* as affording sanctuary only to combatants within their own clan groups, not to every man as we do. They are not as civilized as we are."

Yekwara was beginning to appreciate more and more the Yali expression *wit-bangge*—the cutting-through-of-knowledge. Never had he dreamed there was so much to learn!

"Tell me, father," he queried further, "if those two Kobak women we killed had fled to an *osuwa* in time, would they have been safe?"

Kebel wrinkled his nose in disgust at his son's question.

"Of course not! We could rightfully have dragged them out and killed them! And even if we did not kill them, their own people would have killed them for desecrating a holy place with their female presence. Have you forgotten already the sin of the little girl?"

Yekwara shuddered and quickly swallowed the feeling of revulsion that rose up within him at the memory of ill-fated Nindik bobbing on Deko's shoulder as he bore her down to the Heluk.

"Women," Kebel explained, "are beneath all these sacred things. The *kembu* spirits have not accepted them."

Then Kebel quoted the sixth commandment: *"Thou shalt not attack thine enemy during his sacred feasts!"*

By the time Kebel finished explaining it, Yekwara lay asleep, his head pillowed on his father's knee.

Early next morning Wanla the seer stalked through the mists, hiding a bamboo knife beneath his rain cape. Cautiously he passed behind Kiloho's *yogwa*, cut a length of *pandanus* frond from its new roof, and bore it quickly beyond the village to the house of *Kembu* that stood at Yarino, halfway between Sivimu and Hwim.

Inside the sacred dwelling, Andeng and a grim council of fellow priests awaited his return. Under their close scrutiny, Wanla first dried the severed frond over the fire. Then he handed it to Andeng and rose to his feet. Wanla faced one of the four poles surrounding the central fireplace. Solemnly he gripped the pole with his fingers and toes.

All the priests knew that the pole Wanla held on to was the only one of the four that was anchored down into a piece of sacred pig fat.

"Plant! Plant! Plant!" Wanla chanted fervently, pressing his fingers and toes hard against the pole. "I plant myself into *Kembu!*"

Then Wanla looked beyond the assembly of priests to the wall of split boards at the far side of the interior. Beyond that axe-hewn veil lay the "holy of holies"—the dusty chamber where reclined the sacred black stone of *Kembu*. Only high priests might enter there, and then only on special occasions.

Wanla spoke reverently to the spirit of Sivimu's and Hwim's *kembu* spirits brooding behind the boards. "*Kembu!* I have planted my spirit into yours! Now as this frond is burned in your sacred flame, cause me to see in the smoke that rises from it the truth about the man who lived beneath it. Cause me to know if Kiloho has broken your laws or is innocent!"

Andeng laid the frond in the flame. Smoke curled slowly up between the four poles and enwreathed the head of Wanla.

Silence hung heavy in *Kembu*'s house.

Suddenly Wanla shuddered and stared through the smoke, like a man who has witnessed an unspeakable horror.

"Kiloho—is—*guilty!*" he gasped.

His fellow priests rose as one and filed out of the house of *Kembu*, fury rising in their faces. Wanla remained, as if unable or unwilling to disengage his fingers and toes from the sacred pillar.

With only a slight clicking of wet bow vines and arrows they came. A host of warriors and priests, converging from Sivimu and Ombok, merged with two of the clans of Hwim. They vaulted over stone walls and filtered between *yogwas*, silent except for the squish of mud under their feet. Women and children emerging from their *homias* saw them and scurried, insect-like, back into their tiny shelters.

Deko was the first of Kiloho's clan to sound an alarm. "Sar! Kiloho! Bukni!" he whooped. "To arms!"

They emerged, bristling with arrows, to find themselves surrounded.

"Brothers! Why are you doing this?" Sar demanded, stalking fearlessly back and forth, facing a battery of drawn bows.

"*Kiloho must die!*" someone bellowed through drizzling rain.

"Kiloho committed incest!" raged another. "Wanla the seer has confirmed his guilt in the house of *Kembu!*"

Pale with shock, Kiloho pleaded in desperation, "It is a lie!"

"Why would anyone lie about such a horrible thing?" shouted Andeng.

Kiloho's lips trembled, and his eyes tried to watch in every direction. Then he shrieked, "Some of you have asked to marry my daughter Alisu, and because I refused, you are bringing this false charge against me!"

Then Sar, stricken with horror, added his weight to Kiloho's defense. "My brother denies any guilt. You have recently caused me to slay my own daughter. Do not think now that I will agree to let you kill my brother!"

"Wanla the seer has confirmed his guilt!" roared Andeng. "Wanla had no designs to marry Kiloho's daughter—he would not lie! Kiloho must die!"

More of Kiloho's relatives had arrived now, forming a protective wall around him, glaring defiance at his accusers.

"You protect him because he is your brother," snarled Andeng, "but he has betrayed you as well as us! He has brought this *o-sanim* upon us all. Your gardens as well as ours have gone bad, have they not?"

"Go back to your places!" Bukni commanded, shielding Kiloho with his own body.

As opposing sides maneuvered into position for the impending battle, the overcast sky grew darker. From beyond a high ridge to the south, a black wall of rain swept down upon Hwim. Immediately the same thought occurred to every one of Kiloho's defenders: *The elements are siding with the accusers.*

"Can you stop this rain while Kiloho lives?" taunted Andeng. "Can you bring back the sun to our valley? Can you dispel the sickness and hold back landslides? Are you wiser than the *wene melalek*? Are you more powerful than *Kembu*?

Every question pummeled with terrible force against the intellect of the defenders, weakening their resistance.

"Go back to your places!" Sar pleaded. "Our brother denies his guilt!"

"Then let him also deny that the wrath of *Kembu* is upon us!"

The rain struck with blinding force.

"For your arrogance, I, as a high priest of the *kembu* spirits, will shoot the first arrow in his name!" Andeng roared again and drew his bow.

Fear settled upon every man. Dodging arrows in a blinding rainstorm would not be easy. But incest—the ultimate evil—could not have a delayed punishment. Might not this sudden darkening of sky mean that already the *o-sanim* was giving way to a dread *kulamong*?

Andeng's arrow lofted high in the air and fell toward Kiloho, who dodged it easily and fired back. The battle was on. Angry men weaved among *yogwas* and *homias,* bending and dodging and launching arrows. Frantically they shook raindrops from their eyelashes to keep their vision clear and struggled to keep their footing in treacherous mud.

Outnumbered, Kiloho and his defenders found themselves forced out of the village and down a steep slope. There, one of them took an arrow through his arm. Sar, Deko, and Bukni, seeing they were cut off from their families, urged Kiloho to flee for his life.

"Surely you cannot live here any longer, brother! Go!"

"They will kill my wife and daughter!"

"We will try to protect them. But you must go!"

"Where can I go? No other village will accept me now!"

"Then go to the mountains and live alone! We'll bring you food!"

Kiloho turned and fled through the rain, drawing the deadly hail of arrows away from his brothers.

Eluding his pursuers, Kiloho hid in a clump of bushes, unwilling to go farther until he learned the fate of his family. Well-screened, he peered out through a small gap across a gorge to the village. Through the rain he could see Sar, Deko, and Bukni standing in a group, tensely observing the manhunt.

Determined to find and exterminate the cause of their communal despair, the hunters fanned out through the forest, bows at the ready, each man eager to be the first to restore the purity of his people.

A small bird made a sharp, startled cry as he flew out of the clump of bushes that sheltered Kiloho. Suspicious, one of the hunters, Libeng, crept up the slope, climbed out onto a vantage point of rock and looked down. To his delight, he saw Kiloho directly below him, peering intently across the slopes.

Carefully, Libeng drew his bow.

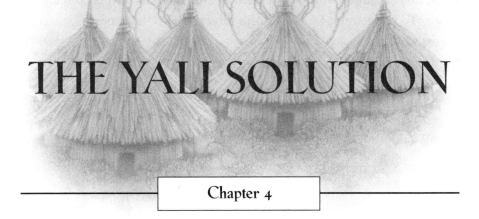

THE YALI SOLUTION

Chapter 4

WITH a hoarse cry, Kiloho leaped to his feet, reached over his shoulder, and yanked Libeng's arrow out of his back. The great depth of the wound reached down into his lungs, and he knew it was possibly fatal. Fleeing to the mountains would render it fatal for sure, so he decided to try breaking through the encircling hunters to the uncertain protection of his relatives in the village.

Thrashing his way through dense undergrowth, he found a trail and followed it at breakneck speed toward his home. Atop the outcrop of rock, Libeng watched him and shouted to other pursuers, directing them toward Kiloho. Rounding a bend, Kiloho startled a teenage boy. The lad bravely drew his bow but, before he could release his arrow, Kiloho pushed him down a steep slope and continued his race for life, splashing blood, rain, and mud behind him.

Wild shouting echoed from the hillsides as a hundred pursuers hurried to cut off Kiloho's escape. Arrows pinged against trees and stumps or sliced into mud and grass around him, but he ignored them. As his breathing quickened, the pain of his wound increased, stabbing through his chest and back.

Atop the village wall, old women waved their digging sticks threateningly as he approached. Three older priests, who did not join the manhunt, leveled arrows at him, but Deko, Bukni, and Sar reached out and tilted their arrows upward before they could shoot. Kiloho leaped the wall, darted through a cluster of houses, and vanished into his own *yogwa*.

Deko, Sar, and Bukni looked at each other and shook their heads grimly.

Within moments, Kiloho boarded up the single entrance of his dwelling as his pursuers thronged around the *yogwa*, spoiling for prey.

"COME OUT TO US AND DIE!"

"Why do you try to avoid the judgment of *Kembu*? You know you cannot live!"

"Spoiler of our gardens! Bringer of sickness and death! Come out and meet your doom!"

"You who have put yourself above the *wene melalek*, come out and take what is right for you!"

But Kiloho did not come out.

Meanwhile Andeng ordered a host of younger initiates to take leaves and wood chips and scrape up every drop of Kiloho's blood that had fallen among the bushes or along the trail.

"Everything that comes from his body is now vile and must be removed from the world along with him," he commanded. "Gather up his blood with the contaminated soil. When we have killed him, it must all be thrown into the river with his corpse."

Then Andeng turned his attention to Kiloho's defenders. "Do you still resist our righteous duty?"

"No," they replied dejectedly. "It is too weighty a matter. Take him as best you can. Only do not destroy his *yogwa* if you can avoid it."

The warriors surrounding Kiloho's dwelling succeeded in breaking open the doorway, being careful lest Kiloho shoot an arrow out at them. The thought of entering the dark interior of the *yogwa* unnerved them. Anyone entering would make an easy target.

"He'll be waiting opposite the doorway with an arrow ready," said one man.

"Perhaps he is in the upper story, where it is even darker, waiting for the first one who dares stick his head up through the ceiling hole."

"Let's tear the *yogwa* apart or set it ablaze. The rain will protect the nearby dwellings."

"His relatives request we preserve it if possible," Andeng interjected. Then he shouted, "Kiloho! Hear me! Do not force us to destroy this dwelling! Come out now!"

Then they heard Kiloho's terrified, pain-stricken reply. "Sar! Bukni! Deko! I have done no wrong. Save me—save my wife and Alisu from these men and their false obsessions."

All eyes turned to Kiloho's three brothers. Sar, who had not smiled since the day he consented to Nindik's death, wore again that harrowed, deep-lined grief his generation would never forget. Deko stared dumbly, like a man overwhelmed with horror beyond human bearing. Bukni huddled helplessly on the ground, staring at Kiloho's tragic house through rain and tear-wet fingers.

Kiloho called to them again, and Bukni's sobbing gave way to high-pitched keening.

"Come out! Come out!" Andeng commanded relentlessly. His voice carried to the nearby *homia* where Alisu had just learned of the heinous accusation brought against her father.

"Mother, what does it mean?" she asked breathlessly.

"It means they will first kill Kiloho—"

"And then?"

"And then you—and me—because we have been with him."

Alisu trembled violently. "Me? Die? Like Nindik?"

Her mother nodded. Convulsed with terror, Alisu fell against her mother, who enfolded her tenderly in her arms.

The drizzle continued, increasing sporadically to a downpour. Most of the executioners withdrew to surrounding *yogwas,* keeping bows ready in doorways lest Kiloho try again to escape to the mountains. Others huddled under overhanging eaves of Kiloho's new roof, barely visible behind the water screening down from its spired summit.

"If you don't come out by the time this rain lets up, we'll tear this *yogwa* to pieces," they called through the stout wall.

Young men began bringing bundles of freshly cut banana leaves to catch the blood from Kiloho and the others when the killings took place. With so much rain, there was danger the blood might soak deeply into the ground, causing permanent contamination.

By the time banana leaves were piled several layers deep over a circular area of ground in front of Kiloho's door, there was a noticeable lull in the rain. The executioners emerged from their shelters. Some now carried sharp stone axes.

Andeng called impatiently. "Kiloho, the time is late. Come out now or—"

With a roar of anger, a large barrel-chested man barged past Andeng with a stone axe raised high above his head. Furiously, he attacked the roof of Kiloho's *yogwa*, chopping through *pandanus* fronds and exposing the vine-bound boards of the substructure itself. Others closed in, shouting and chopping with increasing fury.

"Since you won't come out to us, worker of incest, we are coming in to you!"

"You could at least leave this fine *yogwa* for your brothers to live in! How stubborn you are!"

"Stop! He's coming out!" shouted another.

Immediately the men laid aside their axes and grabbed up bows and arrows. Quickly they formed a line facing the bed of banana leaves and the doorway of Kiloho's home.

Behind them crouched little Yekwara, watching in horror and fascination as Kiloho's shaggy head emerged from the doorway. He saw the livid wound on Kiloho's back and heard the clicking sounds of tautening bow vines as the warriors prepared to inflict more such wounds.

Kiloho straightened and faced his accusers. He hitched his shoulders back because of his dreadful wound and grimaced with pain. Blood frothed on his pallid lips, yet his eyes shone with composure.

Suddenly Andeng's voice rang out, "Drop it!"

Yekwara saw that Kiloho was holding up a net bag adorned with brightly colored parrot and cockatoo feathers. Kiloho's *hwal-sum!* The healing bag he used so often in treating the sick in the village.

"Drop it!" Andeng commanded again. "Why do you keep thinking of ways to frustrate your judgment?"

Then Yekwara felt a hand on his shoulder and heard his father whisper, "Now you are witnessing the seventh commandment, my son: *Thou shalt not attack a healer while he holds his medicine bag.*"

Wide-eyed with awe, Yekwara listened as Andeng cried with anguish, "It is not right to cover evil with a holy thing!"

But Kiloho advanced holding the net bag, shoulders hitched back, mouth grimacing, eyes shining. The warriors retreated, dismayed, flexing their bows and looking to Andeng for direction.

Kiloho saw the spread banana leaves and knew what they were for. He stepped into the midst of them, holding the *hwal-sum* out in front of him. Then he looked sternly around at his executioners and said, "With this *hwal-sum* I healed many of you of your diseases. I made your wives and your children well. And now—"

Kiloho wavered as the warriors jostled for good shooting positions. "And now you are going to kill me and my wife and my child on this false charge. Very well. If that is the way you choose to reward me—" Kiloho took a deep breath, closed his eyes, and dropped the *hwal-sum*.

In their *homia,* Alisu and Lalo shuddered at the thudding sound of arrows striking Kiloho. They envisioned him jerking and spinning under the impact of heavy shafts. They heard the constant uproar of his executioners.

"Stay on the banana leaves, accursed one, and don't splash your evil blood on me!"

Then followed the deep-chested shout of triumph and relief as Kiloho fell on the bed prepared for him.

"Now bring out the two women!" someone shouted above the din.

The sound of hundreds of feet thumping closer, sloshing and splashing mud. The sudden blackness inside the *homia* as violent men crowded in the doorway. Rough hands snatching at wrists and ankles and dragging—dragging—into the dim light which was more to be feared than darkness, into the mud and rain toward the bed of banana leaves where Kiloho lay writhing.

It took six men to wrench Alisu and Lalo apart, and still more to hold each of them in place above the banana leaves until they could be slain. In the midst of her screaming, Alisu saw the first arrow aimed at her midriff. As the bow vine stretched back she shrieked, "Mother! Mother!"

The arrow pierced her through, and the men dropped her across her father. Lalo did not scream for herself. As a Yali woman, she had lived close to death long enough to face it bravely. She died wailing for Kiloho and Alisu, and for little Toli left motherless in the *homia*.

In barbaric societies, hostility tends to discourage free exchange of marriageable daughters between clans. Thus inbreeding threatens to weaken Yali society. Some tribes remedy this problem by maintaining special social rewards for all who willingly wed their daughters into other clans. Yali culture chose a different solution—instill in every heart an obsessive dread of incest. So deeply was this dread instilled that Yali males sometimes suffered recurring nightmares in which they saw themselves committing incest with female relatives. From such nightmares they usually awoke screaming, fearing they had incurred the death penalty. For to be slaughtered by one's friends for committing incest was an ignominy even worse than to be cannibalized by one's enemies!

As the entire population of Hwim, Sivimu, Liligan, and Ombok gathered to view the disheveled corpses of Kiloho, Lalo, and Alisu, the ancient lesson was emphatically reinforced. The villagers watched as Andeng and his fellow priests took bamboo knives and excised from the corpses of Kiloho and Alisu the allegedly offending genital parts. These, along with the bamboo knives used in the operation, Kiloho's gourd and Alisu's grass skirt, and their other personal possessions, were then dropped into the center of two huge balls of grass prepared especially for the purpose. The grass balls were then closed up, bound with vines, and rolled downhill to the Heluk, the grass thereby insulating surrounding gardens from defiling emanations.

The three corpses were laid on their own *pandanus* sleeping mats and carried down to the Heluk. The piles of leaves on which their blood had fallen were bound up and transferred to the river.

The priests then demanded a pig from Kiloho's brothers, slew it, caught its blood in gourd containers, and sprinkled it for atonement wherever some of Kiloho's or Alisu's blood might have soaked into the ground unnoticed.

Then the population stood in the rain along the edge of the swollen, raging Heluk while Andeng and other priests recited the *wene melalek*, commanding the people to obey its ancient laws strictly in every detail.

The people wept because these laws had been broken. Then strong men who had experienced at least three of the four sacred feasts lifted the corpses on their mats, the two huge grass balls, and the bundles of blood-soaked leaves and hurled them as far as possible into the churning rapids.

The people burst forth in rejoicing and looked expectantly for the weather to clear, for they knew the Heluk would well fulfill its cleansing task.

Evil had been flushed from the world of men.

But the weather did not clear.

Even as the people filed back up to their villages, the downpour thickened into another near deluge. The water turned the very trails their feet had worn into the hillsides into streams, washing their footprints away.

Cold, wet, discouraged, and nearly sick with fear, they endured another night of pounding rain, amazed because their stringent measures had not satisfied their *kembu* spirits.

By morning, Andeng discerned what was yet troubling their gods— fat little Toli, Kiloho's son.

"We have allowed the evil man's seed to remain among us!" he thundered. Yekwara cringed when he saw the terrible, merciless expression on Andeng's face. And he wept again as a group of men carried fat, funny little Toli down to the Heluk and hurled him in.

By evening the sky cleared. A brilliant half-moon and a host of stars beamed down upon the obedient people. On both sides of the valley hundreds sat outside till midnight, enjoying the feeling of comparative dryness in the air.

Then, duly impressed with the stringency of *Kembu*'s requirements, they retired to a sweet sleep of relief.

Next morning the sun dawned red and hot in a nearly cloudless sky. Yam gardens began to dry. Women went out to work in droves, gabbling cheerily, and little children swarmed at play among the *homias*. The *o-sanim* was broken.

But in the heart of one man a new storm was brewing. Bukni silently crouched beside the waterfall where Alisu, Nindik, and Toli had often frolicked. He listened for the soft tinkle of their voices through the gurgling streams. He looked for their laughing faces among shifting reflections. Then he climbed the mountains to the high alpine meadows where he and Kiloho had often hunted possum. There he sat among wind-tossed flowers, remembering, mourning, questioning—until cold mists drove him to a shelter far below.

As Bukni questioned, anger swelled within him. Anger against Andeng and Wanla, against—yes, even against *Kembu* and the *wene melalek!* But it was hard to think such strange, forbidden thoughts. His language had no familiar ways to express them. When he tried to voice such thoughts in solitude, he sounded to himself like an insane man. How much more insane would he sound to other men if ever he dared express them aloud?

And yet steadily the conviction grew within him that he *must* express his thoughts. This intense sorrow was more than he could live with. Anger fomenting within that sorrow created an intolerable pressure inside him. Sometime, somewhere, somehow, Bukni decided, he must vent his inner rebellion against *Kembu.*

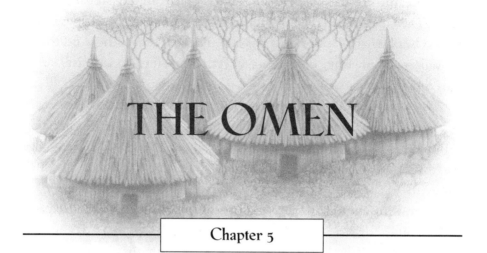

THE OMEN

ANDENG and four of his assistant priests stood at the foot of the ladder leading up into *Kembu*'s cone-roofed temple on Yarino knoll. Around them spread the great, stone-walled enclosure of the Hwim-Sivimu *osuwa*, newly cleared of brush and weeds. Outside the enclosure hundreds of men and young initiates waited in suspense.

Among them stood Yekwara, resplendent again with feather and shell ornaments, trembling with uncertainty as he faced the second stage of his initiation into the mysteries of *Kembu.*

Down from a misty mountainside, troops of women carried loads of firewood for the feast. Timorously, keeping their eyes to the ground, they filed hurriedly in front of the men and boys, dropped their bundles as close to the sacred wall as they dare, and then fled in haste to their *homias.*

Not until the last female entered her *homia*, and boarded her doorway behind her, could the sacred event begin.

"The women are all indoors!" shouted watchmen standing at various vantage points in both Hwim and Sivimu hamlets.

A great shout erupted from several hundred male throats. It echoed from mountain walls above and carried across to the enemy side of the valley, signaling the beginning of a sacred feast. There was no danger of an enemy attack until a final shout later signaled the end of the feast.

First a group of men herded some ten pigs through a gap in the *osuwa* wall. As soon as the pigs set hoof upon sacred ground, they belonged to *Kembu* and could not again be withdrawn for common use. Andeng then touched the largest pig with the end of his bow, and warriors led it aside to be slaughtered and cooked inside *Kembu*'s house for the new initiates. The remaining pigs would be cooked in the open center of the *osuwa* for those already accepted into *Kembu*'s house.

Other men shouldered net bags of sweet potatoes gathered earlier by the women. Bearing them into the *osuwa,* they heaped the produce near the central cooking pits. Finally, the older initiates carried bundles of firewood into the *osuwa.* At once the ten pigs were slaughtered, butchered, and placed among heated stones and sweet potatoes to cook.

All was now ready for the first ceremony—cleaning and anointing the sacred stone *of Kembu.*

With deep solemnity, the celebrants massed around *Kembu*'s hewn-board temple. Then, squatting on their heels, they raised a swelling, deep-chested chant.

Andeng and his four fellow priests climbed slowly up the ladder and entered the structure. With utmost solemnity they approached the forbidding veil of boards that hid *Kembu*'s stone from human view. Judiciously explaining their intentions to *Kembu,* they removed the central boards of the partition. Light from inside the holy of holies streamed through the opening. The light came from a small window in the far wall through which the local *kembu* spirit might freely enter and occupy the sacred stone, his dwelling in this particular village. Through that same window, he could also exit to the mountains, his primary domain.

Hushed with dread, the five priests peered inside the holy of holies. *Kembu*'s stone lay wrapped in a net bag upon a bark pallet. Thick dust obscured the once-bright colors of parrot and bird-of-paradise feathers adorning the protective sack. Tattered cobweb draperies hung down on all sides, for many moons had passed since the holy of holies was last cleaned.

With utmost care four of the priests reached in and gripped the bark pallet by its four corners. With bated breath they lifted it together. To tilt the pallet and send the stone clattering to the floor would provoke *Kembu* to a terrible anger. He would then administer a horrible death to the offending one. For this reason no one was ever permitted to move the pallet alone.

While the four priests held the pallet suspended between the holy of holies and the fireplace of *Kembu*, Andeng opened the dusty net bag and removed the sacred stone with its adorning coils of cowrie shell necklaces. Blowing and rubbing, he removed the dust from the shells and from the stone itself. Then, muttering words of praise to *Kembu*, he anointed the stone with fresh pig fat.

Before the priests' awe-filled eyes, the stone began to gleam anew with the greenish-black sheen that had delighted their forefathers. Generations earlier the stone was selected from *Seima*, one of the sacred places where mankind first emerged from the earth.

Andeng then placed the stone inside a new net bag and set it lovingly on the pallet. The priests carefully returned it to its hallowed bed. And outside, the chanting waxed louder.

Emerging from *Kembu*'s house, Andeng stood on its small, elevated porch and raised his arms, signaling the second stage of the feast. The chanting stopped abruptly.

"You have come into the enclosure of *Kembu*," Andeng began. "You must all obey the *wene melalek!* Hear now the commandments passed on to us from the ancient people! Learn what you may do and what you may not do!"

To a rapt audience, Andeng recited the *wene melalek*. It was then that young Yekwara learned the eighth, ninth, and tenth laws of the ancients.

Thou shalt honor the four sacred feasts for the cutting-through-of-knowledge.

If a woman or uninitiated male beholds sacred things or overhears sacred words, thou shalt make atonement by pouring pig's blood into such a one's eyes or ears.

If a woman or uninitiated male intrudes upon holy ground, thou shalt punish such a one with death.

"If we forsake these laws, the *kembu* spirits will forsake us," Andeng continued. "Our gardens will become infertile. Our women will give birth to stunted children. Our pigs will die of sickness or remain small. Our enemies will overcome us in battle. *O-sanim* weather will darken our valleys. Do you want these things to happen?"

"No!" roared the multitude.

"Then you must honor *Kembu* and keep the *wene melalek!*" Andeng's voice carried like the clear call of a bamboo horn above the sea of up-raised black faces. Andeng was pleased to see all of them nodding assent. Or almost all of them.

Young Yekwara, crouching among the initiates directly below him, sat very still. Pressure to surrender his soul to the overwhelming una-nimity of the august assembly was so strong, so very strong, and yet he hesitated. Poignant visions of Nindik, Alisu, Toli, Kiloho, and Lalo still haunted him, inarticulately pleading for his loyalty to something he did not understand.

Bukni, far back in the crowd, sat glowering, his anger still rising like a slow, irresistible tide. He was beginning to enumerate the multiple risks involved in accepting the *wene melalek* as a rule of life. It seemed to Bukni those risks were almost as grim as the danger of *breaking* the ancient laws.

He knew, of course, that if he voiced his feelings, the men around him would ask, "What alternative do you offer?"

And for *that* question, Bukni had no answer.

But he was angry just the same.

After the men in the courtyard ate their fill of pork, yams, sweet potato, sweet potato leaves, and taro, they gathered up the leftovers in their mats and bore them back to their *yogwas,* lest midday rain should spoil them. Then they returned to the *osuwa* for the final and most im-portant stage of the feast—the feeding of the young initiates.

As yet the two dozen young boys had eaten nothing. Now they were to be fed with a very special food—pork and taro cooked by the priests over the sacred fire within the house of *Kembu* itself.

The priest Lisanik gave instructions. "You will come up in groups of five into the house of *Kembu.* Enter and be seated between the door and the central fire. Do not pass beyond the fire into the holy place next to the room where *Kembu* watches over his sacred stone."

Lisanik's face grew very grave. "Take care, young men, how you climb this ladder. Enter carefully through this door. If any of you stumbles while climbing this ladder, or bumps himself entering this door, it will be a sign that *Kembu* does not accept you and that you are marked for early death.

"And when we, his priests, offer you the sacred food within this house, take it in your hands and do not drop it. If you drop any of the sacred food or, if when you eat it, it makes you sick, we will know *Kembu* has rejected you and that you will not live long in the world of men."

Finally Lisanik pointed to the sky. "There is still one final sign," he warned the initiates. "If thunder peals while any five of you are eating sacred food within this house, it will be a sign that at least one of you displeases *Kembu*. That one will die an early death under *Kembu's* curse."

Yekwara felt his heart quicken in fear. Would *Kembu* know that he still felt sorry for his friends who had died? Would *Kembu* cause him to stumble on the ladder or on the threshold? Would he make the food slip through his trembling fingers? Would the priests discover that Yekwara had not yet sided with *Kembu* in his heart? Was *Kembu* already preparing a peal of thunder to expose Yekwara's hidden duplicity to the world?

Why couldn't he be like everyone else and simply agree that his friends truly deserved to die?

Like a tall, gaunt specter, Lisanik descended the ladder. He approached the huddle of boys and touched five of them on the shoulder. They arose and followed him up the ladder, tensely gripping each rough rung in their toes.

Yekwara was in the last group of five chosen by the priest. A cold chill settled in his stomach as he rose to his feet, shell bands and feather ornaments swaying about him in a quickening breeze. He stole a quick glance at his father and saw the mingled pride and anxiety on the old man's face.

Setting his jaw, Yekwara stood in line with Bengwok, Andeng's youngest son, and then climbed the ladder behind him. It seemed such a long way to the top, and when he stepped off onto the porch facing the low doorway, his heart pounded as if he had climbed a mountain. Bengwok ducked confidently (it seemed to Yekwara) through the open doorway, and Yekwara followed, keeping his arms close to his sides and watching for treacherous loose boards beneath his feet.

Within the temple the five youths straightened and looked around them. The structure's unusually high ceiling was hidden in smoke from the cooking fire. It was by far the largest building they had ever entered. Beyond the central fire, Andeng and three other priests squatted like wiry buddhas behind an aromatic heap of roast pork and taro. Andeng's face was impassive, as if unaware that one of the five young men before him was his own son.

Lisanik gestured to them, and the boys sat cross-legged upon the palm-bark floor. At once the attitude of the priests softened. They smiled at the fearful initiates, eyes twinkling with inviting warmth. Gathering handfuls of pork and taro, they rose to their feet, came around the four-poled fire-place, and bent toward the youths, offering each a portion of food.

It seemed to Yekwara that his were the only hands that trembled as he received the offering from Andeng himself. Gripping the food in both hands, he raised it to his lips.

The wind grew stronger now, blasting across the *osuwa,* chilling the seated multitude. It buffeted the outer boards of *Kembu*'s creaky temple, dislodging dust and stirring the layers of smoke inside. A slow, acrid finger of smoke made Yekwara close his eyes as he bit into the savory pork and taro.

Suddenly the savor turned to blandness in his mouth as he heard it— a low rumble of thunder in the heavens, gathering force and ending in a resounding crack above the *kembu-vam.*

REBELLION

Chapter 6

FRIGHTENED, Yekwara looked quickly at his fellow initiates and saw fear in their faces also. He was relieved to see that all four had already bitten into the food as he had. Suspicion, then, could not easily be focused at once upon him alone.

Yekwara looked at Andeng. The pot-bellied priest stared apprehensively at Bengwok, his son. Then his eyes flicked to Yekwara and the others, his expression changing from concern to suspicion.

"At least one of you is unworthy to partake of this food," he said. "At this moment, we do not know who. Perhaps the unpleasing one himself does not yet know that *Kembu* has rejected him. Later we will all know—in time—in *Kembu*'s time. But for now, continue to eat the food."

"Andeng's house is burning!"

"My home! My home! Bring water! Bring water!" screamed Owu, Andeng's wife.

Awaking with a start, Sivimu village scrabbled dopily for bamboo water gourds in the darkness of *yogwas* and *homias*. Soon an aroused population doused the fire, but not until one side of the *homia* where Andeng and Owu slept stood exposed to the rains of night.

"Who set fire to my dwelling?" Andeng roared, while Owu ranted noisily beside him. No one pleaded guilty, and eventually everyone settled back to sleep.

Andeng went back to his *yogwa* for the remainder of the night. Owu moved to her sister's *homia* until her own could be repaired.

Next night it was Wanla's *yogwa* that mysteriously caught fire. Once again, destruction of the dwelling was averted, but now it was obvious that mischief was afoot. Everyone began to question and to watch.

By the time he had set fire to six dwellings on six consecutive nights, they caught him.

"Why are you doing these things, brother?" shouted a priest. Bukni glowered in silence as they surrounded him. His eyes gleamed red in the torchlight—red from the demon of bitterness agitating within him and from the sleeplessness the bitterness caused.

"You really kept us busy putting out all the fires and repairing the damage!" said someone, trying to be congenial toward the man who in former days spread so much cheer among the villages. "Do you intend to keep on disturbing our sleep like this?"

For an answer Bukni's lip curled in a snarl. His rebellion against the religion of his people had begun. He had little hope that he could make his peers understand why the rebellion was necessary, but that no longer mattered. Rebellion against *Kembu* had become an end in itself.

"Let's beat him!" shouted someone else with a shorter temper.

Some of the men caught up their wives' digging sticks and closed in on Bukni. He raised his arms to shield his head, but Sar and Deko intervened.

"Brothers, we will provide two pigs for all of you who suffered damage or who repaired the damage!"

The raised sticks lowered, and Bukni was released.

"Bukni! You must not do this again!" Sar and Deko warned. "We cannot afford to buy your release a second time!"

On the next dry evening, Bukni set fire to another priest's *yogwa* and fled into the night. Next morning a man named Kongok found Bukni and struck him a hard blow across the back with a digging stick.

Wheeling about, Bukni impudently thrust out his jaw at Kongok and shouted in the hearing of dozens of people, "Go commit incest with your own mother!"

Kongok could not believe his ears, nor could the witnesses. Surely such perverse words had never before been uttered by any member of mankind.

"What?" Kongok asked incredulously.

Bukni repeated his taunt and walked away.

Too stunned to take further action, Kongok stared after Bukni in utter perplexity.

"Did he actually say what I thought he said?" he asked a friend.

"I think he did," came the reply.

"He must be crazy!"

"He's out of his mind! First he sets fire to the homes of *Kembu*'s servants! Now he commands a horrible violation of the *wene melalek*!"

"What shall we do?" queried someone.

Kongok hissed, "If he ever says that to me again, I know what *I'll* do!"

Desperately—and vainly—Bukni's relatives and the priests of his village tried to counsel him. Having rejected the morality of *Kembu* and finding in the world no alternate morality, Bukni had become amoral. The entire universe was meaningless to him, and the only way he could find new meaning was to accept as right anything opposite *Kembu* and the *wene melalek*. He began mocking the four sacred feasts, telling young men not to bother with them. He kept the clans busy putting out fires, and when they beat him, he shouted, "Go commit incest with your mothers!"

Vacillating between anger and confusion, the people kept asking, "Has anything like this ever happened before? What does the *wene melalek* say about such as this?"

Even Andeng had no answer, and he was reluctant to pronounce a death penalty against so popular a person as Bukni without firm legal basis. It was Bukni himself who made the solution easier.

"Unga Woooo! Kolongat woooo! Besal-ma wooooo!"

Every man in the village froze with horror. Women and children looked up in confusion.

"No! No!" growled Andeng. "Not that! Not that!" But it came again.

"Unga woooo! Kolongat woooo! Besal-ma wooooo!"

"Stop him!" Andeng screamed. He dashed out of *his yogwa* screaming, "Stop him!"

"Unga woooo! Kolongat woooo! Besal-ma wooooo!" came the cry.

Frenzied with anger, the aging priest scanned with eyes and ears to locate the source of the shouting.

Bukni stood, spread-eagled atop the temple of *Kembu* on Yarino knoll, shouting first to Hwim village on one side and then to Sivimu on the other. Steadying himself with one hand on the sky-spike anchored in sacred pig fat, Bukni waved his other hand in the air and called again in a loud voice, "Women and uninitiated children! Listen while I teach you these names. *Unga woooo! Kolongat woooo! Besal-ma wooooo!* These are the names of—"

Andeng was now running toward the *osuwa* as fast as his creaky legs could carry him. Out of every *yogwa* men came sprinting, carrying weapons and shouting at the tops of their voices as they tried to drown out Bukni's voice.

"The names of the places where mankind first—"

Quickly they poured into the *osuwa* surrounding the holy structure.

"—came forth from the earth—"

Shouting voices finally drowned out the secrets Bukni was divulging to the women and uninitiated children of the villages.

The men were shocked. No one could remember a time when a man ever dared divulge the secret of those names except to initiates in the sacred feast of *morowal*. Such a violation of the *wene melalek* deserved an automatic death penalty.

Some of the women sensed that Bukni was speaking of things forbidden for women. Those who understood the gravity of the moment screamed to drown out Bukni's voice and covered the ears of small children so they could not hear him.

Others fled crying to the jungle or took refuge in *homias*, covering their ears with *pandanus-leaf* sleeping mats.

Meanwhile Kongok, armed with a heavy stone axe, skirted around behind the *kembu-vam* to the pole Bukni used to climb up onto the tall cone-roofed structure. Hanging the axe over his shoulder, Kongok gripped the pole between his toes and fingers and climbed rapidly up onto the roof. Bukni's back was toward him, and the uproar of hundreds of anxious people covered the crunching of dry *pandanus* fronds under Kongok's feet as he came up behind Bukni, stone axe upraised.

"Kongok!" Andeng screamed. "Do not shed blood within the *osuwa!*"

Kongok hesitated. Bukni whirled around and saw his assailant poised behind him with stone axe upraised. Startled, he lunged at Kongok, and the two men tumbled down the *kembu-vam's* roof. Near the edge, Kongok gripped the thorn-edged fronds to keep from falling. Bukni caught the pole and half vaulted, half fell, to the ground. Springing to his feet, he sprinted toward the far wall of the *osuwa,* pursued by a hundred angry men. Kongok swung himself down under the eaves of the *kembu-vam,* gripped the ends of the rafters, and dropped to the ground. Snatching up his fallen axe, he joined the pursuit.

"Try to kill him without shedding blood!" Andeng shouted after him.

Standing behind the old priest, Yekwara shuddered and buried his face in his hands. Then he heard Andeng mutter into his beard as he followed Kongok, "Why is it so difficult for this generation to keep the *wene melalek?*"

By the time the pursuers overtook Bukni and dragged him to earth, Kongok arrived with his axe and shouted, "Let me do it!"

The crowd gave way before him. Bukni, held firmly by five strong men, nevertheless managed to struggle to his feet when he saw Kongok coming with upraised axe.

"No! No! Don't kill me!" he pleaded. "You don't understand! None of you understand what—"

Hoping not to draw blood, Kongok turned his axe broadside and struck Bukni across the temple. Bukni gasped and tried to raise his arms in self-defense, but the men held him fast. His eyes widened in terror as the heavy axehead swung toward him again. Those who loved Bukni winced at the chilling sound of stone against living bone.

Still conscious, Bukni tried to speak. "May—" A third stunning blow nearly silenced him, but he continued, "the sky—"

Kongok struck again, pleased to see that he had gauged the force of his blows perfectly. The victim was losing consciousness without bleeding.

But Yekwara, watching and listening from a distance, could hardly keep from screaming, "Do it quickly, murderer!"

Bukni murmured, "fall upon—"

With the fifth blow, Bukni's weakened skull cracked. His eyes rolled back in his head. Shuddering, the would-be reformer collapsed. Blood trickled from Bukni's nose and from a small gash on his temple. Whatever blood did not soak back into his matted hair, the people mopped up with clumps of moss.

Later, after Bukni's corpse and the bloody moss were thrown into the Heluk, and after more of Deko and Sar's pigs were slain and their blood sprinkled over the ears of all of the women and small children who had heard anything of Bukni's outburst of "craziness," Yekwara sat pensively beside his father and asked, "Father, was it *Kembu* who caused Bukni to do and say those evil things?"

"Of course not!" said his father.

Moments later, Yekwara asked again, "Then what is the source of that kind of evil?"

Kebel had no answer.

Sitting alone in the darkness of Kiloho's desolate *yogwa,* Deko and Sar looked grimly at each other.

"Brother, we are destroyed!" Deko whispered.

Sar looked around at the *yogwa*'s cobwebbed walls, dimly visible in the fireless dwelling. His eyes probed the darkness as if looking for Bukni or Kiloho among the shadows. The haunting sorrow on Sar's well-seamed countenance was so deep that many people could not bear to gaze steadily at him. All those terrible memories and the sorrow aching within him seemed to come out of him and envelop anyone who looked upon him.

Yet Sar expressed no bitterness. He was himself a priest of the *kembu* spirits. He knew only to accept his sorrow.

Deko knew that he too would eventually accept it. As the one who, with his own hands, helped hurl Nindik into the rapids at *Kembu*'s command, he would not now rebel as Bukni had done.

But for the present, it was hard, so very hard.

The men sensed what they could never have articulated in words—the breaking of *Kembu*'s power, if ever it was to be accomplished (forbid the thought), would call for men with stronger resources than Bukni, Sar, or Deko. Between the three rims of the Heluk people's world, such men were not to be found.

Beyond the western rim of *Kembu*'s world were two men whose resources *might be* sufficient. Among the many disadvantages facing them, they little dreamed of the existence of the *kembu* or the *wene melalek*. Nor could they imagine the disciplined devotion that the Yali, though a stone-age people, rendered to those ancient gods and their harsh requirements.

Nevertheless they had already embarked on a fateful course, a course that would swiftly bring them into bloody life-or-death conflict with the *kembu* spirits and the complex religion they sustained.

One of the two was Stanley Albert Dale.

Part II

BEYOND THE RIM

THE WEAKLING

Chapter 7

STANLEY Albert Dale.

Born June 26, 1916.

His background was not one calculated to produce a missionary. Yet a missionary is what he became, and one with unusual qualities traceable in part to that very background.

His father, Walter James Dale, though raised in a staunch Methodist home, early rejected the faith of his parents to embrace both atheism and alcoholism. In time, after squandering three legacies, Walter settled near Kyogle, a small town south of Brisbane, Australia. He kept a gun and occasionally, during drunken fits of rage, threatened to use it, even against members of his own household.

Stanley's mother, Ethel, was an emotionally unbalanced woman who sought relief from unhappiness by living in a dream world, believing one day she would blossom into a famous actress.

Instead she became the mother of three needy little children: Sadie, Stanley, and Elaine.

Sadie reminisced years later: "Our childhood was hell! Fear! We never knew when we went to school what we would come home to. When Stan was just a tiny thing, if he came in one minute late, Dad would belt him. We were afraid of the drink, afraid of his temper, of the gun, of seeing mother faint before his rage—we were very nervous. Like mother, I wanted to close my mind off to the reality."

Haunted by pain and terror at home, little Stanley also ran a daily gauntlet of abuse at school. Unusually small and angular for his age, he attracted constant taunting and beating from older boys.

The wounds went deep. One day a gang of bullies encircled him on the way home from school. Whichever way he faced, someone pushed him from behind and then laughed as he sprawled, "Weakling! Why can't you stand up straight?"

Bounced back and forth like a squash ball, he finally burst into tears, which occasioned still more raucous derision. But it was not this experience that inflicted his deepest wound. Finally he reached home, clothes thoroughly muddied, and sobbed his sad story to his father, sniffling, "And they called me a weakling!"

Walter Dale sneered down at this muddy, awkward moppet fate had flipped him for a son. "They're right. You are a weakling." Then he turned and walked away.

For a few seconds tears welled afresh. But then something hardened inside Stanley, something that said, "If I'm a weakling, why don't you tell me how I can be strong? You're my father, but you won't teach me how to be strong!"

But his father's very indifference told him bluntly, "Find out for yourself."

And that is what Stanley set out to do. But where could he find an answer? Not from his schoolmates, none of whom would even understand the *question!* Not from his mother, whose only answer to life's problems was to ignore them. From his schoolteacher perhaps?

Well, nearly. At least his schoolteacher drew attention to the answer.

"Students, the reading lesson today is—yes, it is a poem by Rudyard Kipling, the great English poet. You will find it on page 67."

Rude yawning broke out in various corners of the threadbare classroom. Stanley, too, though a conscientious student, felt a wave of drowsiness sweep over him at the thought of reading poetry on such a dreamy, hot afternoon.

"The poem's title is just one word—'If.' Master Stanley, you will rise to read the first verse."

He heard the bullies snicker behind him as he planted his oversize
boots on the rough-hewn floor and stood beside his desk. He focused his
eyes on the first line of the poem. A spitball hit the back of his neck and
rolled down inside his crumpled collar. More snickers. Ignoring the spitball and the snickers, he began to read:

If you can keep your head when all about you
Are losing theirs and blaming it on you;

Stanley was startled. He had the distinct impression that whoever
wrote those words might have understood what it was like to be Stanley
Albert Dale.

If you can trust yourself when all men doubt you,

Tears nearly welled on that one. Amazed at how a mere poem could
speak so directly to his heart, he continued.

But make allowance for their doubting too;
If you can wait and not be tired by waiting,
Or, being lied about, don't deal in lies,
Or, being hated, don't give way to hating,
And yet don't look too good, nor talk too wise;

By now not only the spitball and the snickers but even the bullies
were forgotten. Stanley was experiencing for the first time the power of
poetry to ravish a human heart. He finished his reading. Just as well. He
nearly choked on the last line. He sat down. A girl next to him rose to
read the second verse, but he was racing ahead of her.

If you can dream—and not make dreams your master;

That was the pit his mother had fallen into.

If you can think—and not make thoughts your aim;
If you can meet with triumph or disaster

And treat those two impostors just the same;
If you can bear to hear the truth you've spoken
Twisted by knaves to make a trap for fools,
Or watch the things you gave your life to broken,
And stoop and build 'em up with worn out tools;

When school was out, Stanley slipped that poetry book into his schoolbag, eluded the bullies, and fled across the fields to a lonely hilltop. There, with eager fingers, he fumbled to page 67 and pored again over Kipling's lines:

If you can make one heap of all your winnings
And risk it on one turn of pitch-and-toss,
And lose, and start again at your beginnings
And never breathe a word about your loss;
If you can force your heart and nerve and sinew
To serve your turn long after they are gone,
And so hold on when there is nothing in you
Except the Will which says to them: "Hold on."

Later that afternoon, after chores on the farm, he read it again. And after washing supper dishes, once more, this time by the kerosene lamp in his bedroom.

If you can talk with crowds and keep your virtue,
Or walk with kings—nor lose the common touch;
If neither foes nor loving friends can hurt you;

Stanley pondered long on that line.

If all men count with you, but none too much;
If you can fill the unforgiving minute
With sixty seconds' worth of distance run—
Yours is the Earth and Everything that's in it,
And—which is more—you'll be a Man, my son!

Stanley wasn't sure what Kipling meant by "the unforgiving minute," but no matter—life was to teach him *that* quickly enough. What he did know was that Kipling, through just thirty-two lines of poetry, had filled the vacuum Stanley's own father left untended.

So Stanley memorized the poem. Where formerly he trudged forlornly across the fields to school, now he bounced with spring in his step, shouting his poem to the clouds. When he climbed over the rustic fence back onto the road and saw the bullies waiting by the schoolyard gate, he said it under his breath as his hidden ally helping him to advance, head up, right up to their ugly scowls. And when they beat him, it kept him from weeping.

For Rudyard Kipling taught him how to be strong and even called him "my son."

Stanley Albert Dale found a father.

He was to find still others as his family moved from Kyogle and settled far to the south in Bowral. As he grew, he discovered Henley's poem *Invictus,* and the writings of Matthew Arnold, Oliver Goldsmith, John Masefield, Alfred Tennyson, and Robert Browning. Since his schoolbooks contained not nearly enough of these great men, he soon learned to open the great heavy door of the Bowral Public Library. Before long, Stanley became one of its most frequent visitors, huddling for hours, alone and scarcely ever noticed, at the end of one of the long reading tables close to the small-paned window.

There he discovered books on history—biographies of rugged warlords became his special delight: Alexander the Great, Hannibal, Cromwell, Nelson, Lord Kitchener—men who overcame impossible odds, and whose ideals Kipling later distilled as poetry in "If." At least once a week Stanley would open a new volume and peruse it avidly, grinning as if all his birthdays had come at once.

How Andrew Carnegie would have smiled to see a public library so thoroughly whet and fete a poor boy's thirst for knowledge!

Inspired by his studies, Stanley began to dream of a great destiny for himself. And unlike his mother, he fully intended to make his destiny *fact!* Already, as a child, he was learning to surmount difficulties; what might he do as a *man?*

As a result of his prolific reading, Stanley soon found he could comment aptly on almost any subject, causing some people to deride him as a know-it-all. Even more annoying, according to Sadie, was the fact that investigations proved he really *did* know what he was talking about!

Still, as both sisters agree, Stan was sometimes a little *too* cocksure. "I never knew him to lose an argument," said Elaine with a wry twinkle. But as Stan grew older, both sisters felt their respect for him soar. There was something so intensely appealing in the way he set himself to compensate for every disadvantage fate had thrown him.

"Handicaps are a compliment to a fighter," he would quip.

His smallness of stature, for example. Unable to add one cubit to his frame, Stanley decided to make what there was of him not only far wiser but also far stronger ounce for ounce than any of his peers.

He succeeded.

By dogged cross-country running and hard work on the farm, he transformed himself into a pint-sized Atlas, bulging with miniature brawn. As his strength increased, so also did his courage. He feared nothing and would accept any dare.

Let a playmate mount a sand dune and shout, "I'm the king of the castle, and you're the dirty rascal," Stan would quickly prove otherwise.

And though his father still dismissed him as "weakling," the bullies soon gave him a new title—"Toughie." For at the first sign of provocation, Stanley would always seize the initiative, no matter what the odds, and the outcome was often embarrassing! So they tried new tactics.

"Toughie, see that old house—it's *haunted!* Don't ever go in there or horrible things will happen to you!"

Feigning fear, Stanley asked each boy in turn, "True?"

When they had all committed themselves (confident that at last they had his nerve at bay), he suddenly smiled, sprinted into the house, raced through every room, and laughed hilariously at his would-be intimidators from an upstairs window.

Years later, when dared to swim Sydney Harbor to a certain island, "Toughie" plunged in and struck out through the waves. His mates, perhaps fearing they would be held accountable if he drowned, had second thoughts and went after him by boat. They had to pluck him by force—still swimming—from tossing whitecaps.

Thus did he emerge from his tormented childhood: toughened not only in mind and heart but in sinew as well. Rushing to meet every challenge before him, shoulders squared, chest out, spring in his step, backbone straight as a poker. *Head-on!*

Yet still there were scars.

And setbacks.

For example, his father's bakery—newly purchased at Bowral—quickly went bankrupt. After creditors came and removed all furnishings from his home and business, Walter Dale sat on the floor in a bare room and wept miserably. Then he turned to Stan and Sadie and said grimly, "You must both leave school to help me support the family." His dream of achieving higher education shattered, Stanley also sat down and wept with his father. What could life hold for him now?

For a while, because of his small stature and extreme youth, fourteen-year-old Stanley could find employment only as a golf caddie. But then a neighbor interceded, and Stanley found his path to destiny merging incongruously with an apprenticeship in someone else's bakery.

Long hours of labor by hot ovens threatened to deny him time for private study; however, he managed to steal away to the local library on the few off-hours allowed to him.

Three years later it happened. Someone slipped a *new* kind of challenge in his path, in the form of a little book, *Four Things God Wants You to Know.*

Reading it, seventeen-year-old Stanley found himself on unfamiliar ground. His atheist father had carefully avoided exposing him to a subject like this.

For the first time, the youth who had trained himself to take up every challenge was stymied. Here was a call, not to a test of mere physical strength or cunning but of willingness to surrender oneself to what was evidently the ultimately moral ideal of the universe—the glory of *God!*

Stanley felt his usual rocklike self-possession teeter. For some time he had become increasingly aware that he was not living up to Kipling's earthly standards. And now this.

A sense of gentle warning came to him: "Fail this test, Stanley, and no matter what else you accomplish, still you will be found not fully a *man*. But if you pass this test, even your finest physical exploits will appear paltry by comparison!"

His heart began to pound. Suddenly a new and profoundly exalted view of the meaning of human existence took his breath away.

"So *that* is why I am here—to glorify God!" He read the tract again. One verse caught his attention:

All have sinned and fallen short of the glory of God (Rom. 3:23).

Weighted now with guilt and unworthiness, Stan saw his problem— sin had kept him from fulfilling his true purpose. He read on:

By grace are you saved through faith, not by your own endeavor. Salvation is a gift from God. If it could be earned, men would boast (Eph. 2:8-9).

Faith, then, was the key. Somehow he had to find out how to use that key. Then he remembered! The friend who gave him the little book had mentioned a meeting to be held that evening, Saturday, November 14, 1933.

The meeting was on Mount Gibraltar, a favorite picnic spot jutting above the town of Bowral. As Stanley climbed the hill, he saw a large tent on the crest. He heard people singing hymns. The sound was so sweet, so appealing—every leaf, flower, and branch seemed to assure him that what those people were singing about was really the basis of everything.

It was good.

After all he had been through at home, at school, and at the bakery, he wanted, oh so badly, to be part of something *good*.

He entered and sat on a bench among very plain yet beautiful people. How different were their faces! Neither sullen like his father's nor dull and empty like so many of his acquaintances. How different were their voices! Not hard-edged with curses like the voices at the bakery.

Then a preacher stood up and expounded from an obviously very ancient, well-tested, hence authoritative book.

By the time the preacher called for a decision based on the text of that book—the Bible—Stanley was ready with his own personal verdict.

The preacher, Alex Gilchrist, saw the youth rise to his feet, square his shoulders, step out into the aisle and march forward. Even from a distance, there was no mistaking the look in the youth's eyes—a look that said, "Count *me* among Christ's followers!"

Closer up, Gilchrist could detect fiery intensity of purpose quivering through the small, wiry frame.

Youth and preacher gripped each other by the hand. They looked into each other's eyes. They knelt and prayed together in front of the congregation. Then and there, Stanley sealed his commitment to Jesus Christ. It was not a one-sided transaction. Someone else's pure, sweet joy swept through him, and he knew within himself that God heard his prayer!

His past was forgiven!

His entire life would now be transformed.

Best of all, the transformation had already begun!

"Stanley's conversion was instant and irrevocable," Sadie recalled years later. "We, the members of his family, responded in different ways—not at all as he intended. For example, when he told our atheist father—"

"No!" snarled Walter James Dale. "Not that!"

Stanley braced himself. He chose one of his father's rare sober moments to break the news, but even so there was danger of unpleasantness, perhaps even violence.

"Yes," Stanley replied respectfully, yet firmly.

A sneer curled his father's lip. So the "weakling" had weakened himself further by putting his trust in a God who didn't exist!

After a moment, the words came, slow and deliberate. "I no longer have a son."

Stanley was crushed.

He tried also to recall his mother from her daydreams to faith in God. She tolerated his fervent pleas with placid acceptance, agreeing with everything, comprehending little.

His sister Elaine, ten years Stan's junior, at first resented his conversion. "He became so dedicated to God he almost wasn't a brother to me anymore."

Yet both Elaine and Sadie, who was two years Stan's senior, knew that some very dynamic vision had taken possession of their brother.

"He worked unjustly long hours at the bakery," Sadie recalled. "Yet when he came home, he would spend hours in prayer. Often we found him asleep on his knees beside his bed, even when the temperature was near freezing."

Before many years passed, however, not only Sadie and Elaine but even Stan's mother came to share Stanley's evangelical faith.

As earlier Stanley had devoured poems and histories, so now he gave himself ardently to the reading of patriarchs, prophets, and apostles.

One day his study uncovered evidence that Rudyard Kipling, foremost of his boyhood heroes, also drew inspiration from the Christian Scriptures, as Stanley himself was now doing. In a closing line of "If," Kipling promised those who fulfilled his ideal of absolute, uncompromising manliness, "Yours is the Earth and everything that's in it." Stanley discovered that this expression paralleled a line from King David's twenty-fourth psalm: "The earth is the Lord's, and the fullness thereof" (Ps. 24:1).

So, Stanley reasoned, pondering the poet's meaning afresh in the light of this newly realized background, *Kipling intends us to understand that a truly ideal man will share in God's ownership of creation—he will be, under God, a lord of the earth!*

Could this be true?

Stanley recalled that Christ Himself also proclaimed, in spite of Caesar's evident sway, "Blessed are the meek for they shall inherit the earth" (Matt. 5:5)!

And was not Kipling's ideal man also meek? Doubted by others, he makes allowance for their doubting. Lied about, he does not deal in lies. Hated, he gives no place in his own heart to hating. Talking with crowds, he still maintains virtue. Walking with kings, he does not lose the common touch.

All without looking "too good" or talking "too wise"!

Suddenly everything began to fall into place! *Christ* was the only Man in history who fulfilled Kipling's ideal to perfection!

In the storm on the Sea of Galilee, Christ "kept His head" when the disciples were losing theirs and blaming it on Him!

As the Son of God, He was capable of profoundest "dreams" and "thoughts," yet He crowned them all with practical deeds!

In Gethsemane and on Calvary, He forced His heart and nerve and sinew to "serve His turn long after they were gone."

Throughout two thousand years of history, Stanley reflected, Christ has witnessed the twisting of His truth—particularly by unscrupulous ecclesiastics who make traps for fools. Then, under their very noses, He straightens it out again through the witness of lowly men who get back to His original sayings and those of His apostles.

Repeatedly the church He gave His life for has been "broken" by persecution or corrupted, yet He stoops and builds it again with worn but worthy tools—discipline and instruction.

Doggedly, He "risks" the "heap of all His winnings" in history upon the faltering witness of followers in each new age.

And often, in human estimation at least, He "loses" and starts again at His beginnings, never departing from His original purpose.

All in preparation for the climax of history and the final verdict He is destined to wrest from both critics and enemies.

Stanley gazed intently at the open Bible before him.

Surely Kipling must have used Christ as model for his ideal man! Still more exciting, the spirit of Christ used Kipling's poem as a tutor for Stanley! A sort of interim Old Testament to help an otherwise uninstructed boy see his need for repentance.

How many other "interim Old Testaments" might Christ have at His command throughout the world, preparing otherwise uninstructed men for encounter with Him?

Later, perusing the apostle Paul's first letter to the Corinthians, Stanley found a further biblical source for Kipling's soaring promise: "For all things are yours, whether . . . the world or life or death or the present or the future, all are yours; and you are Christ's; and Christ is God's" (1 Cor. 3:21-23).

He saw it now—the echelon that man is meant to fit into, the echelon that rises above man into the Godhead and descends below him to galaxies and atoms. He saw also the secret of that echelon: *Remain subject to everything above you, and everything below you will be subject to you!*

"Lord, apart from You," he prayed in ecstasy, "Kipling's poem remains just that—an awesome *if* which no man can measure up to! But any man who is united to You can do all things through You, because You have fulfilled Kipling's ideal *and more!*"

Thus did Stanley Dale find insight to complete his transition from Kipling to Christ.

Eventually Stanley accepted an invitation from Alex Gilchrist to join a band of men called the Open Air Campaigners. Reviving the apostolic spirit of British reformers John Wesley and George Whitefield, the Open Air Campaigners preached fearlessly on crowded beaches, in markets, army camps, or skid row. Insistent gadflies, they assailed the consciences of wayward pleasure-seekers. Fending hostility or derision with disarming quips. Piercing the indifference of the world-weary. Nettling men until they decided for or against the Savior.

Often, along the spillways of humanity, the Open Air Campaigners found the nuggets they were searching for—the ones, twos, or threes who, arrested by bold preaching, would be drawn irresistibly by the love of Christ. And whenever such a one came, Stanley and the others would kneel and pray with him before scorning crowds, heeding neither catcalls nor hoots of derision but thinking rather of "the angels in heaven rejoicing more over one sinner who repents than over ninety and nine righteous persons who need no repentance" (Luke 15:7,10).

Soon Stan was in the forefront of the campaigners, shouting his convictions above the noise of traffic, parrying abuse with wit, meeting challenge with kindly counterchallenge. But sometimes the insults were so vile, so stinging! It was hard not to get angry. But whenever the red began to rise above "Toughie's" collar, a calm, steady look from Mr. Gilchrist would serve to cool the fast-heating steel.

About this time the young preacher began to notice that not all who called themselves Christians truly followed the self-denying Nazarene who was Captain of their faith. And so, as he regaled worldlings on beaches and street corners, so now on occasions Stanley addressed himself in no uncertain terms to what he called the "lip service" of modern Christians who were trying to enjoy "the best of two worlds" instead of committing themselves wholly to God.

Stanley's outspoken comments sometimes drew critical reaction. But Mr. Gilchrist, Stanley's "father in the faith," was undisturbed by criticism of his protégé.

"A diamond newly mined is always rough," he would say, with a twinkle in his cool reserve. "But just you wait—"

From "weakling" to "Toughie" to "rough diamond."

What next?

By the time Stanley was twenty-two years old, the necessity of helping to support his family was lifted from him. Immediately he fled the stifling bakery and his apprenticeship. He journeyed to Sydney and enrolled in the Sydney Missionary and Bible College. But before he completed his training for Christian service, Hitler and Hirohito declared war against the Allies.

Stanley took it as a personal challenge. Much as he enjoyed his studies, the challenge had to be answered first. Excusing himself from school, Stan joined the Australian infantry and soon qualified for a commission with an officers' training school. But training dragged on for months, while the Japanese worked their way southward, still virtually unchallenged.

Stanley chafed for action.

Then he noticed that units of a division called "the commandos" shipped out to the New Guinea front more quickly than regular army units. Stanley begged to surrender his officer's commission in order to transfer to the commandos. To his delight, his request was immediately granted.

Suddenly he found himself moving in the midst of a very different breed of men, an elite corps of paratrooper-commandos known as "the suicide boys." They were rugged and ready for anything, like Stan himself, but some of them were embittered against life and seemed to court violence and danger as ends in themselves. They took Stan's measure, found him tough steel from sole to crown, and accepted him.

His religion, however, baffled them. They had never pictured religious people as anything other than milksops. And Stanley was no milksop.

At one point in his army training, Stan and some two thousand other soldiers were barracked in an immense hall at the Sydney showground. Since his conversion, Stan had always adhered strictly to the practice of kneeling beside his bed in prayer every evening before retiring and again every morning before breakfast. Now he faced a rugged test: was he willing to kneel and pray in the midst of two thousand rough-neck soldiers?

Stanley decided he could do nothing else and still be true to God and himself. On that first evening, he dropped to his knees beside his cot. Within a few seconds, he detected it—a shockwave of stunned silence spreading outward in all directions to the far corners of the great hall. Then came aftershocks of raucous laughter mounting into a tumult of derision.

Stanley prayed on.

During training near Sydney, Stanley discovered a recreation center for servicemen, on Goulbourn Street. It was operated by Baptist Christians of the city and opened from 6:00 to 9:00 P.M. each Sunday. So every week he moved back and forth between two completely opposite environments. From Monday to Saturday it was a world of hardboiled sergeants mingling insults with orders, forced marches, belly-crawling under barbed wire, trying to close one's mind to the lewd language of the barracks.

But then on Sunday! Singing Charles Wesley's or Fanny Crosby's hymns with cheery faces and lilting voices; renewing one's dedication to God in times of solemn, earnest prayer; listening to probing expositions from the Bible; urging one's fellow servicemen who had not made peace with God to do so while there was still time; partaking of sandwiches and tea served by bright-eyed, smiling young women.

Stanley's interest in girls was late developing, but thoughts of romance at last stole into his heart. First to draw his interest was a vivacious brunette named Yvonne. But how should he approach her? One thing was certain—Stanley would not imitate what he regarded as the devious, deceptive courting methods used by some of his peers. In fact he was quite outspoken against the practice of leading trusting girls along only to jilt them for another when it suited one's own fickle fancy.

Stanley prayed long and earnestly to find out if Yvonne was indeed "God's choice" for him. When he seemed to receive assurance that indeed she was, he took a deep breath and approached her one day in a quiet corner at the Goulbourn Recreation Hall.

"Yvonne."

She looked up and smiled at him sweetly. "Yes, Stanley?"

"Yvonne," he repeated, struggling to recall the opening words he had memorized, "I have become deeply attracted to you, and after much prayer, I believe you are God's will for me."

The smile on her face quickly faded. Stan continued, "And I want you to know this is a solemn, sacred matter with me, and you can count on me to be true to you as long as I live."

Yvonne blanched. But then she remembered to be polite to this staunch young soldier who would soon fight and maybe die to defend her freedom to say no, so, in company with others, she invited Stanley for two or three Sunday afternoon visits to meet her family. Gradually after that, she made herself more and more elusive.

Stanley took his disappointment like a man. "Ah, me!" he sighed. "Next time I'll try a less direct approach." But indirect approaches to *anything* would not come easily to Stanley Albert Dale.

Sudden transfer to the war zone cut his romantic agonies short. His last good-bye at Goulbourn Street was a solemn one for his friends. They were all certain of three things: one, Stanley would never return from the war; two, he would sell his blood as dearly as possible; three, they would never meet another person like him.

Stanley's unit landed at Port Moresby, on the island of New Guinea, with orders to resist the Japanese advance southward from Lae on the north coast of the island. This meant foot-slogging through mud and tropical heat into the rugged Owen Stanley Mountains, spine of New Guinea's eastern end.

Stanley was surprised (and delighted) to find that almost all natives along the track to the Owen Stanleys were already Christians. At least every village seemed to center on a church, and the people were extremely friendly.

"Good thing the missionaries got here first," Stan remarked to his bone-weary mates, "or we'd be watching out for these boys as well as the Japanese."

Some of the commandos mocked the hymn-singing Papuans but had cause to eat their own words later. For hundreds of allied soldiers were to be wounded in the Owen Stanley fighting. These very Papuans bore the wounded on stretchers (or on their own shoulders, if necessary) down the muddy Kokoda Trail to Port Moresby and hospital care.

They called them "fuzzy wuzzy angels" then.

But when he encountered villages of the negrito tribes dwelling far up in the mountains, Stanley was shocked by the difference. The people there struck him as furtive, haunted. Their eyes lacked expression, like little holes leading to nothingness.

"The church of Jesus Christ has failed these people," Stan thought to himself.

Later, on patrol, he and his buddies crested a high pass of the Owen Stanleys and looked down upon a wide vista of the Markham River Valley. Near the river mouth, Japanese barges were unloading supplies for their forces. His buddies had eyes only for the barges, but Stan's gaze wandered farther afield. Beyond the valley to the west and north, still other mountain ranges jagged the horizon. And others. And others. Ranges beyond ranges beyond ranges.

A sense of the vastness and mystery of New Guinea settled over him. He understood better now the awe which had caused Rudyard Kipling, in another of his inspiring poems, "The Explorer," to write:

Something hidden; go and find it;
Go and look beyond the ranges.
Something lost beyond the ranges,
Lost and waiting for you. Go!

What was it that was lost beyond *these* ranges and possibly waiting for *him*?

He remembered the wild people they had passed along the track, and reflected that probably they were scattered all through those far ranges as well. Perhaps hundreds of thousands of them. In hundreds of unexplored valleys. Warring and struggling to survive. Disease-wracked and demon-haunted.

When Jesus died on the cross, was it not for them as well?

When He arose from the dead, was it not to give new life to them *also*?

And when He said, "Go into all the world and preach the gospel to every creature" (Mark 16:15), did He mean to exclude them?

No. They are included, Stanley reasoned. *But the church of Christ had failed.*

It followed logically that he, as a responsible member of that church, should—

Stanley chewed his lip, deep in thought. *What would such a task involve? Learning their languages, probably.* He gulped. That alien mixture of gibbles, gabbles, and gobbles he had heard along the track—how could any white man ever learn it? And even if one learned to speak it, would its grammar be developed enough to express spiritual concepts?

The task would call for a man with a keen, versatile mind. Stan surveyed the rugged peaks and gorges around him and added, *And a strong body.*

Stanley looked down at his legs, which scarcely seemed to tire of the track. He filled his chest with the rarefied mountain air, which often left his heavier mates gasping, weak as kittens.

"Lord, You may have better men for such a job," he whispered in prayer, "but if they're not willing, try me."

A punch on the shoulder jolted him. "Snap out of it, mate. It's a long way back to camp before dark."

During a lull in the fighting, Stanley sauntered over to a nearby Yankee unit just to look them over. As he passed a cubicle, he heard a loud, gushing sound, followed by a long sigh.

Stan cocked his head at a Yank passing by and asked, "Excuse me, mate. What was that noise? You blokes got some sort of animal caged up in there?"

"Mister, that was a toilet flushing."

Stan took a long stride backwards, feigning surprise. "Flush toilets on the front lines!" he exclaimed with a hurt expression, as if the reputation of fighting men everywhere had just been irreparably besmirched.

Stan strode away, shaking his head. But then he passed a mess hall and saw an American soldier spreading jelly on a slice of buttered bread. Thunderstruck, he returned to his tent in the Australian camp, muttering to a fellow commando, "I thought we had a chance against the Japanese. Now I'm not so sure."

"Dale!"

It was the commanding officer's gruff bark. Stan fell into line.

"You and these others have been chosen for a special mission. Be ready to leave at dark."

Stan thrilled inwardly, though his set jaw betrayed not a trace of emotion. But later that night, for no apparent reason, Stan learned that his name was withdrawn. Another commando was put in his place.

His replacement never returned from the raid.

"He's the second man to die in my place," Stan observed. "My life is far too dear to waste on myself."

Stanley opened a letter from Sadie and read, "Dear Stan, after you joined the army, Dad went back to the merchant navy—he wanted to help in the war too. He signed on a ship called the *Ceramic*. I've just received word it was sunk in the Atlantic. Dad went down with it."

Stanley sat for a long time with Sadie's letter in his lap, gazing wistfully out across sweeping lowlands toward the Gulf of Papua.

In 1944, Stan completed his term of military service and returned to Australia. With his manly duty to his country well discharged, he could now with clear conscience return to his first love—the Bible and the preaching of the gospel. He studied at the Sydney Missionary and Bible College until graduation. Then he set out on an evangelistic tour of Tasmania with William Tate, under the auspices of the Tasmanian Gospel Campaigners.

Stan's contribution to the campaign was lively indeed! Drawing nuggety illustrations from his deep knowledge of history and his personal experiences as a soldier, he held audiences rapt.

In the town of Launceston a young nurse-in-training, Patricia McCormack, attended one of Stanley's evangelistic meetings.

Stanley was not trying to charm anyone. He didn't have to. He simply came to the pulpit and faced his audience, perfect in posture, with a bold, honest countenance, small in stature but very large in character. Patricia McCormack found herself paying especially close attention to everything he said as well as everything he did.

When afterwards, on November 18, 1945, an acquaintance introduced Stanley to this fair and gentle young woman, Stanley could sense deep within her a kindredness of spirit he had not encountered before in any woman. Their acquaintance deepened into friendship and friendship soon ripened into love.

This time there was no awkward groping for the right approach. This time, romance and the will of God were *truly* in alignment for Stanley Albert Dale.

But Patricia was several years Stanley's junior and had still to complete her nurse's training. Stanley, meanwhile, uncovered an exciting prospect for fulfilling his desire to return to the interior of New Guinea as a missionary.

Alex Gilchrist, his old friend and spiritual father, had by now become the Australian secretary of an international missionary society called the Unevangelized Fields Mission. And unevangelized fields were exactly the kind of place Stanley longed to be!

Stanley applied for membership, was accepted for service in the wilds of New Guinea, and soon found himself touring the churches of New South Wales, Tasmania, and Victoria to announce his mission and to encourage financial backing for it.

Late in 1947, he set foot once again in New Guinea, this time as a commando for Christ, armed with a Bible instead of a Vickers machine gun.

THE UNFORGIVING MINUTE

AT WASUA, the Unevangelized Fields Mission's headquarters near the mouth of the Fly River, Stan received his first assignment: village school teaching among the Suki and Zimakani headhunters who lived in a region of swampy lagoons some two hundred miles by river from Wasua.

It was not an easy assignment. Suki youngsters, it turned out, regarded anything more than two or three days of school per week as an outright imposition on their way of life. Stan's 1948 diary abounds with entries that prove this.

They stole from him: knives, plates, pots and pans, and then something very close to his heart, his Returned from Active Service badge. On three consecutive days he went searching for it in vain.

To compound his problems, Stan lived in almost total isolation from fellow missionaries. For long periods of time, he received supplies and mail only once a month, or whenever a riverboat happened to stop by his lonely island in the Daviumbu Lagoon.

Sweltering days and long oppressive nights passed in endless succession, while he subjected himself to the tyranny of his near-impossible task as a teacher. Afternoons and evenings he kept his mind alert studying the Bible, the Zimakani and Motu languages, and moral philosophy, or penning letters to friends and supporters in Australia.

He also read and reread endearing letters from Patricia McCormack, who by now had completed nurse's training in Tasmania and enrolled as a student in Stan's alma mater, the Sydney Missionary and Bible College.

At times he wondered if Zimakani antagonism toward his unpopular duty might result in danger to his own person. Still, he ventured out every weekend to preach in villages around the lagoon, though few would listen.

Stanley took heart and pressed on, but by now problems of a different nature were beginning to gather around his head. Some of Stan's fellow missionaries, returning from rare visits to his lonely outpost, carried critical reports to Wasua that he was sometimes "too hard on the natives" or that he erred in not relying more heavily on local chieftains to help him settle grievances with the tribespeople.

But as Stanley had not allowed isolation, loneliness, oppressive climate, malaria, or wild tribespeople to daunt him, so also now a few critical words from fellow missionaries would not faze him either. Standing alone was something he had already learned to do quite well. Nevertheless his troubles in this particular quarter were to increase.

By September 1948, George Sexton, the mission's field leader, decided it was time Stan had a break from school teaching at Daviumbu. From the time Stan arrived in New Guinea, he had voiced his desire to follow the mighty Fly River to its source in the unexplored Star Mountains, searching for tribes that had not yet heard the gospel.

Sexton gave the go-ahead to Stanley, Ted Hicks, Fred Dawson, and Nigel Gore, a New Zealander. Within a few days they had stowed their gear in the mission's new riverboat, *Maino II,* and set out for the Star Mountains.

Stanley exulted. This was closer to the destiny he envisioned in coming to New Guinea. When they sailed as close to the mountains as rapids would allow, Stan and Nigel left the *Maino II* and struck out with carriers into unknown hinterlands. For weeks they trekked into the foothills, joyously pitting their strength against steep ascents and reeking swamps of guru palm, slashing through forests of giant fern, plunging through masses of snare-like roots and vines, and probing corridors of alpine forests, heavy with cloud-wet moss. Even so, at the apogee of their journey, Stanley and Nigel were still more than three days' trek from the fabled Star Mountains, with their twelve-thousand-foot peaks and their more populous, never-before-contacted tribes.

Along the way they encountered small bands of furtive tribesmen from whom they elicited with great difficulty scattered samples of tribal vocabulary as a guide to tribal boundaries in this unknown area.

Early in the trek, Stan wrote, "My feet were soon blistered from new boots. From then on I walked in bare feet, which were soon cut severely by the sharp grass. As every cut became a painful sore, walking became—" and here is a characteristic Dalean understatement "—uncomfortable."

Meanwhile their colleagues who remained with the *Maino II* faced a different problem. The level of the river dropped suddenly one night, leaving the launch stranded on a gravel bed! Thinking the river might remain at a low level for a long period of time, or that a flash flood descending rapidly from the mountains might swamp the *Maino II* before it could be properly uprighted, the captain dispatched Fred Dawson in a small accessory skiff for the three-hundred-mile return journey to Lake Murray, to radio Wasua for help.

But the next night the river rose, floating the *Maino II*. The captain decided to head downstream at once, before the water dropped again, endangering the mission's only large vessel. Weeks later Stanley and Nigel returned from their jungle odyssey and found a note advising them to make their way home as best they could by raft or canoe. Which they did!

Lashing trees together to form a raft and carving themselves paddles, they set out, sometimes navigating, sometimes simply drifting, along interminable bends of the crocodile-infested Fly. Weeks of strenuous exercise had conditioned every muscle to maximum efficiency. Beaching on the evening of November 25 at one end of an expansive wilderness sandbar, Stan and Nigel heaved their packs ashore and stood gazing wistfully over the smooth, inviting sand. Instantly the same thought occurred to both of them. Exchanging glances of mutual challenge, they were off. Limbs flailing, shouting for sheer exhilaration, bounding with incredible strides, they raced to the far end of the beach and back. After cooking their evening meal, they slept under the tropic stars.

Beginning December 1, the Fly bore them for some one hundred miles along the border of Dutch New Guinea, a land that entranced Stanley even more than Papua New Guinea, for it was said to be equally vast and even more mysterious.

Nigel and Stanley went ashore at a village named Boset. "A bamboo fife and drum band came out to meet us," Stan wrote. He came away from Boset with an unmistakable feeling that some day, he could not say when, he would bear the gospel of Christ to Dutch New Guinea also.

On December 3, unshaven and sun-bronzed South Pacific versions of Tom Sawyer and Huckleberry Finn, Stan and Nigel moved into Obo, the mission's northernmost outpost. Nigel dropped his pack on the porch of the mission house and laid down his paddle. A great weariness swept over him.

But not Stan! Someone handed him letter number 104 from Patricia. Grinning ear to ear, Stanley strode briskly away to a quiet place.

Stanley's next endeavor was to convince his colleagues that now was the time to extend their missionary operations into the areas which he and his colleagues had explored, and beyond them to the Star Mountains and across the border into Dutch New Guinea. To this end Stanley wrote eloquent reports based on his various explorations, urging the mission to contest at once "the previously undisputed sovereignty of Satan over lost tribes still under his sway." Some of his reports were published in the mission's Australian periodical, *Light and Life.*

But colleagues on the field found it a difficult decision to make. "Already we are stretched too thinly," reasoned some. "The ministries newly begun in these lowlands need to be strengthened first. Later, when we get reinforcements—"

To Stanley, such objections were merely excuses that indicated a lack of either vision or faith, or both. He continued to urge, even to agitate.

Stanley once delivered a sermon he titled, "God's Agitators." In it he quoted from *The New Acts of the Apostles,* by A. T. Pierson, regarding a reformer named Baron Von Welz: "Such men are God's agitators, sent to marshall the conscience of the church, to mold the law of its life, and the methods of its work, in conformity to His Word and will."

Stanley felt that the mission needed such a man for this hour, and he aspired to be such a man, if only they would hear him. So he pleaded verbally and by letter. When colleagues on the field would not heed him, he began writing home. And that is what finally precipitated action, but not the action he wanted.

On December 8 Stanley began translating the Gospel of Mark into the Zimakani language. Some of his schoolboys, responding to him now as a friend, helped him in the difficult task. Through these intense labors, insight into the meaning of the gospel at last broke through into the minds of some of these young men. On January 8, 1949, seven of them, deeply moved as Stanley preached, opened their hearts to Stanley's God.

Stanley wrote, "They seemed sincere as they prayed. I believe they are truly converted." And so he took heart. The first signs of a Zimakani harvest had appeared!

By April 8 Stanley and his apprentice translators rejoiced. They completed a first draft of the Zimakani Gospel of Mark!

On April 24 he baptized one of the seven in the lagoon.

Next day the blow struck.

Midmorning a riverboat chugged into Stanley's lagoon, bringing mail. Opening one of the letters, Stanley was stunned by the words: "We, the field council, have voted to terminate your membership on this field, and the home council in Australia has confirmed our decision. You will pack your belongings and leave at your earliest convenience."

He read on. The letter expressed appreciation for his various notable contributions. At the same time, his "marked individuality, bombastic attitude toward leadership, and attitude toward nationals" (a reference to the earlier criticisms leveled against him) had weighed the balance in favor of his dismissal.

There was another reason. The field council feared, perhaps justly, that Stanley's frankly critical letters to friends in Australia might undermine public confidence in their administration of the mission's Papuan field.

Stanley swallowed. Then he closed his eyes as hopes and dreams fell in shattered pieces around him. He looked down at the newly completed draft of the Gospel of Mark on the table and out across the bay to the village, where the Zimakani Christians would soon meet for prayer.

He had so hoped to lead those young believers through to maturity in Christ and to perfect that fledgling translation. But now—

Stanley squared his shoulders, took a deep breath, looked straight ahead, and whispered, "So this is what Kipling meant by 'the unforgiving minute.'"

He left Papua without saying a word against those who had dismissed him.

It seemed an interminable journey. From Daviumbu to Suki to Torerema to Mugu Muga to Wasua. Then out through the Toro Passage to Daru and across the Torres Strait to Thursday Island. There he stopped to work in the Public Works Department, chipping rust to earn pocket money for his onward journey.

June 13 he reached Cairns. It was a public holiday, and a band played, as if to cheer his lagging spirits.

In Sydney, Alex Gilchrist was waiting, hoping Stanley would stop by to see him at the mission office. He had been part of the council that felt compelled to confirm Stanley's dismissal.

The decision distressed Alex. It had not been easy to vote against this fiery young man whose tormented youth had conditioned him more for quick reaction and independence than for the diplomacy, gentleness, and teamwork required of a missionary.

Alex recalled the times he heard Stanley pour out his heart in prayer, wanting to *be* something for God, to attempt great things for God. If only he could pray together with Stanley again, counsel with him, remind him that men who never make mistakes usually never make anything else either.

But Stanley never got to the mission office. He found himself a job in Queensland and set to work at once. He needed more passage money, this time for passage to Tasmania.

November 5, 1949: Married. The service commenced at 4:30 P.M. Pat looked radiant in white and cream satin. Reception commenced at 5:45 P.M. Forty telegrams.

She had understood and loved him still.

"It's a boy, Stan."

On that cool August day in 1950, Stanley looked past the doctor through an open door. Pat, pale but smiling proudly, looked up at her husband from a hospital bed. With one arm she encircled a bundle of downy blankets, their edges opened like petals around a bright pink face. Stanley moved forward, buoyant with gladness, magnetized by the poignant beauty of mother and newborn child. And to think that God had given both to him, to cherish, to protect!

He smiled down. With utmost gentleness he touched tiny, wrinkled fingers curling and uncurling beside a dimpled chin. He thought of the future, of the days when he would teach his son the thoughts of God and of noble men, the wisdom of prophets and poets. "David—my son," he breathed, his heart welling with joy.

One month later David fell ill. The doctor labored. Stanley and Pat anguished in prayer beside the bed of their tiny son.

But David died.

" . . . triumph and disaster," Kipling had written. But for Stanley Albert Dale, the formula seemed to be reversed, and not only reversed but weighted heavily in favor of disaster.

"Our light affliction," he recalled from the New Testament, "works for us a far more exceeding and eternal weight of glory" (2 Cor. 4:17).

That hope he knew he could always fall back on. Yet he dared to believe that he actually trusted God to work a triumph of grace through him in *this* life as well. A triumph visible not only to heaven-secured saints and angels but to residents of this world also. Not that anyone should admire Stanley Dale, but rather his God.

Stanley sighed and, through his tears for David, looked down at a diploma he had just earned from the Summer Institute of Linguistics for completing a concentrated ten-week course in the SIL's technique of analyzing the grammar and sound systems of unwritten languages, such as those found in New Guinea.

Armed with this new training, Stan set out again for New Guinea, seeking a second chance to lead a truly pioneer mission to "a Christless tribe." Pat, meanwhile, remained with Stan's mother, Ethel, in Sydney.

Less than two months later, word came from Stan: "Please come at once, darling! I've found a place for us far to the west, along the Sepik River."

Together Stan and Pat pioneered a new work at Lumi and Eritei, among the Wapi tribespeople. Later they offered to place their work under the aegis of a mission society known as Christian Missions to Many Lands.

Christian Missions to Many Lands, or CMML, is a foreign arm of the Brethren Assemblies, an international fellowship of Christians that countenances no ordained or salaried pastors but propagates itself solely by lay leadership. Patricia and her family had been followers of the Brethren movement for many years, and Stanley, even apart from their influence, likewise found the Brethren ideal of hardy, grassroots independence from ecclesiastical domination exactly to his liking.

And so the Brethren and the CMML accepted Stanley and his fledgling work by the Sepik as part of their worldwide mission responsibility. They did so without querying the reasons why his earlier term of service with UFM had lasted only two years instead of the usual three or four. Nor did they ask UFM for a reference on him. Stanley impressed them very well indeed, and their own judgment was sufficient.

Soon the CMML dispatched still other missionaries to join Stan and Pat along the Sepik, and the work grew.

Stanley worked hard in the western Sepik. In addition to his regular physical labors and wide-ranging patrols in the task of evangelism, Stan learned the Wapi tribal language, spoken by a few thousand people around Eritei. Gaining fluency, he first authored several hymns as an aid to worship for newly established congregations. Then, even more strategic, Stan put his recently improved linguistic skill to work in translating assorted passages of the Bible into the Wapi language.

The experience of contemporary missionaries, as well as his own study of the history of the Christian church, convinced Stanley that translating the Scriptures into every man's mother tongue was a sacred obligation.

In a sermon delivered in 1950, Stanley proclaimed, "Four hundred years ago, William Tyndale was strangled and burned for giving the English people their own Bible. But as a result of his labors, English plough-boys came to know the gospel better in some instances than bishops in their cloisters! Tyndale could lay down his life a happy man!

"And so today also hundreds of young men and women count it worth any sacrifice of time, money, or life itself to give God's Word to all of earth's tribes in their own languages . . . Restless millions await the Word that makes all things new."

But once again Stanley was not to complete the translation he had begun. Nor would he remain to perfect the faith of the Wapi tribesmen he led to Christ.

After four years of service on the Sepik River, Stan and Patricia returned on furlough to Australia, joyfully presenting to Stan's two sisters near Sydney and to Patricia's family in Tasmania their two fine sons, Wesley and Hilary, born in New Guinea. Then Stan and Pat set out on deputation for CMML to Queensland. They were quickly recalled in mid-journey, however, by a letter from CMML spokesmen in Tasmania.

Later the spokesmen explained, "Stan, I'm sorry to inform you that you and your dear family will not be able to return to our work in the Sepik."

Stan gazed steadily at his friends, waiting for what was to follow.

"There are those on the field who object to your return, saying they disagree with your manner of disciplining the natives."

Once again a work Stan pioneered was taken from his hands and given to others.

Nothing is more difficult to understand about Stanley Albert Dale than his philosophy of discipline. As far as this biographer can discover, Stan never put his philosophy into writing. Nor did those of us who knew him ever hear him explain it verbally. Some of his critics assumed that there was no philosophy to be explained. He simply never learned to control his temper. Others, including some of his admirers, discerned behavior patterns deeply ingrained since childhood and tried to make allowance for him, acknowledging that all of us have our weaknesses.

But still others felt there was more depth to Stan's actions than mere background or habit could explain. They would credit his penchant for stern discipline as part of an incisive strategy for shaping human raw material into something more distinctly Christian in shorter periods of time. There is some evidence for this view. Stan had studied well the methods army sergeants use to traumatize raw recruits into toughened soldiers who would obey orders no matter how thick the battle. His writings and conversations, moreover, show that he regarded his missionary work as the spiritual equivalent of a life-or-death military conquest.

It must be acknowledged also that many of his converts *did* manifest a remarkable sense of soldierly responsibility. Saiga and Donoma, for example, were two of the Zimakani schoolboys who at first resented Stan's determined attempt not only to shape their morals but also to schedule their daily lives. Yet both came to acknowledge Stan as their "spiritual father." After Stan baptized him, Saiga remained true to the faith until his death in 1968. Donoma went on to become a leader of the evangelical movement in Papua.

But for Stan's Brethren colleagues along the Sepik River, his frequent sharp reprimands to errant natives were too much.

"It is a missionary's glory to rely upon example and moral persuasion only," they argued.

And so Stanley Albert Dale lost his second venue for serving Christ in New Guinea.

For most missionaries one dismissal from foreign service, added to the acknowledged inconveniences and frustrations of the vocation, would be ample persuasion to abandon any further pursuit of a missionary career. And for the remainder, a second successive dismissal would invariably squelch any last, lingering desire to make a go of such an exacting task.

But there was one missionary who was, as usual, an exception: Stanley Albert Dale.

After a season of work as a schoolteacher in Tasmania (made possible by a letter of recommendation from the director of education in Port Moresby), Stanley applied again for active missionary service, this time in Dutch New Guinea, that vast and inscrutably mysterious territory lying west of regions Stan previously explored.

His choice of a mission this time was the Regions Beyond Missionary Union (RBMU), one of at least four interdenominational sending agencies established in the nineteenth century upon principles laid down by J. Hudson Taylor, a pioneering spirit of modern Christian missions.[1]

Founded in 1873 in London, England, RBMU became the first mission to answer David Livingstone's famous 1878 plea from the heart of Africa, "Send me your young men!"

In the same year, RBMU sent eight young missionaries, trained by serving five years in the slums of East London, to the disease-ridden Congo. Within a matter of years, half of them fell victim to the Congo's voracious fevers, but others went out to take their places. And others. Wave after wave of them, young, spirited, undaunted by the certain knowledge that at least half their number were marked for early, hideous death from tropical disease.

As a result the church of Jesus Christ was established in a wide swath of northern central Congo.

The work in the Congo was only the beginning. With the turn of the century, other deputations ventured out to India and Nepal, across the Atlantic to Peru, and in the lapse between the two world wars, to Borneo.

Always the emphasis of the mission paralleled the words Paul the apostle wrote to the church he established at Corinth: " . . . hoping . . . to preach the Gospel in *the regions beyond* you" (2 Cor. 10:16)—that is, in virgin territory where others had not yet labored.

Finally, after the Second World War, a new vision—the interior of Dutch New Guinea, western half of the immense, largely unexplored island called New Guinea.

As RBMU's outreach widened, new offices were opened in still other cities of the developed world—Philadelphia, Toronto, and finally Melbourne, Australia. It was to the executive secretary of this latter office that Stanley Albert Dale presented himself in October 1958.

W. M. Jarvie looked Stan over. The need for reinforcements for RBMU's fledgling work in Dutch New Guinea was urgent. Thus far the mission's task force penetrating Dutch New Guinea's vast interior wilderness consisted only of young Canadian and American recruits.

Mr. Jarvie was eager to see his own motherland, Australia, contribute some of her young strength to this new frontier so close to her own borders.

This man named Dale, Mr. Jarvie mused, *small frame, but obviously very strong, and with eight years total experience in soldiering and missionering in Papua New Guinea; could he and his wife form Australia's first contingent for RBMU's Dutch New Guinea operation?*

For an hour or more, the friendly mission statesman and the would-be applicant chatted in the former's living room. They sipped tea on an outside porch. They strolled together in Jarvie's garden. Then Mr. Jarvie handed Stanley a set of application papers.

W. M. Jarvie is dead now. It is too late to ask him if he ever ferreted out the reasons why Stan was applying for membership in his *third* foreign mission society. Nor do the letters Jarvie left in the mission's file shed any light on the matter. We know simply that he did not ask either UFM or CMML for written references on Stan. He did, however, obtain verbal references through his own widespread personal contacts, some of which may have included associates of UFM or CMML.

At any rate, Stanley submitted his written application. And in May 1959 the Australian Council of RBMU gathered in Melbourne to make a fateful decision: to accept or reject the application of Stanley Albert Dale for service in interior Dutch New Guinea.

"I have spoken to some who have reservations about him," Jarvie confided, "and to others who praise him highly as a man of boundless dedication."

"What is your own evaluation?" a council member asked.

Jarvie spread out the papers on the table before him, papers covered with Stan's large, uneven scrawl.

"Dale may have more rough edges than we would like," he began, "but then the interior of Dutch New Guinea is no place for delicate men."

So the discussion began, a discussion which concluded that although Stan might not be a man for the "finishing work" in RBMU's mission, he could obviously make an immense contribution in the punishing initial phase, with its weeks of trekking into the unknown, its grueling labor in mud and rain, and its constant confrontation with danger.

By the time Jarvie finished his evaluation, there was no doubt in anyone's mind; God had given the young ex-commando a special gift for *that* kind of ministry, even if for no other. And by the time that crucial first stage of the work in Dutch New Guinea was finished, they would know if he had gifts for other kinds of work.

"I think this man is worth a try," Jarvie concluded, "and afterwards we'll see."

Fourteen months later, backed financially by Brethren Assemblies and other Christian friends in Australia, Stanley, Patricia, and their four children—Wesley, Hilary, Rodney, and six-month-old baby Joy—landed at Hollandia, a tiny enclave of civilization on the north coast of Dutch New Guinea.

Stanley emerged from the aircraft and planted his feet squarely on the famous Sentani airstrip, built first by Japanese occupation forces, seized later by General MacArthur, and now used as a commercial airport. He gazed around him.

Beyond the airfield the jungle-covered slopes of Mount Cyclops soared majestically into cloud and reappeared in jumbled peaks above the cloud, floating in a world of their own.

Then he gazed southwestward, where deceptively low foothills belied the jagged fifteen-thousand-foot ranges hidden some distance behind them. He thought of the many lost tribes living wild among those ranges, still unaware of man's true destiny, and of the unknown thresholds he now dared to cross with his wife and children.

It's my third opportunity, he thought, *and by the grace of God, I'll make it good!* If his goal eluded him again, there would not be another chance. The years were slipping by too fast.

This time, somewhere among those uncharted ranges, he must find a tribe, his own tribe, some lonely place where there would be no meddling critics to descend upon him and cut short his work before he had time to bring it to fruition.

With Pat by his side, he would put both his faith in God and his theories of missionary practice to the test against who knows what odds. With every last sinew, he must struggle against those odds until the most meaningful wonder on earth, a New Testament church, shone forth in the most unlikely setting on earth, the stone-age hell of interior Dutch New Guinea!

And in the process he would prove to all his critics that he was indeed a man for all seasons. Not just a foot-slogging pioneer, but a perfecter of the thing pioneered as well.

He would prove this time that he was a man with a genuine call from God and not just a crank with an obsession for working among primitive people, as some of his critics had begun to suspect.

Stanley set his jaw, musing again on Kipling's lines "Something lost beyond the ranges, lost and waiting for you—go!" *He was on his way!*

Note

1. Regions Beyond Missionary Union (RBMU) is now known as World Team.

SOMETHING LOST

| Chapter 9 |

FROM Pat's diary—July 13, 1960: *We said good-bye at 6:30 A.M. to friends at RBMU's coastal base. Pilot Paul Pontier flew us over miles of sago swamp.*

Next a wilderness of broken ridges forced the single-engined aircraft higher. Then the ridges dropped away again into a vast interior swamp called the Lakes Plain. Through its center the Idenburg River roiled like some awesome prehistoric python, looping and coiling from horizon to horizon.

And beyond the Idenburg, the *real* mountains! Unnamed sawtooth ridges challenged the tiny craft to eleven thousand feet. Like a bright yellow fly, it buzzed through a gap in the ramparts, then dropped with dizzying speed into a valley called "Swart"—after a Dutch explorer who discovered it two decades earlier. A postage-stamp airstrip beckoned from between green ridges. It was known as Karubaga—RBMU's main base in Dutch New Guinea.

The pilot banked still more steeply. For several minutes the airplane spiraled downward, while peaks, cliffs, waterfalls, luxuriant yam gardens, and ridgetop villages of tiny cone-roofed houses whirled in profusion past the windows.

When finally the little craft touched turf and rolled to a stop, its six passengers looked out at an awesomely unfamiliar landscape and the most alien-looking beings one could imagine! It was as if the little aircraft had somehow spirited them through time as well as space, back into some long-forgotten world. Milling hordes of stone-age men, women, and children—thousands of whom had newly embraced the Christian faith—blinked back at the Dale family in mutual astonishment. The pilot swung open a door and a tumult of voices crashed in, all exclaiming in strange polysyllabic words.

Then, abruptly, voices in English, with Canadian and American accents, welcomed the Dales to their new home. The North Americans looked Stan over as he alighted with a bounce from the Cessna. By now he was a crusty forty-four-year-old veteran, brusque-mannered but appealingly honest—and very much his own man. His right eye squinted nearly shut, in deference to his many years under a bright tropical sun. It opened wide only in moments of rare emotion. But his left eye, green and bright, pierced you with a sharp gaze that could take your measure in a moment. Crested with fiercely tufted brows, both eyes narrowed at their corners into furrows that continued downward past his ears to his jaw.

When Stanley Dale shook their hands, his grip was strong. One thing was obvious: a man of set purpose had been added to their number. Stan's every conversation, his movements, and his bearing indicated that purpose burning in him like a flame in a lamp.

And so the new mission began. After he helped Pat and the children get settled in one of the local mission residences, Stan reported for work with hammer, saw, and a carpenter's apron bulging with nails.

In spite of his forty-four years, Stan worked as hard and as steady as the youngest of his colleagues. Moreover he knew how to brighten a dull job on a rainy day with Aussie puns and aptly chosen quotations from Wordsworth, Masefield, or Blake.

The Yanks and Canucks were impressed. They liked him. Friendships began to form.

But at times—early in the morning or under the stars at night—Stan would draw apart from the missionary community and look away to the wild horizons of the valley, communing alone with God and with his own private vision of some other valley even more remote than the Swart. Already the Swart Valley was too thickly populated with missionaries for his liking. Missionaries, according to Stan Dale's creed, must always be scattered as thinly as possible over the earth, each one doing, ideally, the work of three or four people. As soon as they began to concentrate their numbers for their own fellowship and comfort (except for brief conference periods once a year or so), they were drifting away from the Great Commission of their Master, who had commanded that they go into all the world.

But the mission force the Dales joined in Dutch New Guinea was itself hardly lacking in idealism. Reconnoitering other branches of the sprawling Swart Valley, which was more thickly populated than many areas of Dutch New Guinea, they opened two other outposts with airstrips: Kangime in September 1960, just two months after the Dales' arrival, and Mamit in April 1961.

Stan himself shared in the expansion. With his commando experience in the use of dynamite, he was frequently called to new airstrip sites to blast room-size boulders out of the way, earning himself the nickname "Dynamite Dale."

As the younger missionaries trekked back and forth between Karubaga and the new airstrip sites, competition developed to see who could log the fastest trekking time between Karubaga and Kangime, or Karubaga and Mamit.

A would-be record-breaker would first check his watch with that of someone remaining at Karubaga and then set out, racing over high ranges and deep gorges until at last he reached the radio shack at the new site.

Then someone at Karubaga would hear a nearly breathless voice gasp over the wireless, "I'm here!"

Inevitably Stan was drawn into the competition. Could the rugged old veteran match the speed and stamina of the younger men?

Determined to prove that he could, Stan set out one day for Mamit. Dani carriers laden with dynamite fell far behind as Stan, with one burly-limbed Dani escort to carry his salt and a flask of drinking water, struck out ahead. Unfortunately, even the lightly laden Dani could not maintain the pace. When Stan began to feel weak from loss of sweat, he paused to ask the carrier for an invigorating lick of salt and a refreshing drink of water. The escort was nowhere in sight. Rather than lose precious minutes, Stan pressed on in spite of weakness and thirst.

By the time he reached Mamit, Stan was delirious. Swooning to the floor of the radio shack, he lay there reciting great facts of history to concerned colleagues who gathered around to offer him salt and water. When at last he recovered, they had good news for him.

He had broken the record by far!

Stan spent much of his free time pouring over a five-foot-wide United States Air Force map of Dutch New Guinea, drawn almost entirely from aerial photographs. Carefully he noted the known details of the land, as well as the unfilled blank spaces.

Stan listened one day as Missionary Aviation Fellowship (MAF) pilot Bob Johannson described a certain valley he had sighted from the air. It lay in a particularly rugged region of the Snow Mountains. Later Stan located it on his map. The river flowing southward through it was unnamed, like so many hundreds of other rivers in Dutch New Guinea. The valley was well beyond the proximity of any established mission or Dutch government post, yet not so distant that it would be infeasible to reach it on foot.

For a reason Stan could not fully understand, the valley seemed to call him. He pondered, and prayed. Finally he mentioned his interest in the valley to Bob Johannson. Bob responded, "I can take you there for an aerial survey, if you desire."

Stan desired. He approached his colleagues about the matter early in 1961. "We have established ourselves well in every main branch of the Swart Valley," he reasoned. "Yet we have a new missionary family arriving, on the average, every three months. Should we not now launch a probe to new areas of operation?"

It was an intriguing proposition. They liked it, and they believed the Spirit of God was behind it.

As Stan wrote, "In March we held our annual conference, which was a time of great blessing . . . At this conference Pat and I expressed our desire to go to a completely unevangelized tribe, and the conference agreed that this seemed to be the Lord's leading."

So, on March 20, 1961, Stan's colleagues in the Swart Valley granted him his dream. They officially commissioned him and Pat to occupy in

Christ's name that unknown and unnamed valley that called to Stan from the surface of his air force chart.

But Stan and Pat were not to go alone. The conference decided that Bruno de Leeuw, a soft-spoken bachelor recruit newly arrived from Canada, should share the new outreach alongside them. Stan and Pat agreed to this.

Stan notified his supporters in Australia, "Mr. Bruno de Leeuw and myself will trek toward the new area in about a week's time. Pray for us as we make this move. The tribe to which we are going is uncontrolled and its language unknown. The only thing we really know about them is their location."

The first step was a reconnaissance flight.

In the unknown valley, sunrise fell softly upon the village of Balinga. From its lofty position at the head of the Heluk Valley, the village surveyed both the enemy slopes east of the river and many of the friendly ridges and gorges of its allies on the west.

In the dim light of dawn, Sunahan and his brother Kahalek, armed to the teeth, descended a slope to their garden near the Heluk River. With utmost care they scrutinized the river for any sign that enemies from Kobak might have bridged it during the night, for the season of war that began many moons earlier with the killing of Selambo was still in full sway.

Detecting no sign of enemy incursion, the two men advanced to the center of their gardens, laid down their weapons, and began digging for sweet potatoes. Occasionally they looked up warily at the enemy slopes towering above them across the river. On those slopes they could see every Kobak garden penciled in by its own stone walls and every enemy village outlined in the smoke of its own cooking fires.

But the enemies themselves, to Sunahan and Kahalek's relief, were nowhere in sight.

A moment later it seemed to Sunahan that a flock of swallows darted past him. In the next instant, one of the "swallows" buried its head in Kahalek's side.

"Ambush!" Kahalek shrieked, yanking the bloody cane-shafted barb tip out of his flesh. As if spurred by a single mind, both brothers snatched up their weapons and bolted through a savage hail of arrows toward a low stone wall at the far edge of their garden.

"I'm hit again!" Kahalek shrieked, and then added, "Mobahai—Mobahai—I must reach you!"

Sunahan leaped over the stone wall. Instantly he whirled to see if Kahalek—

To Sunahan's utter anguish, Kahalek lay dying just three strides from safety. Enemy warriors swarmed like bees, shooting still more "reeds" into Kahalek's body. Another enemy, wearing a heavy rattan war vest, stood just outside the wall, with his eye on Sunahan and an arrow fitted to his bow.

But he did not release the arrow, for Mobahai, the ground upon which Sunahan stood, was the *kwalu* refuge for the northwestern corner of the Heluk Valley, as Ninia was for the central region. He merely stood ready, lest Sunahan step out of the refuge to try to avenge his brother's death.

But in the heat of his anger, Sunahan forgot for the moment that he, too, was forbidden to wage war while he stood upon holy ground, even though his brother's killers stood within easy range of the bow he held in his hand.

With a cry of rage, he drew bow and released an arrow at the lone enemy who stood watching him. The enemy's eyes opened wide in unbelief as Sunahan's bow twanged.

Did not this youth from Balinga understand the wene melalek?

Sunahan's arrow struck the enemy's war vest and stopped dead.

"Lucky for you!" the enemy shouted above the roar of the nearby river. "Had your arrow drawn my blood, your own friends would have hurled you into the Heluk!"

Sunahan shuddered, realizing what he had done. For a moment he expected the enemy to match his violation of the *wene melalek* with return fire. But the enemy simply retreated, remaining true to the code of the ancients.

Sunahan burned with shame.

Other men from Balinga were coming now, streaming down a high ridge overlooking the refuge. The raiders melted away toward the river, leaving Kahalek's corpse a bloody, arrow-riddled heap upon the green leaves of the garden.

Sunahan climbed quickly to a nearby vantage point. He was curious to see how the enemy would escape across the river without a bridge. With unbelieving eyes he watched as they walked calmly across, apparently treading on air above the white rapids! But then he focused his eyes and saw under their feet what had not been visible to him from higher ridges in the dim light of early dawn—a white bridge!

Later he discovered how the ingenious Kobak people camouflaged the bridge in white. During the night they jerry-rigged a span of poles across a narrows of the Heluk and covered it with large leaves from the kobak tree (which grows in profusion east of the Heluk, giving the area its name). The underside of kobak leaves is a whitish-green color. Binding leaves to the bridge with their undersides up rendered the bridge virtually invisible against the foaming water, especially in the dim light of early morning.

Sunahan's anger mingled with admiration. He thought he was undeceivable, but they had deceived him. And the deception cost Kahalek his life.

Now he wondered what his own sin would cost *him*.

"It is said you released an arrow while standing upon holy ground!"

The priests of Balinga surrounded Sunahan, their brows lowered in consternation.

"It is true, my fathers," he confessed, looking at the ground. "My heart was swollen because of my brother's death. I forgot part of the ancient words and released an arrow. But it did not draw blood. It deflected from my enemy's war vest and fell to the earth. What shall I do?"

The priests consulted together in the house of *Kembu* and then returned their verdict.

"You are still a youth who has not yet been put into the mystery of either *kwalu* or *morowal*, and you have not yet learned the sacred words perfectly. Our judgment is that you must sacrifice a pig to *kembu* spirits for your sin."

As the smoke of Sunahan's sacrifice ascended toward the heavens, the Yali heard it—Bob Johannson's small, yellow plane spiralling down from the Mugwi Pass.

Through a portal framed in glowing cloud, Stanley and Bruno glimpsed a great triangular bowl basking under an open sky—the valley's northern end. Bob Johannson, the pilot, banked again, and suddenly they were through the portal and spiraling down between the three serrated rims which until now had kept this valley a world apart.

Stan noted the confluence of two mountain streams that joined at the head of the valley to form its main river. The formation of gorges surrounding this, the valley's central aorta, suggested a gigantic letter *Y*. Henceforth, until its true name was known, Stan and Bruno called it the "Y" Valley. Here, in the confluence of that massive *Y*, they saw a prospective airstrip site.

Near the junction of the *Y*, a plume of smoke drew their attention to a sprawling ridgetop village—Balinga. Frightened warriors scattered as the aircraft swooped low overhead.

"That will be the first village we'll reach when we walk down from the pass," Stan said to Bruno. They turned down-valley looking for an alternative airstrip site. They could see only one possibility, a slope between two contiguous villages. In the center of the slope was a small knoll peaked with a curious, tall structure surrounded by a circular stone wall. Everywhere else they looked, sharp ridges and horrendous gorges ruled out other airstrip sites. At this second site, Stan and Bruno dropped gifts of steel cutting tools for tribesmen living adjacent to the area. Then they returned over the pass to Johannson's base at distant Wamena.

In the valley behind them, a shaken population emerged from a thousand hiding places and gathered in open spaces in gardens or villages, gazing steadily toward the high Mugwi Pass, where clouds now closed behind the droning intruder.

"What does this mean, brother?" Wanla asked Andeng. "That roaring spirit-bird dropping strange objects from the sky—"

Andeng had no answer. Did even the spirits know what this strange phenomenon signified? And if they knew, would they show the priests what should be done, if anything?

Andeng trembled.

BEYOND THE RANGES

Chapter 10

THEIR aerial survey completed, Stan, Bruno, their five Dani carriers, and their two guides threaded their way up the Mugwi Valley, a branch of the famous Balim Gorge. Doggedly they labored across slopes scalloped with sweet potato gardens, passing village after ridgetop village of pointy-roofed Dani huts ("humpies," Stan called them in his terse Aussie idiom).

In each village they tried to enlist interim carriers but with little success. Men in each successive hamlet seemed afraid of men in the next. The further they climbed, the steeper the mountains rose before them. Finally, gasping like distance runners, they passed beyond the last human habitation and faced the mist-caressed slopes that led upward into remote alpine forests.

The Mugwi River, which at lower elevations drowned their voices in its thunder, now dwindled to a muted trickle, like a worshiper descending hushed from the presence of a god.

Climbing into a heavy rainstorm, they penetrated the alpine forests. Gnarled trees, dripping with rain and draped with moss, orchids, fungi, and twisted lianas, overhung their path in ominous shapes. At still higher elevations, the moss grew more dense, deadening all sound. The two explorers and their helpers had to raise their voices to be heard clearly beyond a distance of a few meters.

After the rain, cold mist descended upon them, surrounding them in thick gloom and chilling the sweat in their shirts. Bruno stopped to unpack an extra sweater. He slipped it on, shivering, then hurried to catch up to the party lest he lose them in the mist. They could not hear him call if he lost his way. This silence was unlike anything he had ever experienced. It seemed unnatural.

Hour by hour they pressed upward. Mist, amoeba-like, thickened around them. By midafternoon Yamwi, a Mugwi dweller and the party's main guide, quickened his pace to reach a cave where he knew they would be sheltered against the night's freezing temperatures. Some of the Danis likewise quickened their pace to keep Yamwi in sight, but Stan and Bruno and the remaining Danis fell behind and soon found themselves in falling darkness with a tent but no sleeping bags! The other Danis had borne most of the packs on ahead, not realizing that night would fall so quickly.

And so, while the other Danis and Yamwi snuggled by a warm fire in a limestone cave, Stan, Bruno, and their remaining escorts spent a sleepless night shivering in bitterly cold rain and wind. Next morning Yamwi and his party came back and found Stan and Bruno, befuddled with cold and bedraggled with lack of sleep. Needless to say, Stan had a few sharp words to say to them. The Danis were mortified, even though the mistake was not intentional.

Warmed by the morning sun, the party climbed still higher ridges, crossing Mugwi Pass at ten thousand feet. But as they started down into the Heluk, cold rain struck again, chilling them to the bone. Stan used kerosene to make damp wood burn, and everyone was warmed for the onward journey. The trail, however, led now through deep bogs treacherously disguised with a heavy turf of alpine grass. Whenever they stepped on weak places in the turf, it gave way, plunging them into slimy mud below.

Beyond the bogs, they descended again below treeline. Yamwi and young Emeroho, a Yali youth who had ventured out of the Heluk a few months earlier, still led the way. Stan and Bruno could hardly keep from quickening their pace. The unknown valley and its unknown people were now only a few hours' walk below them.

And yet, one by one, each member of the party endured his own private moment of doubt. What had he gotten himself into? What kind of people might be waiting below, and what might they do? That last night at an outpost called Hetigima, the local tribesmen gestured ominously toward the Mugwi Pass, warning of the implacable hostility of the people who lived beyond it.

Several thousand feet below the trekkers, four Yali women from Balinga, Kopai, Yal, Mul, and Wo, found themselves surrounded by warriors from Yabi, a village allied with the Kobak people. Even though it was useless, they tried to flee.

The more the laughing enemy shot arrows into their bodies the slower the women ran. One by one the four toppled and lay still among the yam plants they had tilled.

Last to fall was Kopai. Just before she died, she lumbered, arrow-heavy, to within sight of the weed-covered stone wall of Mobahai. But unlike Sunahan, she did not seek refuge there. Instead she turned aside from the wall with a horror almost as great as that which made her flee from her enemies.

For the *kembu* spirits of that place were not her gods. They were the gods of only half the Heluk population—the male half. In fact, the glory of the *kembu* spirits who haunted that place could increase only to the degree that women were excluded from their presence. The *Kembu*'s holy ground, therefore, offered no refuge to Kopai. For her to enter that holy ground, even to escape death, would only assure her death at the hands of her own relatives.

She preferred to die at the hands of enemies.

Although it was too late for Nindik, Alisu, Kopai, and others, the ambassadors of a God who wanted to shepherd the *whole* population were now close at hand. It had taken a long time, a very long time, for such as they to attempt that high cold rim.

But they were over it now and coming down as fast as their weary limbs could walk.

Bruno suggested sending Emeroho ahead to prepare the people of the valley for their coming, but Stan advised against it. Such guides had at times, in the history of European-Melanesian contact, been known to turn traitor at the last moment, proclaiming instead that their employers were evil men who should be killed before they had a chance to cast a baneful spell upon the people.

Sometimes it took so little to precipitate a change of heart in one's guide—a disappointment in trading at a distant post years earlier or even a childish hankering to observe a spectacle. On one occasion a native forerunner reportedly advised a certain group of Papuan warriors that two white travelers passing nearby were immortal. "If you shoot arrows at them," he expounded, "you will see the arrows deflect away." Eager to witness this phenomenon of indestructibility, the warriors fired a volley of arrows. The two travelers died from their wounds.

So Stan and Bruno chose to risk a sudden, unannounced appearance. The choice, however, was taken out of their hands, for on the final night of their descent from Mugwi Pass, Emeroho, their Yali boy guide, slipped away to warn his people.

"We continued down the mountainside," Stan wrote later, "in seemingly never-ending fog, past peat-black bogs and through a dripping moss forest. Our carriers, awed by the unnatural silence, filed noiselessly among twisted, moss-draped trees. About midday the clouds lifted, revealing cleared country below us. At 2:30 P.M. we emerged from the forest."

The four cremation pyres were ready. Wailing relatives bearing the torn and blood-stained corpses of hapless Kopai and her three friends filed down from Balinga's lofty ridge. Meanwhile, across the Heluk, swarms of Yabi men, joined by their Kobak allies, kept up a howl of exultation, taunting the mourners, even daring them to try to cross the river and take revenge. But of course Balinga villagers would not be so foolish. They simply said in their hearts, "Your exultation will be short-lived, O enemy! For the time will come when we will be upon the ridge and you in the valley."

One of the favorite and most stinging challenges that the Yabi shouted was, "Fools! Why cremate all that delicious flesh? Bring it here and let us dispose of it for you!"

Tenderly the mourners laid the four women upon their final beds of gnarled and knotted wood, then kindled fire beneath them. A gust of wind billowed smoke from the four pyres. The tempo of wailing increased with the staccato of crackling flame. Some relatives, crying and wiping tears from their faces, pushed protruding hands and feet back in among the flames. Others embraced children left motherless by the killings and tried to explain why it was necessary for their mothers to be burned.

And while the little ones shrieked in horror, their mothers vanished in flame and smoke. Those who were old enough to understand what was happening covered their ears, trying not to hear that horrible, loud sizzle.

High above, an old man of Balinga crouched on a stone wall, watching the cremation. Suddenly a shout behind him caused him to turn. A boy—Emeroho—was approaching swiftly from the direction of the Mugwi Pass.

Tersely Emeroho communicated his news to the old man, "*Duongs* are descending from the Mugwi Pass!"

Duong was Emeroho's corruption of *tuan,* an Indonesian word the Dani tribe used to describe Europeans. Emeroho had learned the word at Hetigima.

Before the old man could ask what a *duong* was, Emeroho hurried on past him, eager to warn his own people down-valley at Hwim and Sivimu.

Duong? the old man pondered, trying to remember if he had ever heard the term before. Shaking his head in confusion, he rose to his feet and jogged creakily downhill toward the site of the cremation. Barging in among the mourners, he pointed with his walking stick back toward the Mugwi and repeated Emeroho's warning:

"*Duongs* are descending from the Mugwi!"

Decibel by decibel, the tumult of a hundred mingled dirges subsided. Then abruptly all was silent save the dying crackle of four cremation fires and the distant exultation of enemies from Yabi and Kobak.

"*Duongs* are descending from the Mugwi!" the old man repeated.

"What on earth are *duongs*?" someone asked.

"*Duongs* are spirits in the shape of men!" called an authoritative voice from the edge of the crowd. Everyone turned as a tall youth named Suwi rose to his feet. Suwi also had crossed the Mugwi and heard Dani warriors babble excitedly about strange beings who had newly come down through the Balim Valley to Hetigima.

Meanwhile relatives of the four slain women were growing impatient at this preposterous interruption to the funeral of their loved ones.

"Go and see if it is true!" they commanded. So Suwi and his friends set out immediately toward the Mugwi. Behind them wailing for the dead echoed afresh. Before long almost everyone had forgotten the old man's arcane pronouncement. A few hours later, when the priests had completed their disposal of the ashes, came a sharp reminder.

Suddenly a strange commotion broke out among the enemy across the Heluk. From their position they could see past the bluff below which the Balinga mourners gathered. They were all pointing at something in the direction of the Mugwi.

No further warning was needed. The mourners disbanded. Women and children scurried uphill and popped into tiny *homias* like rabbits into their burrows. Men and youths, forgetting their sorrow, swarmed uphill and lined along the far village wall, weapons ready.

A revelation in a floppy Australian bush hat, Stan stood spread-legged, hands on hips, and looked up fearlessly at the ridgeline blackening suddenly with armed warriors. Beside him an ashen-faced Suwi, newly conscripted as guide in Emeroho's place and still uncertain whether he was privileged or doomed, awaited his "supernatural" employer's next unfathomable whim. Stan, with prayer in his heart, adrenaline in his veins, and spring in his step, stretched his hands out palms up as a gesture of peace and advanced boldly straight toward the nearest warriors.

Confused shouting broke out among the men of Balinga. Stan came straight on, light-footed and dashing, as if for all the world he was playing Mercury to Bruno's Jupiter! Weak-willed youths melted into hiding. Only the bravest men dared stand before his advance, and even they were trembling!

"*Nakni!* My fathers!" Stan called, using a term he had learned from Emeroho. Suddenly Suwi found his tongue and did his best to explain the inexplicable. The Balinga men, recognizing Suwi as one of their own, gradually came closer. The initial contact was established! Stan later wrote of this moment in his typically romantic style:

We had come into the forgotten valley. Our journey had ended. Our task had begun!

Next Stan and Bruno descended past Balinga toward the Heluk, intending to measure the first of the two prospective airstrip sites that lay just beyond it on a gentle slope below Yabi's beetling brow. Round a bend of the valley, they noticed warriors of Yabi and Kobak lining up fully armed along the far bank. Balinga, meanwhile, thronged downhill behind Stan, Bruno, and their carriers, shouting at full cry.

The impression the Balinga warriors wanted to convey was, of course, that these strangers had come to ally themselves with Balinga and were now leading a full-scale punitive attack, presumably with awesome supernatural power in attendance, against Yabi and Kobak!

As far as the Yabi and Kobak warriors could see, it appeared to be the truth. Uncertainty swept through their ranks, but still they prepared to make a stand. War cries went up. Arrows came level. Black palmwood bows were flexed in readiness.

Stan and Bruno, of course, still had no inkling of the political situation they had stumbled into. But one thing was clear: the warriors across the river were warning them not to cross. This, of course, constituted a challenge. And for Stanley Albert Dale there was only one thing to do with a challenge: meet it.

"All right, mates!" he barked. "I'll call your bluff!"

Stan advanced boldly toward the Yabi-Kobak horde. Bruno, Suwi and the five Danis, and the host of Balinga warriors watched in amazement. (It was the latter who were bluffing! Balinga did not really want the strangers to lead an open attack; they hoped merely to put the enemy to flight by the *appearance* of one!)

To reach his challengers, Stan crossed the tributary, which led down from the Mugwi, on a low-slung Yali suspension bridge. Then he walked past a low ridge to the foaming Heluk. Here there was no bridge, for it was the edge of enemy territory. Stan judged the river low enough to ford, and he plunged into the white water, right under the bows of the highly agitated Yabi and Kobak warriors.

Bruno's heart sank as he prayed desperately for Stan's safety. Stan was now completely beyond human help.

The Balinga hillside became as a massive colosseum, awed spectators straining to see the lone martyr stride forward to take the lions by their beards!

Thigh-deep in surging water, Stan looked up at the Yabi-Kobak host. Some already had their bows ready. Others waved their arms at him in one last warning: "Go back!"

"Go back?" Stan mused to himself. "Sorry, mates—it's too late for me to turn back, eighteen years too late! I have not come all this way to turn back at the word of men."

He waded forward. The current was stronger than he expected, and he took his eyes off his antagonists on the far bank in order to find sure footing.

Looking down at Stan, the Yabi and Kobak men were stunned. What sort of man is this, they asked, who would advance alone and unarmed (for they had no idea that the stick slung over his shoulder was a weapon), placing himself at the mercy of men on high ground?

He certainly did not look insane or demon possessed. Rather his face radiated the confidence of a priest arbitrating a dispute. Simultaneously several of the Yabi men discerned the truth. The stranger was not advancing as an ally of Balinga but as a neutral agent who desired to align himself with both sides of the valley.

"Don't kill him!" someone shouted. Bowstrings relaxed.

Stan later wrote, "When I reached the bank, most of the men had disappeared! Those remaining apparently decided to be friendly."

Bruno, Suwi, and the others saw Stan beckon them to follow. With a sigh of relief, they joined Stan across the river. They set up camp on the edge of a wide slope below Yabi hamlet, couched between the Heluk and one of its eastern tributaries.

"Suwi says these two villages on either side of us are at war," a Dani confided to Stan. "That's why the Balinga men are afraid to come across to our campsite."

"We'll see about that tomorrow morning," Stan replied.

"Suwi!"

Suwi came running.

"Go tell the war chiefs of your village—Balinga—and of Yabi up there to come down here to our camp *and make peace!*"

As Stan's words filtered through Swart Valley Dani into the Mugwi dialect and finally into Suwi's understanding, Suwi was stunned. Him? A mere youth? Relay a command to his own elders and his enemies to end a war that had continued so long it was virtually a way of life? Who did this green-eyed stranger think he was?

But one look at the green-eyed stranger convinced Suwi that he had no choice. Such an incredible authority came through that gaze!

What shall I say? How can I persuade them? he started to ask. But the words never got through to Stan. Seeing Suwi's hesitation, Stan gripped the lad firmly by the shoulders, spun him around, and sent him on his way with no uncertain assistance.

Somehow Suwi kept going, with his heart in his mouth, right up that dreaded slope toward Yabi, even within bow range. Truculent men came out to meet him, a subtle grin on their faces.

Quickly Suwi blurted his message: "The strangers are spirits called *duongs*. Whenever the *duongs* enter a valley, everyone in that valley must stop fighting!"

To Suwi's surprise, something of that green-eyed *duong*'s authority seemed to flow through his words, gathering momentum as he continued. "Now that these *duongs* have arrived, they command us all to make peace. You are to come down to their camp and make the necessary arrangements."

As if to emphasize Suwi's point, Bob Johannson's yellow Cessna darted again through the Mugwi Pass and spiraled rapidly down into the valley, guided by two signal fires lit by Bruno and the Dani carriers. Banking close to looming mountain ridges, Johannson swooped low over the signal fires, and in one fleeting instant, Stan and Bruno caught a glimpse of RBMU colleague David Martin energetically kicking bundles of provisions and tools out of the aircraft's open side.

Crash!

A five-gallon drum of fuel struck a table-sized rock square on, producing a dramatic pillar of flame.

"See!" Suwi pointed with a shudder. "We must make peace today!"

"Amazing!" the Yabi men agreed. "We'll send word to our allies and meet you down there today."

Suwi went back down the hill grinning. It was amazing what one could accomplish with a little help from a *duong* or two!

Now to persuade his own elders from Balinga.

Not men to waste time, Stan and Bruno spread out over the Yabi-owned plateau and stepped off the length of every angle that could possibly serve as an airstrip site. They soon determined that it was impossible to attain the minimum length required by the missionary pilots for their single-engine aircraft.

"So it's that other site down-valley or nothing," Stan observed, recalling the conclusions they had drawn from the aerial survey.

"Look, Stan!" Bruno pointed at the slopes below Yabi's ridgetop position. Armed Yali men were streaming down.

"Here's more coming from this side," Stan added, pointing to an equally well-armed host of Kobak men descending from the southeast.

"And here come the Balinga men led by Suwi," offered a Dani in his own tongue.

"Our peace move better work, Bruno," Stan said calmly, "or there's going to be one terrible battle fought right where we're standing."

Bruno prayed as Stan advanced to meet the warriors.

Balinga men and their allies, reassured by the previous day's peaceful contact with the *duongs,* crossed the river first and massed behind Stan and Bruno's camp. The Yabi and Kobak horde, not yet so reassured, kept their distance, squatting along ridges like the points on a hundred picket fences. Often they called to each other across the gorges with strange yelping cries. "Like dingoes," Stan commented.

Eventually a few august, befeathered war leaders from Yabi and Kobak descended. Stan abruptly asked through Suwi if they were ready to make peace with Balinga. His tone of voice, by design, implied that they had no choice. But thousands of Yali, together with Bruno, doubted that this small stranger, who still had no knowledge of Yali language or ways, could persuade such confirmed enemies as the two opposite alliances of the Heluk to make peace. At least not during his first twenty-four hours in the valley!

Using young Suwi as an interpreter, Stan engaged the old Yabi and Kobak war chiefs in a brief but highly animated discussion. This in itself was a difficult operation, for Stan could wield only a few dozen Dani terms to communicate his thoughts through the Danis to Suwi. But he used them with amazing energy. Suwi likewise translated with stirring zeal. The old war chiefs responded as if making peace was the very thing they had intended all along. The leaders of Balinga also assented as if they had no choice, even though they were the ones who normally would have desired time to even the score first. But somehow the shock of Stan and Bruno's bizarre third-person presence enabled them to see their war problem in a new light. One side, after all, would have to be content with a lower score of victims if ever peace was to be made. And it would be pleasant for a change to work one's gardens without fear of ambush. In any case, it seemed very likely that these two odd beings were spirits whose command one dare not refuse!

With a spectacular fanfare of shouting and oratory, the war chiefs of Balinga, Yabi, and Kobak met on the now-neutral ground of Stan and Bruno's camp. With an awesome release of emotion, they first laid down their weapons and then gripped each other's arms, nearly weeping in mutual forgiveness. Bruno was amazed. Hundreds of young Yali warriors perched rank upon rank on successive ridges of surrounding hills could hardly believe their eyes. For the first time, an inkling dawned upon them that a highly persuasive spiritual force had entered their valley.

By early afternoon the war chiefs of the eastern and western sides of the valley's northern end had dispersed to prepare for a mutual exchange of "peace pigs"—the accepted Yali means of sealing a new peace agreement as a formal treaty. Wild rejoicing now broke out as younger warriors from both sides followed their leaders back up to their hilltop villages.

"Bruno," Stan mused. "This peace treaty was initiated in a day." And then he added meaningfully, "It could have taken years."

Bruno weighed Stan's point. *Some problems diminish in proportion to the gumption, not necessarily the superior skills or knowledge, of those who tackle them. Or increase in proportion to the timidity of those who lack daring. Some problems,* Bruno reflected, *but perhaps not all.*

Still amazed at Stan's utter fearlessness in confronting these unknown, unpredictable people, Bruno pondered carefully the possibilities of the future. Working with such a bold colleague among such a warlike people certainly could not be boring! And it might even be dangerous. Nevertheless, Bruno remained fully committed to sharing the mission with Stan. Tactfully he tried to suggest to Stan that perhaps a little more caution would be advisable until they both understood the Yali people better.

But Stan replied, "Among people like these, Bruno, a bold approach and a firm hand is always the safest policy."

Bruno held his peace, and together they fell to their noon meal.

After eating, Stan rose to his feet and gazed intently down-valley.

"While you watch our things, Bruno, I think I'll just slip down and eyeball that other airstrip site. I'll leave the rifle here with you."

Bruno, a tireless trekker himself, was amazed at Stan's energy. This long-dreamed-of entrance into the "forgotten valley" seemed to have charged him with a god's strength—and happiness! There were only four hours of daylight left, and the trekking time to the down-valley site was unknown, yet with a bound Stan was off, plunging back across the Heluk and striding along a down-valley trail, with Yali teenager Suwi barely keeping ahead of him as a guide. The Dani named Wandawak followed Stan as an aide.

Hurrying past the ashes of the four cremation fires without noticing them, Stan stopped to survey the lay of the land.

"What is the name of this down-valley area we are going to?" he asked Suwi in halting Dani.

As they were then standing close to Mobahai, the *kwalu* refuge that had saved Sunahan's life not long before, Suwi decided to categorize the down-valley region by the name of its own corresponding *kwalu* refuge—Ninia, where little Nindik had gone astray.

"You could call it 'Ninia,'" he replied.

"Ninia," Stan repeated, memorizing the name. And he struck out once more with swift, steady strides.

Startling hamlet after hamlet, Stan and a swelling crowd of escorts broke out at length on a ridge near the children's hidden waterfall. As word of his coming spread through the Sivimu area, Yali men chased their womenfolk and small children along side trails into the forest. "If you even so much as see him, we may have to rub pig's blood in your eyes or even kill you!" they warned. It was enough. Women and children fled with speed born of terror; Stan glimpsed not a single woman or small child during the entire trek. Drawn by the waterfall's whispering voice, he first cooled his brow with a dash of its clear, cold water and then followed the trail out onto the huge rock overlooking Sivimu and Hwim villages and the Yarino knoll between them.

He looked down. Sivimu village was first to catch his eye. Its swirl of humpies ensprawled a ridgetop to Stan's left. To his right the houses of Hwim arched along the crest of a higher hill like armor plates on the spine of some hulking dinosaur. And between the two villages—

Stan gasped.

Could this be what he and Bruno had called "a prospective airstrip site"? From a height of several hundred feet, in the comfort of a smooth-flying aircraft, it had indeed looked like one. But now, with his feet on the rough terrain, Stan wondered if anything less than sheer presumption could ever dream of making it into an airstrip.

For one thing, the site began with an 18 percent downslope. Stan had seen steep airstrips in other parts of New Guinea but never *that* steep!

For another, the 18 percent downslope ended in a *swamp*, which neither he nor Bruno had noticed from the air. Beyond the swamp the downslope reversed and became an upslope for two hundred feet, forming the knoll crowned with that conspicuous lone dwelling surrounded by the high stone wall.

Curious structure, Stan mused. *Probably some sort of men's clubhouse.*

Beyond the knoll the downslope resumed again at what appeared from a distance to be at least a 14 percent grade, leveling out just slightly, like the end of a ski jump, before plunging off into the Heluk gorge.

As if for good measure, the site was obstacled also with a dozen or so table-size boulders!

Stan sighed. *Lord, You haven't exactly made this easy for us, have You?*

To measure the length of the site, Stan unwound a tape measure, gave one end to Wandawak, and started down the slope, laying the tape repeatedly as he progressed. Skirting the swamp, he headed straight toward the *osuwa,* still measuring. He was totally unaware of the sudden tension that gripped the crowds of wondering Yalis gathering on ridges and slopes around him. The priests especially felt their stomachs contracting in hard knots of anxiety.

"Who is this man, if he is a man?" Andeng queried.

"Who can tell who or what he is or where he came from," Lisanik replied.

"The important thing is, has he been dedicated to the *kembu* spirits?" Wanla interjected. "Because if he hasn't, and he crosses, or even touches, that stone wall, we have a responsibility, brothers."

"Hurry!" Andeng commanded, and started down the slope to intercept Stan.

"What are we going to do?" the others asked, following Andeng uncertainly.

"We must question this young man, Suwi; perhaps he knows the answers."

Suwi saw the priests coming, followed by armed warriors from Sivimu. He knew already the questions they were going to ask. Quickly he ran in front of Stan and pointed to a trail that would bypass the sacred wall.

"Please, my father," he pleaded, "let's take this trail; it's shorter!"

"Not for where I'm going," Stan replied, and brushed past him.

"Where are you going?" Suwi queried nervously.

"Over that stone wall," Stan gruffed, trying to keep his mind on his measuring.

Suwi chewed his lip, and tried again. "Please, my father, do not touch that wall!"

Holding his count, Stan paused and turned. "Why not?"

"Because—" Suwi's mind reeled. How could he make him understand? His Dani vocabulary was so sparse, and it was difficult to convey his thoughts through Wandawak, Stan's Dani helper.

"Because there is a *kembu* spirit in there! It is a bad place for you!"

"What is a *kembu* spirit?" Stan probed. For in the Swart Valley, where Stan had learned Dani, *kembu* was only the name of a certain mountain.

"A *kembu* spirit is like a *mugwat*," the youth replied, using a Dani word for *ghost*. "Only a *kembu* spirit is a much more powerful *mugwat*."

"A ghost, eh?" Stan took another look at the *kembu-vam*. Suddenly it reminded him of that "haunted" house back in Bowral and of the specious attempt of the bullies to make him afraid.

Very well, he reasoned. *If these people are ever to be set free from their fear of ghosts, someone will have to show them that there is nothing to be afraid of. That someone might as well be me, and now is as good a time as any!*

The priests and their escort of armed warriors were hurrying closer. Stan still had not noticed them.

"To show you that I am not afraid of ghosts, I'm going inside that wall. Watch and see if anything happens to me."

Stan turned. Pressing his old Australian army hat down around his ears, he strode briskly toward the wall and with a hop, skip, and a jump handsprung himself over it.

Suwi turned pale, as Andeng, Wanla, and Lisanik arrived, their faces clouding.

"Who is this man?" Andeng hissed as he approached Suwi. "Has he been dedicated to *Kembu?*"

"He—" Suwi began, but for once the facile youth was tongue-tied. Andeng's question left Suwi's intellect groping vainly in darkness. He felt a growing fear that the priests might blame *him* for the *duong's* transgression and kill him too!

"Andeng!" It was Wanla who spoke, his voice hushed with awe. "Have you noticed how much this stranger—" Wanla's jaw moved uncertainly, hardly daring to voice the incredible "—looks like—"

Wanla was staring hard at Stan, his eyes growing wider, more alarmed.

"Looks like who?" Andeng asked impatiently.

"Like—like—Kugwarak!"

Andeng's shaggy brow furrowed. He, too, gazed hard at Stan. Then he started as the resemblance struck him like a landslide. "You're right!" he gasped. "His jaw, his nose, that squint—even his very frame. Just like Kugwarak before sickness shriveled him up!"

In another moment the same shock of recognition swept through Lisanik. "It's uncanny!" he squeaked. "He popped over the ridge and walked straight down here without needing any to show him the way, as if he knew exactly where he was going. As if he had been here before."

None of the Yali guessed that this same *duong* had already studied the lay of the land from inside that roaring sky-spirit that circled overhead some ten days earlier.

"My brothers," Andeng queried, deep in thought, "if this is Kugwarak, why is his hair so straight and his skin so colorless?"

"Perhaps," Wanla offered, obsessed now with an urge to expand the dramatic new theory he had conceived, "when Bukni cremated him, the fire melted the kinks out of his hair and bleached his skin white! And now that he's alive again, he remains that way!"

"Makes sense." Lisanik leaped excitedly into the air, shouting loudly to the mass of Yali men and boys from all the surrounding villages. "Our brother Kugwarak has returned to his own place, and to the *kembu-vam* which he rebuilt for us before his death!"

The crowd moved toward Stan to check the resemblance for themselves, but not close enough to risk too much involvement with a visitor from the dead! The air was filled with a chorus of raptured exclamations of those who had known Kugwarak in his prime. They confirmed the striking resemblance and accepted Wanla's explanation of the odd color of his skin.

Still stretching his tape measure across the sacred ground beside "his" *kembu-vam*, Stan little dreamed that Wanla's sharp memory for faces had, during those very minutes, saved his life.

But neither did the Yali know that their returned Kugwarak determined, on the basis of his measurements, that the hallowed structure that bore his name would shortly have to be demolished to make room for a new kind of *osuwa*—an airstrip!

Winding up his tape measure, Stan called Wandawak, his Dani aide, to his side. "Tell Suwi we'll return in two days' time to buy this land and these buildings from the people."

Wandawak did his best to make the message clear to Suwi, but by the time it was passed on to the Yali elders, the word "buy" had changed to "claim." The elders simply nodded their heads in agreement. Naturally they must expect Kugwarak to reclaim the property that had belonged to him in life. After all, no one had ever paid him for it.

The Yali, in common with many other tribes in Dutch New Guinea, believed implicitly that early mankind possessed immortality symbolized by a lizard or snake but later fell prey to death symbolized by a bird. Some tribes portray the transition in the figure of a race between the lizard of life and the bird of death. In the Yali version, the bird, having won the race, mocked mankind by saying, "*Fong! Fong!*—Too bad for you! Too bad for you!"

But since man once possessed immortality, by implication he might one day recover it again. Some tribes easily identified this prior hope with the Christian gospel's promise of regeneration of character now and resurrection of the body later. As a result, three tribes living west of the Yali had already responded to the gospel with a gusto perhaps unprecedented in the two-thousand-year history of Christianity.

For example, the Ekari tribe called that ancient hope *ayi*—the return of a "golden age." Not long after the first missionaries began proclaiming the gospel among them, Ekari sages announced that the gospel was the fulfillment of *ayi*.

Tremors of excitement swept through Ekari villages. Overnight the presence and the teachings of the missionaries took on immense significance for the Ekari. Learning the secret of their markedly peaceful lifestyle became an absorbing preoccupation.

"Has it ever happened this way before?" missionaries asked each other. Seeing thousands of Ekari faces uplifted to wait upon one's every word made it easy to imagine this was a first event of its kind in creation, if indeed it could ever repeat.

It could. And it would. For *ayi* was a concept known to other tribes—for example, the Damal.

Mugumenday, a Damal chief, lay dying. Den, his son, sat by his side in the dimness of a Damal roundhouse. Weakly the old man reached out and touched Den's arm. "All my days I have waited for *hai*," Mugumenday croaked. (*Hai* was the Damal word for *ayi*.) "I hoped *hai* would come before my death—" The old man's touch tightened into a grip. "But it has not come. Now you, my son, must watch in my place. Be ready, in case *hai* comes within your lifetime."

Soon Den cremated his father's corpse upon a funeral pyre. But years later he still remembered.

Widi-ai-bui, an Ekari trader who had found Christ in the earlier movement among his own people, accompanied missionary Don Gibbons on pastoral visits to Damal homes in the Ilaga Valley. By careful use of bilinguals, Don managed to squeeze Widi-ai-bui's testimony through chinks in the Damal linguistic barrier. The Damal listened inquisitively. Previously, strange-tongued Ekari had come only to trade, but what was *this*?

"O my people!" Den, now a mature adult, had risen to his feet. "How long our forefathers waited for *hai*! How sadly my father died without seeing it! But now—don't you understand?—these white friends are offering *hai* to us. And this Ekari proves it is for regular men like ourselves and not just for exotic beings from the outside world. We must obey their words, or we will miss the fulfillment of our forefathers' ancient hope!"

Neither earthquake, hurricane, nor fire from heaven could have wrought a more dramatic effect upon the Damal spirit! Within a few years, 80 percent of the tribe's ten thousand members embraced the gospel and forsook the fetishes that, until that moment, linked them to a hierarchy of baleful spirit beings. Wars, killings, adulteries, and thievery became shocking exceptions to the joyful tranquility that now flooded Damal valleys. Even sickness and death became rarer as missionaries with their medicine eradicated illnesses and stemmed plagues in wide areas.

The golden age had indeed arrived. The Damal were high on the *hai* of the gospel!

The Dani, political overlords in the Damal Valley, were enraged by their Damal neighbors' radical departure from "the old ways." "Now the spirits will destroy us all!" they predicted. When destruction did not come, the Dani began to examine the logic behind the Damal decision. For the Dani also expected the fulfillment of something they called *nabelan-kabelan*—the belief that one day their tribe would forsake warfare, treachery, and black magic and enter a state of blessedness, with implications of immortality to follow. Could the message that was *ayi* to the Ekari and *hai* to the Damal become *nabelan-kabelan* to the ferocious, unpredictable Dani?

It did not take long. Once again the gospel proved to be what God intended—a master message conveying not only the redemption of individual people (its prime concern) but also the fulfillment of their highest ideals as well! Generated by the teaching of the gospel under American missionaries Gordon and Peggy Larson, a spiritual-cultural shock wave developed spontaneously among the Dani. Once generated, it could not be contained. From its epicenter in the Ilaga Valley, it swept eastward, rocking the population in valley after valley.

Like their colleagues among the Ekari and the Damal, younger missionaries among the Dani found themselves asking, "Has it ever happened this way before? Look! Thousands of stone-age people! Singing, dancing, thronging!" And asking, "What must we do to welcome the message you bring?"

The missionaries were unprepared. For one thing, two thousand years of Christian theology had not warned them to expect *this*! It seemed impossible that savages steeped in paganism could manifest such a fervent desire for the gospel! Plagued with doubts, some missionaries favored quenching the movement.

"Quench this awesome explosion of joy?" others countered. "What if God is behind it? To reject it might cause irreparable harm! Enthusiasm like this, once quenched, may never again be kindled."

The movement swept on. Tens of thousands of Dani men, women, and children embraced the Christian faith—including the five carriers who now shared the dangers of the Heluk Valley with Stan and Bruno. Hundreds of congregations were established under the leadership of Dani elders. Perhaps no other culture in history had welcomed such momentous change in so brief a period of time.

Stan and Bruno, quite naturally, hoped for a similar response among the Yali (though they understood but dimly the cultural factors that had triggered the response among other tribes).

At any rate, it was this same expectation of *nabelan-kabelan* (the Yali call it *habelal-kabelal*) that made it possible for the Yali to believe so readily that even cremated old Kugwarak could rise from the dead. Unknown to both themselves and Stan, the Yali of the Heluk were quivering at that very moment with the potential of still another epochal reception of the Christian gospel.

Before returning to camp, Stan turned aside to survey a semicircular bench of level land adjoining the airstrip site and facing the *kembu-vam* and its *osuwa*.

"Here's room for two houses," he mused. "One for Pat and me and one for Bruno." Already, in his mind's eye, Stan could see the two frugally structured dwellings plus a clinic, school, and church spaced about the bench-land and surrounded by gardens.

Throughout those moments a sense of exultation filled Stan. For the mettle within him yearned to be tested to the full, and this valley and its people promised well to call forth his supreme effort. Here, around this tiny bench of land between the three lofty rims, would be enacted the drama that would justify, if anything could, the existence of Stanley Albert Dale.

Already his muscles tensed and his jaw was set. For Stan had what few men possess—the ability to see the mud beneath his boots for what it could be, a seed-plot of history.

With a gruff command, Stan called Wandawak and Suwi away from their translation teamwork and struck out for camp.

That evening Stan's diary reflected slightly the tension he had sensed among the Yalis during his down-valley excursion. He wrote, *I located the possible airstrip site we had seen from the air, and with some relief—for I was totally unarmed—got back safely at sundown.*

"How does it appear?" Bruno asked.

"Rather rough in spots, mate," Stan understated. "But at least it's long enough. With a little grit and three or four months of hard work, it can be coaxed into an airstrip."

Bruno sighed and relaxed. Stan's estimate of time was, of course, predicated upon the cooperation of several hundred Yalis in the project. But if they wouldn't help—

Throughout the following day, Tuesday, May 23, 1961, Stan and Bruno were occupied with the "peace feast" helping to cement a new relationship between Balinga, Yabi, and Kobak. On May 24 they broke camp and, with the help of carriers from Balinga, moved down-valley to Ninia.

Stan later wrote, *We arrived in a drizzling rain, wet, muddy and tired. I dropped my pack on the best camping place I could see, turned to my companion, and said, "Well, Bruno, this is it." Long afterward he told me that when he looked around the site, his heart sank to his boots!*

But for the moment Bruno simply swallowed his despair and helped set up the tent. There was no use complaining, for there was simply no choice! If there was to be an airstrip in the valley, it *had* to be here! And if he and Stan were to fulfill Christ's Great Commission in the Heluk—without the costly ordeal of backpacking tons of supplies across that desolate Mugwi Pass—there would *have* to be an airstrip. If not for Stan and Bruno's sake, then at least for Pat's sake and the children's, for as Stan later wrote, *Families cannot be maintained in these isolated valleys without airstrips.*

As for the Yali, they still had not the slightest inkling of what the two *duongs* and their five tribal helpers intended to do. Their major concern for the moment was *Bruno!*

If the smaller *duong* was Kugwarak, who could the taller one be?

Wanla stared long and hard at Bruno. Sure enough, there was something familiar about him. If he could just recall—

A sudden realization burst upon Wanla. "Why of course!" he shouted. "Don't you remember Kugwarak's protégé, the one he trained to be priest in his place? His name was Marik! He was tall, with a sharp pointy nose and twinkling eyes, just like this man. Marik! That's who he is! Marik has come back from the dead with his teacher, Kugwarak!"

"Let me ask one question," Andeng interrupted. If there were any questions that could be asked, Andeng would ask them. "How did Kugwarak and Marik—now turned white through cremation—get linked up with these five others who are still black like real men?" Andeng continued, pointing to the five Danis now busy building themselves a shelter.

Wanla lapsed back into deep thought, scrutinizing the Danis. Slowly, laboriously, he unearthed an answer. "Years ago, five men related to Kugwarak died high upon the mountains. Their bodies were not found until only bones were left, so there was no point in cremating them."

The same thought occurred to both men at once: *That explains why the five helpers are still black—there had been no cremation fires to bleach them white!* Now everything was so logical, so watertight, that even skeptical Andeng was convinced. And so it happened that the theory spread widely and was accepted as fact. Unexpected new developments, however, would shortly strain the theory's well-soldered joints almost to the breaking point.

From one of the highest ledges of Hwim village, the boy Emeroho looked down wistfully as Stan, Bruno, and the five Danis set up camp. He wanted so much to go down and present himself to see if they were angry because he had deserted during that last night on the Mugwi. And if they were not angry, he wanted to work for them again.

"If you are thinking of going down to help those men, forget it!" Emeroho's father had still not recovered from the shock of finding that his son had consorted to bring living dead men into the Heluk Valley. It wasn't safe to let one's children cross the ranges these days; you couldn't tell what strange relationships they would get mixed up in!

"But, father!" the youth protested. "I'm not afraid of them now like I was at first. They were all kind to me."

"For who knows what purpose!" his father spat. "I will hear no more of this. You will not go near those—whatever they are! If everything starts going bad, men may blame you for leading them to our valley. You know what that could mean."

Emeroho understood his father's warning and trembled. He hadn't thought of *that!* Fear stole through him. And yet, in spite of his fear, he still wanted to go down to the *duongs*. He knew that he understood more about them than anyone else in the valley, more even than Suwi, and he sensed that soon these impetuous *duongs* would need all the understanding they could get—desperately! But Emeroho stayed where he was, in obedience to his father. Perhaps later.

By the next afternoon, Stan and Bruno had carefully listed the names of the owners of all the gardens and dwellings that stood in the way of the airstrip.

"We will give you a downpayment in salt now," Stan promised, "and when our work is completed and the great bird lands on this ground, we will pay you in full with axes and shells." Shells were, of course, the only currency the Yali could use in their economy. Stan was too wily to give full payment in advance, lest the Yalis, having received payment, should later renounce the agreement. The promise of payment, however, did not get through the linguistic barrier to the Yalis. Because of their own presuppositions concerning Stan and Bruno's identity, they understood only that Kugwarak and Marik and their five relatives were reclaiming the land that had been theirs.

On this basis they nodded in obvious agreement and were startled when Stan and Bruno promptly divided out a considerable quantity of brilliantly white salt to the owners of the land and dwellings. Fearful to taste this gift of food from returned dead men, the recipients stood holding it in embarrassment, until the five Danis dipped their fingers in and touched the salt to the lips of a dozen or more Yali.

They licked it and sighed with pleasure as an exquisitely appealing taste nipped their tongues. Not even the salt wells among the limestone peaks of the high rim could produce salt that tasted like this! It was out of this world!

As Stan, Bruno, and the Danis fell to the task of dismantling the nearest Yali *yogwas* and *homias,* no one paid much attention. All were hungrily nibbling the *duongs'* salt as if they had never tasted true salt before and might never have the privilege again.

The dismantling of the local *yogwas* and *homias* caused their occupants little concern, for almost every Yali man and woman possessed alternate dwellings they could resort to. If not, they simply found a welcome in a relative's quarters. Stan, Bruno, and the Danis, meanwhile, found the Yali's stone-hewn boards to be of excellent quality and promptly used them to begin new and larger dwellings for their own need: a hut for the Danis, a hut for Stan and Bruno, and a common cookhouse for both. Since Stan and Bruno could still resort to their tent, priority was given first to the Dani quarters and the cookhouse. When these were completed, few boards taken from the local dwellings remained.

"No matter," Stan said. "We'll dismantle that spirit house on the knoll tomorrow. It has to go because of the airstrip, in any case. And it will yield plenty of good, large boards to finish our own dwelling."

Bruno and the five Danis became grave. They had noticed that the Yalis seemed to treat the knoll and its entire surroundings with deep respect. It was not to Bruno's liking—this proposal to dismantle a center of the valley's animism during their first week in the valley! How he wished they could wait until the Holy Spirit through the gospel moved the Yali to do it of their own accord, if indeed it had to be done! But Bruno kept his thoughts to himself, for by this time he had learned that Stan possessed an intensely practical mind; what had to be done, must be done, and sentimental wishes to the contrary would be dismissed as childish.

"Lord, You knew," Bruno prayed, "when You created this valley, that this conflict of interests would arise. You could have provided a slope for an airstrip somewhere else, or You could have prevented the Yali from choosing this site for a spirit house. Since You didn't, this conflict of interests must be part of Your plan. Perhaps You intend to work through it."

The Danis, meanwhile, pondered an even more down-to-earth problem—would the Yalis use force to defend their sacred house? As an initial test of Yali attitudes, they told the Yali elders of the *duongs'* plans.

"Tear down our *kembu-vam*!" Andeng gasped. "Why on earth would Kugwarak and Marik destroy the sacred house they restored with their own hands?"

Silence ensued, while the other priests pondered Andeng's weighty question.

"Perhaps they intend to destroy it first and then rebuild it."

"Hmm . . ." Andeng murmured, "and yet the boards have not decayed. Why not simply replace the roof?"

Wanla struggled with the problem. Once again, the credibility of his magnificent theory was at stake! But this time, what could he say? Suddenly he had it!

"Ahaa! My brothers!" he exclaimed. "I think I understand! Naturally, Kugwarak, Marik, and the five others, having returned from the spirit world, no longer require ordinary *kembu-vams* or *osuwas* as we who are still mortal. They need a new kind of sacred place suited to their new condition, and they want their boards back for the purpose!"

"Of course!" someone else chimed. "They want us to relocate our *kembu-vam* elsewhere!"

"Then we must move all our sacred objects out of the *kembu-vam* tonight," Andeng reasoned. "We will use the *dokwi-vam* at Sivimu as a temporary repository."

And so that night, while Stan, Bruno, and the five Danis slept, the elders, with utmost care, transported the large *Kembu* stone on its bark pallet to its new repository. They moved also the *yali* and *hwal* fetishes that hung in their respective net bags about the walls. By morning the *kembu-vam* was bare.

"There's just one thing," Andeng murmured the next morning, as Stan, Bruno, and the Danis came out of their shelters armed with machetes. "None of us may help them do what they intend to do. Just in case—" and he gazed steadily at Wanla "—just in case our brother is mistaken."

In spite of himself, Wanla shivered inwardly. If only he had guessed it might come to this, he would have chosen to seem less wise.

"Fall in!" Stan quipped. Bruno, having served in the Dutch army, stepped forward, snapped to attention, and saluted with a grin. The five Danis simply gathered around, testing the blades of their machetes, and keeping an eye on the hundreds of Yali now standing or crouching on nearby ridges to watch. Although the Swart Valley Dani knew nothing in their culture as sacred as the Yali's *kembu-vam,* they had long ago heard rumors of tribes in other valleys whose customs and beliefs were far more rigid than theirs. Could the Yali be one of those tribes? And if so, what might happen when "Tuan Dale" led their assault on that ominous-looking spirit house?

None of the seven members of the mission had the slightest inkling that Wanla's elegant theory had, for the moment, raised a tenuous umbrella of protection over them.

Sensing their concern, Stan faced the five helpers squarely, like a sergeant briefing his men before a mission. "Remember this!" he said firmly in the Dani language. "We have not come into this valley at the word of men but at the command of our Lord Jesus Christ, who said, 'Go into all the world and make disciples among all men!' He also said, 'And lo, I am with you always, even to the end of the world!' That means He is with us in this very place and nothing can stand in our way, not even the demon they say lives in that hut."

Stan and Bruno knew that the Danis, like the Yalis massing on the ridges above them, had not the slightest doubt that spirits were real. To argue against the existence of such spirits would have been pointless. In fact, Stan and Bruno themselves, though they would not have believed every tribal account of demonic manifestation, believed implicitly the

New Testament record of apostolic encounters with real demons.

Stan continued: "In fact, if that demon knows what's good for him, he'll be high-tailing it for some other valley before we even cross that stone wall!" And then he translated into Dani the immortal promise of Jesus: "'I will build my church, and the gates of hell shall not prevail against it!' And that goes for hell's stone walls too!"

Bruno thrilled inwardly as he saw the five Danis beam with renewed courage and determination. It was clear they were willing to die, if necessary, to help win this new valley. They could never forget that season of glory at Karubaga, when their own night of fear gave way to dawn.

And Bruno could feel his own pulse racing. There was no doubt about it—Stan could be a very inspiring person!

Stan and Bruno set out together. The Danis fell in beside them. Steadily and calmly they advanced toward the *osuwa*, a brave little band of seven. They could feel the gaze of hundreds of eyes following them and a heavy sense of foreboding—or was it suspense? or anger?—curdling the very air within the valley.

Over the wall they went, never halting. Live or die, they had a job to do, and before sundown it would be done, or else.

"Take the roof off first," Stan commanded. The five Danis filed up the *kembu-vam*'s stairpole, ducked inside, and clambered up into the rafters of its conical roof. *Whack!* Wandawak sliced through a knot of rattan binding, and the first ancient *pandanus* frond, heavy with congealed smoke, slid off to the ground. *Whack!* Tuanangen—also one of the five—cut another knot and a second frond slid down. Both men could feel the invisible demon glaring at them in utter rage. They prayed for protection and swung their machetes again. And again.

Stan and Bruno, standing on the ground, began loosening the binding holding the hand-hewn boards against the circular framework of the wall.

And on the crest of a ridge, near the center of Sivimu, Andeng brooded tall and dark against the clouds, looking down. His muscles flinched involuntarily as the sound of the machetes reached him. It was almost as if his own flesh was being cut. If it were not for the assurance of his brother Wanla's interpretation of these strange events, he would have thought that not only his own flesh but also the very tendons of time and space itself were being severed.

At one point, as the boards Kugwarak and Marik so carefully hewed toppled one by one from the temple wall, emotion welled up within Andeng, almost to a frenzy. *What if Wanla was mistaken?* Barely did he restrain himself from signaling an attack. But he did not signal. He waited. It would be better for the people—if Wanla was mistaken—to see how *Kembu* himself would deal with these imponderable strangers.

In less than two hours, the *kembu-vam* was leveled to the ground. The sky-spike anchored in sacred pig fat, the four poles of the sacred fireplace, the veil of boards, and the dusty sanctuary behind it were now only a heap of boards, severed rattan, and old *pandanus* roofing.

As Andeng had commanded, not a single Yali helped in its destruction. That very afternoon the Danis carried all of the usable boards out of the *osuwa* to the adjoining bench of land. There they began erecting a sturdy rectangular hut for Stan and Bruno.

"Work! Work!" Stan called in his most winsome tones. "Come and work with us! We'll pay cowrie shells if you want cowrie shells. Or bush knives. Or axes."

No one moved. Andeng's prohibition was still in effect. And so the missionaries' potential labor force simply squatted by the hundreds along their preferred ridgetop perches, staring down like a forum of black ghouls at the two white men and their five helpers. It was awfully spooky, not only for the mission party but also for the Yali, who in turn took the missionaries and their helpers for ghouls.

Staring back up in astonishment, Stan quipped to Bruno, "Makes you wonder what you've struck!" He called again, "Work! Work! Come and work with us!"

Again no one moved.

Stan saw a group of men squatting on their heels near his camp. He started toward them with a wide smile, hoping to put a shovel in their hands and show them what he proposed was really quite a simple operation. They jumped to their feet and fled, cowering as they ran.

"They're a different kettle of fish, these Yalis," Stan muttered as he returned to Bruno. "Back in the Swart, you only have to say 'work,' and you are nearly knocked over in the rush. Here they crouch down and run!"

He tried to approach two boys (Yekwara and Bengwok) watching from another direction, but they, too, fled.

Stan swept his green left eye again along the entire twisting, uneven length of the 450-meter strip site. Then he squinted at Bruno, sizing up this unexpectedly improbable situation.

At this point Stan and Bruno had a choice. They could build a small cabin and devote several months to winning the confidence of the Heluk Yalis with a "trading partner" approach, a practice long accepted by the Yali. They could trade out such items as medicine for illnesses common to the Heluk. Or they could go ahead constructing the airstrip, trusting that the watchers on the ridges would soon take pity and come down to help.

The first option would have been easier, perhaps, for Bruno as a bachelor. But Stan had a wife and four children who needed him. Building an airstrip would keep him separated from his family long enough. He could not, therefore, relish more months of separation to engage in diplomatic approaches to recalcitrant tribesmen. Besides, he was already pushing forty-five, and time, for him, was running out.

He made his decision. Every other tribe from the Paniai Lakes eastward had accepted the building of airstrips and expressed no regrets afterward. Surely the Yali would be no exception, if they could just get it started.

"Alright, mates!" Stan gruffed. "We'll make a start ourselves and see what happens!" And he thrust a shovel into each man's hand.

"We'll drain that billabong in the low place first, and then fill the hollow with boulders from this stone wall," he added, pointing to the osuwa. "Every man choose a place!"

Brawny forceps bulging, Stan laid another shovel across his own shoulder and walked briskly down to the edge of the swamp.

Grimly, Bruno and the faithful Danis, suppressing a feeling of numb despair, followed. Then one of the Danis whooped as if he were marching out to war, and raced toward the swamp, brandishing his shovel above his head. The other Danis and Bruno followed suit, whooping in unison. They dug in along one edge of the swamp, laughing hilariously at themselves for attempting the impossible.

Even Stan, though he seldom laughed, chuckled for the occasion. Yet within he was struggling to summon up every last ounce of that Kipling spirit he learned in boyhood, for he needed it now as never before, just to fight back the dread that this, his long-dreamed-of mission—the very thing he hoped would justify his existence on earth—might shortly end up a fool's lark!

There were even more grounds for dread than either Stan or Bruno realized. Both men, during preceding months in the newly responsive Swart Valley, had gained an impression that Dutch New Guinea cultures were rather easily persuaded to abandon animism for a new faith. Had not Ekari, Damal, and western Dani, in their tens of thousands, received the gospel with open arms?

Surely the Yali, a neighboring people, would not prove totally different in this respect! For in their lard-and-soot cosmetic, their net bag, cowrie shell, marsupial fur, and feather trappings, their diet, their phallic gourds, and their weaponry, the Yali of the Heluk could easily pass for Dani of the Swart.

And Stan and Bruno were already finding evidence that the Dani and Yali languages were about as closely related as English and French! They noted also, of course, certain obvious visible differences: Swart Valley Danis fenced villages and gardens with split board; the Yali erected stone walls. Yali dwellings, to conserve heat in a colder climate, were smaller. Their spirit houses, conversely, were larger. Herein lay a subtle clue to a vast underlying disparity between Dani and Yali culture—one that portended a grim future for Stan and Bruno's mission.

The western Dani, living on less precipitous northern slopes of the Snow Mountains, farmed a comparatively gentle terrain with a correspondingly balmy climate. Basking in longer periods of sunshine, Dani sweet potato and yam crops could ripen in only three months. Gardens could lie fallow for years because arable land was plentiful. Earthquakes and landslides were infrequent and less severe.

The western Dani could be confident, therefore, that even if they did not honor their gods in a meticulous manner, nature herself would still favor them like a doting mother buffering the wrath of an angry father. Hence, for the western Dani, *one* initiation—and a rather formalistic one at that—was sufficient to induct young men into the knowledge of the spirits. And never would western Dani shamans exact a death penalty for violations of religious secrets by women or uninitiated children, if indeed the Dani had any secrets that should be kept from women and children!

The Yali of the Heluk, by contrast, were a people condemned by their own mysterious prehistory to eke a bare existence in a completely different terrain—the chaotically upheaved southern flanks of the Snow Mountains. Here they built their tiny "humpies" on cold, knife-edge ridges and tilled their hummocked gardens in rain-leeched beds of cliff-side clay. And while they worked and warred, cantankerous monsoon storms, trapped by towering twelve-thousand-foot escarpments, condensed their oceans of vapor almost daily, as if determined to flush the gorges below until every last vestige of human habitation disappeared.

And yet somehow the Yali survived in the Heluk, as they did in equally hostile neighboring valleys. They survived even though their gardens, languishing for sunshine, often took ten months to produce sweet potatoes one quarter the size of those grown by Danis!

They survived even though they could ill afford to let their gardens lie fallow for renewal; even though heavy rain and earthquakes often triggered landslides, destroying some crops before they were ready for harvest; even though their pigs—runty at best—easily died of pneumonia during seasons of protracted darkness and cold. (Little wonder Yali women allowed pigs to share one side of their own warm dwellings and even suckled them on occasion just to keep them alive!)

Harried thus by the elements, Yali tribesmen, over centuries, developed an extreme dependence upon the *kembu* spirits, for in the Yali view of things, the *kembu* spirits and they alone could strongarm nature on man's behalf. The "protection money" the spirits exacted was often grievous: frequent offerings of pig, total obeisance to fetishes, and rigid punishment of taboo breakers. The requirements were so harsh, in fact, and at times demanded such total suppression of normal human instinct, that Yali men eons earlier found it necessary to exclude women from all matters of religion; when it came to a choice between obeying the spirits and yielding to some natural instinct such as mother love, women were undependable. Yali religion, therefore, had long ago been purged of all relation to the feminine psyche, which otherwise would soon undermine man's resolve toward the spirits, thus forfeiting their help and betraying both men and women to their doom.

This suppression of female religious instinct, of course, had its drawbacks. Yali women, deprived of all feelings of religious exaltation and sensing constantly the *kembu* spirits' enmity toward them, lived in perpetual psychological depression. Sanguine personalities were never in evidence among them. Their suicide rate was ten times greater than that of Yali men and many times greater than that of their western Dani counterparts, who were vivacious, cheerful—even bold!

Hence there were fewer Yali women to bear children and, of far greater concern, to till the gardens!

And so it evolved that religion, to the Yali, became inextricably fused with instinct for survival, which made it a very serious matter indeed! In order to impress that utter seriousness upon each successive generation, they developed not one but four initiation ceremonies, each designed to give young men an increasingly heightened awareness of religious mystery. And the Yali articulated their ancient code—the *wene melalek*—with a clarity and concern seldom granted to parallel dogmas of other stone-age tribes. Their death penalty, moreover, was automatically inflicted for many breaches of tribal law that western Dani shamans would punish with little more than a scolding.

For these reasons anyone who dared propose the slightest departure from Yali religious tradition appeared to the Yali a harbinger of doom, not a prophet of salvation. And if any would advocate total abandonment of the *kembu*, the sacred stones, the *osuwa*, and the *wene melalek*, there are no words to describe the trauma of horror with which the Yali would react!

That, in effect, was what Stan and Bruno, without the advantage of insights that could have forewarned and guided them, were preparing to do! If ever a pair of missionaries needed a profound strategy to help a harried, desperate people transfer their survival dependence from an old to a new basis, it was Stan and Bruno.

In the absence of crucial cultural insights, what *was* their strategy?

The young girls of the Yali were never told of sacred things

A Yali boy fords a small stream

A slope of gardens and mounded yam plots

Sar and Ongolek, Nindik's mother and father

A Yali hunter draws his bow

Yali tribesmen

A Yali village

Warriors dancing at Sivimu village

Women of Kibi village (Seng peaks in the background)

Stan and Pat Dale with Wesley, Hilary, Rodney and Joy, in Irian Jaya

Stan, Pat and the children start on a trek to Balinga village

Yarino Knoll, Stan's prospective airstrip site (kembu-van *at left center near the tree*)

Bruno de Leeuw's calling was to mountain people

Pat Dale with Wesley, Hilary, Rodney and Joy, outside their grass hut

Bruno's house on a cold, cloudy day in Heluk Valley

A plane rolls down the completed airstrip

Phil and Phyliss Masters with Becky, Crissie, Robbie and Curt

Phil unpacks a trunk dropped by aircraft to his remote outpost

Phil talks with one of his friends, a Kimyal "pygmy" boy

Costas and Alky Macris replaced Stan and Pat at Ninia during the Dales' furlough

Hulu, a priest of Kembu, knocked Stan to the ground four times

The gorge that Stan walked through at night with five arrow wounds in his body

Phil Masters lets a villager from Kimyal look through his camera lens

Nalimo made a loud popping noise in his throat when expressing astonishment

Don Richardson walks across a suspension bridge like the one Yemu wanted to cut down

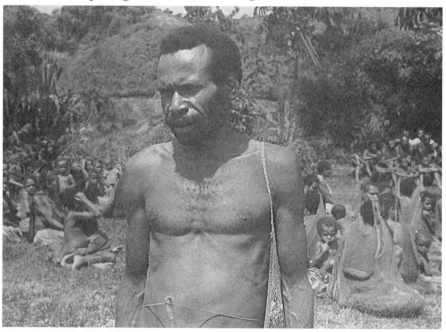

Emerho, who led Stan and Bruno into the Heluk, listened to their words even under threats against his life

Kusaho welcomes Costas Macris and Don Richardson

Warriors tell Don Richardson about the attack near Ilia

Luliap preaching

Pat Dale, treating the sick and counseling Yali women

Don and Carol Richardson and family

The village of Ninia in 1977

Part III

FOOTHOLD
BEYOND THE RIM

A LONELY PLACE IN WHICH TO DIE

Chapter 11

BOTH Stan and Bruno had been duly impressed by "the awesome power of the Holy Spirit of God" in bringing tens of thousands of Ekari, Damal, and western Dani tribespeople to Christian faith after less than a decade—and in some places after only two or three years—of concerted missionary endeavor.

They knew also that the Holy Spirit had not evoked this unusual response out of a vacuum. Inside facets of tribal culture, including tribal anticipation that a message of immortality would one day ease human suffering, seemed to "simplify" the Holy Spirit's task, leading first to a general reformation of tribal conduct, followed later in thousands of instances by personal commitment in Christian faith.

Most missionaries at the time, however, still regarded the contributing cultural factors as more or less incidental. The Holy Spirit intended to achieve the same effect regardless. The cultural factors "just happened" to align themselves with Him, much as a sea current may help a ship on its way even though the ship has sufficient power to reach its destination if the current flows against it.

This view of the phenomenal response seemed to find support from the fact that missionaries among the Ekari, Damal, and Dani tribes did not have to discover those mysterious *ayi*, *hat*, and *nabelan-kabelan* concepts beforehand. They simply preached the gospel. The tribesmen themselves made the association with their own ancient beliefs and responded accordingly—which meant explosively! Gathering in the thousands of converts was a relatively easy operation, like a rich strike in a placer mine.

It had not yet occurred to anyone that the cultural factors might actually be indispensable facilitators of that particular kind of response, and that parallel touchstones in still other cultures might require the equivalent of deep-earth mining to uncover them. Or that workers elsewhere might have to connect such factors with the gospel *manually*, as it were, to arouse otherwise recalcitrant cultures to response.

As for Stan and Bruno, they intended to learn the Yali language well and to observe Yali culture carefully in the course of their daily lives. Beyond this, neither man considered himself an in-depth researcher of tribal culture. And neither, in any case, considered a cannibal culture a promising place to search for elements helpful to the gospel. If such elements ever existed, surely the prince of darkness, exploiting an age-long absence of the Word of God, would have erased them by now.

But both Stan and Bruno were very wise in a message long renowned as a catalyst of compassion in human affairs—the gospel! And they trusted implicitly that the same Holy Spirit who created receptivity among Ekaris, Damals, and Danis would somehow create it again among the Yali in spite of the limitations of His servants. Yes, He would create response again, even here in the hearts of those hundreds of Yali who now looked on, seemingly aloof, while two sweating white men and a handful of helpers tried to shift a swamp and shape two ridges into something called an airstrip!

Theirs was an ancient confidence, Stan's and Bruno's, and a well-tested one. No doubt it would work again to the winning of the Yali tribe. Or would it?

Yekwara and Bengwok, having fled from Stan when he approached them offering shovels, settled down again now on a slightly more distant vantage point to continue their curious scrutiny.

"Did you notice how Father Kugwarak smiled when he came toward us with those digging things?" Yekwara asked.

"Perhaps *he* thinks *we* look funny!" Bengwok quipped.

"Be careful, friend! If they are spirits, they may be able to hear us!"

"I think they must be just plain human," Bengwok countered. "See, they are starting to make a new *osuwa* for their *Kembu*—that means they must still be human!"

Yekwara pondered Bengwok's suggestion. "If they are making an *osuwa* for their *Kembu*, why does Andeng forbid us to help them? Do not all our villages help each other in such things? Surely our refusal will make their *Kembu* angry."

Now Bengwok in turn pondered the reasonableness of Yekwara's thoughts.

Yekwara continued, "Already these seven returned dead men have stopped the war between Balinga and Yabi. And now our Kobak enemies reportedly are trying to make peace with us so that they can safely come across and see these strange wonders! These men are bringing peace to our valley, and this is how we reward them!"

For the next three days, both boys pleaded with their fathers and older brothers for permission to help the strangers. Andeng would not yield. But eventually Bengwok's older brother, Dongla, a spirited, strongly independent young man, agreed that help ought to be given. Dongla spoke with his friend Luliap, who also agreed, as did another youth, Aralek. All three, confident that no actual breach of taboo was involved, boldly ignored Andeng's command and marched down to the white man's camp with Bengwok. And of course Kebel then permitted Yekwara to join them. And Liakoho allowed Foliek, who had nearly been executed over the mushroom affair, to go down and work as well.

"Why shouldn't we help our own forefathers?" they shouted to those who objected. It seemed a reasonable question. At least temporarily, the objectors were silenced.

Stan chuckled as he gave out shovels to the new crew.

"It reminds me of the line of that hymn you were singing early this morning, Bruno, 'A noble army, men *and boys!*' "

From the edge of Sivimu, Andeng looked down and scowled. But he did nothing, for it would be beneath Andeng's dignity as a high priest to enforce his ruling in a brutish, personal manner. A high priest controlled situations by charisma, hardly ever by personal use of force. And for the moment the charisma of the new white Kugwarak and Marik proved stronger than his own, even over his own two sons. It was a stinging blow, but Andeng took it quietly. He did not care to draw the white beings' attention to himself. Not yet and perhaps never. There were still too many unknowns. If anything had to be done, Andeng and his hundreds of fellow priests would do it later, working behind the scenes. Meanwhile let the young satisfy their aching curiosity.

Encouraged by the slightly larger crew, and eager to demonstrate to the watchers on the hillside galleries that progress was being made even without their help, Stan drove himself to the limit. In the late afternoon, when Bruno returned to the little tent to prepare an evening meal and make radio contact with Karubaga, Stan still continued with shovel and pickaxe, chatting with Yekwara, Bengwok, Dongla, Aralek, Luliap, and Foliek in the few Yali phrases he had earlier gleaned from Emeroho, until the sun went down and the crew slipped away, leaving him alone beside the swamp.

He looked around. The patch they had cleared still seemed so pitifully insignificant. Would the task ever be accomplished? Suddenly overcome with weariness, he staggered back to the tent, took a plateful of food from Bruno, gave thanks to God, and ate it with a little extra salt (advice he remembered from a tough army sergeant many years ago).

Then he rolled over into his sleeping bag with a great sigh. The next thing he knew, someone was unlacing his boots and removing them. With a start Stan jerked his head up and saw Bruno leaning over him, outlined against a rare starry sky above the valley.

"Thank you, brother," he groaned. "I must have forgot to take them off."

And as Bruno massaged his feet, Stan fell asleep.

Cold rain and mist did not stop them, nor burning sun. Bending their backs to their shovels, they worked, their vision blurred by sweat one hour, rain dripping from their noses the next. Meanwhile Yali watchers on the hills, looking down from under protective pandanus frond capes, began to see humor in the situation. They developed a new kind of contest among themselves. Its object was to see who could invent the most imaginative or hilarious idiom to describe the doggedness of the new white Kugwarak and his strangely inspired little crew.

Young Yekwara, although enthused by the camaraderie of the work, complained to Bengwok, "If only their *Kembu* didn't require such an immense *osuwa!*"

Stan and Bruno, who might otherwise never have noticed these particular young men among thousands of Yalis, soon learned to know each of them by name and treated them with special regard. Day by day, one or two more watchers would find themselves inexplicably moved to join the strangers in their jovial madness, to the further consternation of the priests. The crew increased, ever so slowly. But yet the amount of work done, compared to that still ahead of them, resembled only the scratchings of a few ants in the center of a sandbox.

They needed help, and on their third Sunday in the valley, it looked as if they might get it. On that day a horde of men from villages of the eastern alliance, drawn by news that gourdless wonders returned from the dead were trading exotic cutting tools made of some unknown substance, finally succeeded in concluding a peace treaty with Hwim and Sivimu in order to gain safe access to the area.

And so the killers and devourers of Selambo came to see Stan and Bruno. They came armed to the teeth, but minded their *p's* and *q's* very well, lest they give their newly placated Sivimu enemies the slightest cause to renew war.

They were big, barrel-chested, wild-looking men, awesome in bearing, resplendent with nose tusks, shells, and feathers, and powerfully scented with old pig grease. At first they paid no attention to Bruno and Stan, who inspired their visit. Instead they gave their attention wholly to the diplomatic concern of properly greeting their hosts, the men of Sivimu, Hwim, and Ombok. Of course after such a long period of war and estrangement, only the fondest, most ardent scatological greetings would suffice. Stan and Bruno would have turned green had they understood what those fervent exchanges meant!

But when the scatological muttering, the fervent forearm gripping, and the affectionate chin scratching were finished, they all turned toward Stan and Bruno, who were sitting calmly in their little camp, all washed and shaved and Sunday-rested.

"It's true! They wear no gourds!" sniffed one Yali. "How unmanly can you get!"

As the multitude gathered around, staring in wide-eyed awe, Stan, out of the side of his mouth, quipped to his mild-faced companion, "It's Sunday afternoon at the Ninia zoo, Bruno, only it's you and me in the monkey pit, instead of chimpanzees."

Then Stan, rising slowly to his feet, added, "I'll show 'em something no chimpanzee ever did!"

With consummate perk, he sauntered forth into the tightening circle of warriors, opened his mouth wide, plucked out his upper and lower plates, and clacked them manually before several hundred unbelieving eyes! Did ever a single action so quickly drain composure from a host of august countenances! And did ever an assembly of bold men bolt in more instantaneous fright?

But at the sound of Stan's loud, reassuring guffaw, they slowed their headlong retreat, regained composure, and gradually returned, chiding each other for their cowardice.

"Imagine you, Nemek, fleeing like a frightened child!" said one of the men to Selambo's killer.

"What do you mean? I ran only because you did!"

"We bolted like a herd of startled pigs," someone else chuckled. "Under and over each other and all in different directions!"

"How embarrassing," another blushed. "Our enemies are all covering themselves with their rain capes to hide their laughter. You can see the rain capes shaking!"

"Never mind. He probably pulled the same trick on them. Watch out for this man. He's unpredictable. Who knows what other tricks he's hidden in the tip of his gourd, so to speak."

Even if he never impressed them again, Stan was already a legend.

After the visitors satisfied their curiosity by observing Stan and Bruno closely for about an hour, and examining the various utensils in their camp, Stan urged them, using his young Yali aides as interpreters, to return the next day and work on the airstrip. They left discussing this proposal (still looking back over their shoulders, amazed to see that Stan had somehow fused his teeth back into his mouth).

Bruno commented, "Where else in the world could you rout a veritable army simply by taking out your false teeth?"

Stan replied, "I'll tell you of someone who's done me one better, though, Bruno. A missionary named Bill, back in Papua New Guinea. Bill had several hundred tribesmen working on an airstrip. Whenever he left them, they all sat down. So one day Bill shouted, 'Look here! I'm going away for a while, but I'm leaving one of my eyes on this stump!' So saying, Bill plucked out his glass eye, set it on a stump with the pupil facing toward the work gang, and with his one good eye walked over the hill. When he returned some time later, he found the entire crew still working hard and still shuddering!"

The two companions chuckled. They passed the afternoon in relaxed conversation, while Yali men and boys of all ages squatted on ridges and rocks, just watching. Then, as Stan was cooking the evening meal—

"Bruno!"

Bruno turned and saw Stan doubled over in pain. He hurried to his side and heard him gasp, "This sudden terrible pain in my lower abdomen! No, dear God! Don't let it be—yes, Bruno, surely it could only mean one thing—appendicitis!"

Pale with shock, Bruno hurried to the little trail radio and called Karubaga for medical advice. But Pat, who chatted with Stan just an hour earlier, had by now turned off the Karubaga radio. Angry static mocked Bruno's urgent call.

Stan, meanwhile, staggered into the tent and lay down on his sleeping bag. Almost immediately nausea that seemed to tear his body apart forced him out of the tent again. He knelt on his hands and knees, praying and retching at the same time. Hovering in helpless anguish, Bruno saw Stan raise his head and look up at the cold stars, just now beginning to emerge above the Heluk Valley's black mountain walls. And in his expression Bruno could almost read what Stan was thinking.

It's a lonely enough place in which to live, but it's an even lonelier place in which to die!

ANOTHER LISTENER

Chapter 12

STAN and Bruno knew that it would be impossible even for the willing Dani helpers to carry Stan by stretcher over the treacherous alpine swamps and rock bluffs of the Mugwi Pass. If even one carrier slipped, Stan would fall, rupturing his swollen appendix.

They would have to wait and hope that Stan would live until somewhere a doctor could be found who was willing and able to trek across the pass with equipment suitable for an operation in the wilderness.

While they waited, still another problem loomed, for at the sound of Stan's groaning, Yali men came running. In utter astonishment, they saw a man whom they regarded as having been blessed with immortality doubled over with pain, retching violently. Simultaneously, the same question occurred to all—how could Wanla's theory account for this?! There was only one way to find out. Ask Wanla.

Wanla sighed. Bolstering his once elegant theory was fast becoming a taxing chore. Should he simply admit that he didn't know the answer? Or was there a way of rationalizing this contradiction also?

Meanwhile his brother Andeng's mind was working too. *Only days ago,* Andeng mused, *this "Kugwarak" ordered the destruction of our* kembu-vam. *Now, suddenly, he falls sick, as if struck down by some invisible force. Could it be that he was not Kugwarak but some mere mortal? Were the spirits now in fact inflicting their judgment upon him, as in the past they had similarly punished even Yali priests who erred in sacred matters?*

Bruno, too, though unaware of the inner working of Yali minds around him, wondered if the people would interpret Stan's illness as a judgment from the supernatural world and side with the spirits against them. Indeed, could it be that spirits hostile to the gospel were hereby seeking to frustrate Stan's and his mission?

A feeling of deep loneliness, compounded with awesome responsibility, swept over Bruno. *So much depends upon Stan's recovery,* he reflected. *What can I—untrained in medicine—do to keep him alive until help arrives?*

To begin with, he decided, *I can pray!*

And pray he did. Hour by hour. Fervently. And with faith that increased despite multiplying odds.

Through the long night, Bruno watched over Stan, who lay sleepless, grimacing with pain. With the first light of Monday's dawn, Bruno began calling on their small trail radio. By 6:00 A.M. he had contacted not only Pat but also Myron Bromley at Hetigima, whose new bride, Marge, was a medical doctor. She confirmed Stan's own diagnosis of probable appendicitis and prepared injections of penicillin for an airdrop to Ninia. MAF pilot Bob Johannson immediately canceled his schedule for the day and flew to Hetigima to pick up the penicillin. By midmorning Johannson found a gap in the clouds above the Heluk and swooped down over the fledgling airstrip site, dropping the precious vials and a thermometer by tiny parachute.

Recovering the package from nearby rough terrain, Bruno opened it in suspense, but found the crucial contents still intact. He trembled as he lifted the formidable-looking syringe with its long sharp needle, for Bruno never before had given an injection! Still, bravely following Marge Bromley's detailed instructions, he filled the syringe with the prescribed one million units of penicillin, rolled the patient over on his side and, gritting his teeth, thrust in the needle. Stan winced. Opening his eyes, Bruno drew back the syringe slightly. No blood appeared in the syringe, so he knew he had not struck a vein. Still trembling, he pushed down gradually on the syringe, withdrew it, and wiped cold sweat from his forehead.

Just then he heard the radio crackle again. One of Bob Johannson's fellow pilots, George Boggs, had contacted Dr. van ten Brink at a Dutch government hospital beside the Paniai Lakes, two hundred miles to the west. The doctor was willing to trek over the Mugwi Pass.

Bruno breathed a sigh of relief. Now there was hope, if only Stan could hang on to life for a few more days.

Then Pat called again from Karubaga to say that RBMU missionary John McCain from Florida volunteered to accompany Dr. van ten Brink over the mountains. Bruno turned up the radio volume so that Stan could hear Pat's loving words of hope and encouragement to her stricken husband. Later that afternoon George Boggs flew Dr. van ten Brink, a medical orderly, John McCain, and a handful of Dani carriers at treetop level, in blinding rain, down the sprawling Balim Valley to Hetigima. Descending from the aircraft, they quickly sorted their packs, drank down a thermos of hot beverage, and set out along that same precarious trail toward the Mugwi. And in the Heluk Valley, day merged into night and night into day as time, for Stan Dale, drifted slowly by in a fog of pain. After what seemed an eternity of enduring, Stan asked, "Bruno, what day is it now?"

"It's Thursday evening," Bruno replied. "You have been five days without food."

"And without sleep," Stan added. "Bruno!"

There was a sharp edge of desperation in Stan's voice.

"I can't stand any more of this. Pray for me again, Bruno. Pray that the pain will stop so I can sleep. If it doesn't stop, I can't last more than a few hours."

Trembling with emotion, Bruno placed his hand upon Stan's head according to a biblical injunction of the apostle James, and prayed for Stan's healing. It was a moment such as he never before experienced. In the absoluteness of his concern for Stan's life and for the welfare of Stan's wife and four children, Bruno found himself able to believe implicitly in the reality of God's love for Stan, and God's ability, on Stan's behalf, to contradict His own creation, a universe of natural cause and effect. It seemed to him suddenly that the very matter around him, through God's power, became subordinate to his desire, that there was no longer any probability that Stan could die. Surely God did not give his pure and simple trust to Bruno in order to disappoint it! But then, almost as quickly, came the stabbing doubt: *Have not others before you felt this same degree of trust and still been denied?*

And while Bruno's hand lingered on Stan's forehead, John McCain and Dr. van ten Brink were forcing their weary legs to hurry down the slippery trail from the Mugwi Pass. Grimly determined, they plunged through bogs and penetrated labyrinthine moss forests, thankful that at last they were descending from those bare heights where two days of rain at near freezing temperature kept them continually chilled to the bone.

Bruno removed his hand from Stan's forehead, crawled out of the tent, and stood looking up-valley toward Balinga, scanning darkening ridges for some sign of approaching help. But there was still no sign. Had some injury forced the medical team to turn back? After a minute he looked back at Stan and saw that he had fallen into a deep sleep. There was no sign of pain on his relaxed features.

His heart pounding with gratitude, Bruno lifted his hands in praise to God.

Then he returned to constructing an operating table.

Not until ten hours later did Stan awaken. Bruno saw then that the mist of pain had truly cleared from his eyes. Stan said he felt refreshed and ready to continue his fight for life. That afternoon, June 9, 1961, John McCain, the doctor, and the medical orderly came over the ridge and strode anxiously down into the camp.

Now it was Bruno's turn to sleep.

And while Dr. van ten Brink attended to Stan, Yali men in the *yogwas* of Hwim and Sivimu were rapidly narrowing down their diagnosis of "Kugwarak's" plight.

"The night before he fell sick," one informant offered, "I saw a giant fruit bat feeding in the yelep tree behind their camp. When it finished, I heard it flutter downward in the darkness. In the next instant I saw him—Kugwarak—walk out of the shadows and enter his strange little house. I'm certain—almost certain—that the bat and the man were the same being. He had changed into a bat to feed in the tree, came back down, and changed into a man again. I was so frightened, I ran!"

Fear of the unnatural settled over the elders. "Are you suggesting," one of them asked, "that it was the yelep fruit that made him so sick?"

"That's my guess!" said the informant. And so the story spread, and was used by many to bolster Wanla's original theory. Others, Andeng included, adopted a wait-and-see attitude. "If he dies, I'll say it was *Kembu* and not the yelep fruit that killed him!" they said.

And so the Yalis awaited the outcome of Stan's illness, while Dr. van ten Brink studied Stan's blood pressure and pulse and administered further drugs.

Seeing that Stan's condition was steadily improving, Dr. van ten Brink decided not to attempt an operation in the tent. Instead he waited beside Stan in the Heluk for several days, until he was sure the infection had subsided. Then the doctor and his orderly returned over the Mugwi to Hetigima and from there, by aircraft, to the Paniai Lakes. Later Stan judged himself ready to trek out at a slow pace for an appendix operation. Bruno, weakened also by an attack of malaria, accompanied him. The treacherous journey was accomplished with considerable suspense, lest either Bruno's malaria or the inflammation in Stan's abdomen be reactivated by the exercise.

John McCain, meanwhile, remained at Ninia and worked with the Dani crew and the handful of Yalis until a few weeks after Bruno returned. The work crew by this time had dwindled to as few as nine members. After John McCain left to begin still another RBMU venture to tribes in the southern lowlands, Missouri-born colleague Bill Widbin trekked into Ninia and worked with Bruno for some four months. During this time the stones from the sacred wall of the Yarino *osuwa* were carried down and deposited in the swamp as fill. And once again Wanla's theory protected the mission party from massacre.

Stan's appendectomy was delayed until October, lest the doctor's incision serve only to spread the still latent infection. Finally, however, doctors in Hollandia completed the operation successfully, and on November 9, Stan, fully recovered, set out on his return trek to Ninia.

He was accompanied this time by Oscar, a native carpenter whom Stan hired to construct a family-size missionary dwelling at Ninia.

Later Stan described the last day of their journey:

"As I came down from the ranges, the morning mist lifted and I could see the Heluk Valley spread out beneath me. A great longing came over me to see groups of Christians in all its villages and to hear them sing songs of praise to God! I stood still on the trail for a few moments and claimed the valley by faith for Christ!"

And so the Yali looked up to see their would-be spiritual conquistador returning from the gates of death with sure and steady tread. Once again priests of the *kembu* spirits huddled in *kembu-vams* from Balinga to Sivimu and beyond, endlessly debating the significance of dead Kugwarak's dramatic return to the world of men. In general Stan's recovery was taken as further confirmation of "the Wanla theory," giving Stan and Bruno still more time to establish their beachhead in the valley.

Stan's recovery also caused Andeng to relax his prohibition against Yali participation in the project, with the result that a larger number of workers were available—when the weather was good!

There was a danger, of course: the longer the Wanla theory lasted, the more severe might be the backlash when finally it crumbled.

"I hope Stan will be pleased," said Bruno. He and Bill Widbin had made excellent progress, considering the ruggedness of the terrain and the scarcity of workers, during Stan's four-month absence.

There was only one hitch; they had chosen to make the excavation through the Yarino knoll about twenty feet narrower than Stan had directed. The reasonableness of their decision was plain enough to themselves.

"We can widen it later," they assured each other, "but our initial goal must be to complete something an aircraft can land on in case of further medical emergencies, like the one that nearly cost Stan his life. Each foot added to the width now will delay that crucial first landing by a week or more!"

Later that day, over the ridge Stan came, followed by Oscar the carpenter. The greetings were cheery enough as Stan dropped his pack and wiped the sweat from his brow. But then he walked over to check what Bill and Bruno had done.

"Whatever happened here!" he gruffed. "This is far too narrow."

Without another word, Stan yanked out the stakes Bruno and Bill had set and marked out a new, much wider border for the already immense hand excavation. Bruno's heart sank. He tried to explain his reasons to Stan, but Stan would hear none of it. His orders as "commanding officer" had been disobeyed, and that was that!

But there was an even more serious area of disagreement.

"Come and get it!" Bill Widbin called. Interrupting their animated discussions about the airstrip, Stan and Bruno headed for "the camel's hump"—as they affectionately called the hut they had fashioned earlier with hand-hewn boards from Kugwarak's ill-fated *kembu-vam*. Stan was hungry as a wild boar after his long trek over Mugwi Pass, yet he stopped short when he saw the meal Bill had prepared. Expensive tinned vegetables complemented the plain boiled rice, and a more costly canned meat replaced Stan's favorite—bully beef. Worse yet, sweetened tinned fruits and jelly waited for dessert!

Stan bristled. Memories of the "extravagant diet" of American soldiers in the New Guinea war theater flashed through his mind. "How can God's soldiers on the front lines of this spiritual warfare afford such luxuries?" he demanded.

Bruno and Bill looked at him. They already knew that Stan was not merely content but actually *happy* with an almost unvarying field menu of bully beef and rice. But they hadn't expected him to raise such a forthright objection to their enjoyment of more appetizing food.

"Stan," they countered, "we've scoured these grim hillsides and found no fruit at all. Even banana plants never bear because of the high altitude. We'd prefer fresh fruit, of course, but since none is available, except for a few things Pat sends in airdrops from Karubaga, we thought—"

"My family and I cannot afford to pay for such expensive foods," Stan interjected, "so I'll thank you not to serve them to me. I'll share the cost of the rice, bully beef, tea, the things Pat sends in airdrops, and other basics, but nothing more."

Bruno and Bill looked at each other. Stan's proposal meant complex bookkeeping. They had ordered enough of everything for Stan as well as themselves, and counted on him sharing the cost. Bill thought Stan had promised to share, but Stan denied this. Finally, it would be awkward day after day to continue eating the food they had chosen under Stan's disapproving gaze.

Tension increased and finally broke.

"You can cook for yourself and eat with the Danis!" Bruno said firmly. This never came to pass; nevertheless Stan was hurt. Nor was it easy for Bruno to stand up to him, for if Stan's greatest problem was the extreme boldness he had learned in childhood, Bruno, conversely, struggled against a deeply ingrained shyness. Throughout his boyhood in Holland, he had leaned heavily upon his older sister, Rinske, who first helped him face the great, cold world beyond the end of the quaint cobblestone street where they lived. Then came the German occupation, abduction by military police—harrowing months digging trenches in Holland and Germany, forced labor in a submarine yard—followed by four postwar years in the Dutch army. Through it all, the shackles of Bruno's shyness began to fall away, preparing him for his next great adventure—emigration to Canada and, following his conversion to Jesus Christ, to Dutch New Guinea.

The road to inner confidence had been rough and hard, but Bruno had come a long way. Nevertheless, whenever Stan, archetype of the born leader, turned his stern, authoritative glance toward him, Bruno could feel his spirit receding into that old shyness. Only now, steeling every fiber of his being, had he summoned the strength to resist Stan's will.

It was a rare experiment for Bruno, and it worked. At least until the day Bill Widbin, having contributed immensely to the Ninia project, returned over the mountains to his own work in another part of Dutch New Guinea. Once again Stan and Bruno found themselves alone in the valley with their black-skinned partners. Disagreement over diet, by this time, had subsided.

Missionaries, though they may differ among themselves as strongly as other men, have this in their favor: on the average, they resolve their differences more quickly than others whose circumstances make it easier to ignore those with whom they disagree.

And what did they eat? Mainly bully beef and rice, of course! For though Stan could not budge from his principles, Bruno found grace in Christ to subordinate his personal tastes to the dictates of his colleague's conscience. Nevertheless he could not resist the temptation, months later, to indulge in a mildly sarcastic comment to an acquaintance elsewhere. "I have a deep, dark secret to confess." He sighed forlornly, but his eyes twinkled. "One night at Ninia, I opened a tin of Mandarin oranges and ate them under my blanket!"

"Hurry that bucket brigade!"

As Stan and Bruno kicked away burning logs from a massive monolith of rock, shouting Danis and Yalis moved in, sloshing buckets of cold water upon the heated stone.

Crack! Pop! To the intense delight of the workers, the rapidly contracting surface began to shear away from the still expanded interior, reducing the size of the monolith. A few more cycles of heating and rapid cooling and the rock would be small enough to roll down into the swamp as fill.

Where did Stan get the idea? Out of his deep knowledge of history! One of his boyhood heroes, Hannibal—descending the Alps to attack Rome—had used the same method to reduce the size of rocks blocking the path of his army.

It was another small bit of progress in a mammoth undertaking. Whereas initially Stan and Bruno hoped to complete the project in three or four months (counting on a much larger work force), they now revised their estimates to seven or eight months. Unknown to them, the task was to require a full ten-and-a-half months of bone-jarring labor, an unprecedented duration for the construction of a single airstrip in the interior of Dutch New Guinea.[1] Three more missionary men were later sent in with fresh crews of Danis to try to speed up the work, but all to little avail. The mountain seemed determined to levy a full tax, not only of effort but of time as well, before it would consent to its final taming under the wheels of an aircraft.

And, of course, every extra day of labor for the married men was another day of separation from their wives and children, which added a special test of patience. Yet at no time did the missionaries try to compel unwilling Yalis to join in the work or vent anger against the watchers on the hillsides for their seemingly inexplicable reserve. Even though every missionary on the project was convinced that the building of the airstrip would bring incalculable spiritual, medical, educational, and eventually economic help to the Heluk Yalis, each acknowledged the Yali right not to participate in its construction.

Those relatively few Yalis who *did* sign on the project, however, were expected to work at a steady pace, following the example of the missionaries themselves. And this expectation, among a people not accustomed to taking orders from outsiders, led to occasional moments of tension. At one point a missionary colleague looked up to see a number of Yalis turn upon Stan with upraised shovels. The colleague rushed in among them in time to prevent harm to Stan. Later he remarked, "I can't be sure, but I think I may have saved Stan's life."

But Stan, though grateful, brushed the incident aside as hardly worth mentioning. For those who regard absence of fear as a measure of manliness, Stan Dale was one of the bravest men you could ever hope to meet.

Certainly the pressure of trying to complete an airstrip under bad weather conditions and in extreme isolation was not the most ideal context for a first meeting of two very opposite cultures!

Indeed, all members of the project, including Stan, showed signs of strain as months of hard labor accumulated. But for one member the stress proved intolerable.

From the beginning of his venture into the Snow Mountains, Oscar, Stan's handpicked Papuan carpenter, had been under pressure. The long trek across the Mugwi in sleet and mist, the unnatural silence of the moss-hung forests, the strangeness of these Yali people and the rumor of their awesome supernatural powers, the "impossibility" of constructing the Ninia strip with so few workers, Stan's brush with death—which Oscar suspected may have been caused by Yali witchcraft—and the almost unbroken inclemency of the Heluk weather kept his nerves taut as steel wires for some three months.

By late 1961 Stan and Bruno began sharing news reports that Indonesia and the Netherlands were on the brink of war over possession of Oscar's homeland, Dutch New Guinea, plunging the carpenter into still deeper apprehension.

Then, with the coming of the westerly monsoons in January 1962 Heluk weather worsened into a full-blown *o-sanim,* as the Yali called it. This meant calling upon their helpers to work in oppressive rainstorms. The Yalis refused, saying, "The rain eats us!" The Danis, though willing, lacked waterproof clothing and soon became so chilled they had to be sent back to their warm fires. Oscar, who was responsible for constructing the Dale family's residence, was better clothed, but long hours of work in the rain were crumbling his spirit faster than the flood was eroding the soil at his feet.

Soon Oscar heard rumors that Yali shamans were blaming the *o-sanim* on the foreigners. "The *kembu* spirits are displeased because the foreigners are not subject to them!" was the complaint. And Oscar began to believe that the entire mission was doomed. He could see no way that these two foolhardy white men could even complete their impossible airstrip, let alone plant the church of Christ among such a sinister, inscrutable people!

By January 19, 1962, Oscar could bear it no longer.

At Karubaga, Pat recorded in her diary a terse radio report from Stan: *Oscar is mentally affected by our situation here.*

Two days later, Oscar was suffering hallucinations, believing Yali shamans had placed a curse on him. Stan cocked a grimly tufted eye and looked around at the mysterious misty villages huddled on their bleak ridges.

Perhaps they have, too! he thought to himself. It was easy to believe in curses in such a place and on such a cheerless day.

By January 26, 1962, Oscar became almost uncontrollable. It was clear that he could no longer stay in the Heluk Valley. Bruno and three of the original Dani escorts set out from Ninia, accompanying Oscar back to civilization. On this his fourth crossing of the freezing Mugwi Pass, a weary Bruno looked down through black cloud layers at the distant Balim Valley, awash in sunshine. Involuntarily, as if drawn by a magnet, he quickened his steps toward the sunny valley. Not until that moment did he realize how heavy had been his own depression, building up steadily over six months of labor on that horrendous airstrip. Inclement weather and an uncanny sense of demonic resistance in the atmosphere of the Heluk increased the pressure.

But there was an even more serious problem for Bruno—Stan.

Bruno sensed that Stan did not want him to return.

"You've had a hard six months in here, Bruno," Stan had said. "After you see that Oscar gets medical help, why don't you just take a vacation?"

But the way Stan turned away after speaking seemed, to Bruno, to say, *And after your vacation, if you have somewhere else to go—*

Bruno had agreed to Stan's way of building the airstrip, and he was learning to live on Stan's frugal diet. Yet the two men found themselves poles apart on another sensitive issue—is it really necessary to scold Yali workers for sitting down on the job? Why not simply try to *humor* them back onto their feet?

Stan, in true soldierly tradition, believed that an overly diplomatic approach would lead to an unmanageable breakdown of morale. And Bruno, in fact, often did find it difficult to persuade the Yali with good humor. Bruno, gentle pragmatist, feared that too much discipline would discourage workers, driving them from the project.

Half-hearted help is better than none at all, he reasoned.

But in a wider sense, Bruno thought, *perhaps Stan, dyed-in-the-wool individualist, truly needs to work alone. Perhaps he's a John the Baptist who has finally found a wilderness wild enough to be his proper setting. Here in this wilderness, Stan must now fulfill a special kind of lone ministry on a meager diet, and I'm just a regular guy who wants to eat regular food and do things a regular way!*

Bruno found encouragement in this line of thought. *Probably not even Saint Paul could have fully shared John the Baptist's life; perhaps I shouldn't feel too bad because I don't enjoy working with Stan Dale!*

Bruno might have felt more encouraged had he known that he was by no means the first missionary colleague to experience serious disagreement with Stan.

Bruno respected Stan for the years of seniority Stan had accumulated in eastern New Guinea. This respect kept him from disagreeing with Stan on all but the most painful issues. And now it made him willing meekly to move himself out of Stan's way.

Bruno looked back over his shoulder at Oscar, who trudged abjectly behind him, haunted by some incredible nightmare that would not end. *There,* Bruno sighed, *but for the grace of God, walk I.*

Far behind Bruno, in the Heluk, Stanley Albert Dale stood alone in a howling rainstorm, water streaming down from the brim of his old Australian army "digger" hat. Grimly he surveyed his beloved airstrip, now a sloping sea of mud. Never had it looked more desolate. Never had his spirit felt more eroded. The remaining Danis and all the Yalis had fled to their warm fires, but still Stan waited, brooding, shivering.

"Aw!" he bawled suddenly into the wind. "Two hills and a swamp for a strip site. People who won't help! Appendicitis in me own carcass! A near deluge! And now lunacy in the crew! What next, Lord?"

For a moment, like a hairy spider out of a chink, the thought intruded that perhaps Oscar was the sane one! But only for a moment. The words of Rudyard Kipling, like an echo from the heavens, came to Stan again in his hour of need:

If you can force your heart and nerve and sinew
To serve your turn long after they are gone,
And so hold on when there is nothing in you
Except the Will, which says to them: "Hold on."

"Get thee behind me, Satan!" Stan bellowed into the rain. "I have already claimed this valley and these people for Jesus Christ, and I haven't changed my mind, you hear?"

He leaned into the howling wind, while water-borne mud rippled over his boots.

"And I'm not complainin' about any of this! It's not what I hoped for, but God allows it, and I'm glad! You hear?"

The wind swept a blast of rain at his face, but he gritted his teeth against it and exulted, "What's more, these Yalis are going to know their Creator through Jesus Christ. You hear? And His church is going to be established in this valley and beyond because God the Father, Son, and Holy Spirit, and Pat and I and Bruno and all of us in this mission will it! You hear?"

With renewed determination, Stan struck his shovel into the mud again, as if planting a flag. Then, as he looked around him, both eyes opened wide. For on the higher and lower hills, wherever he and the others had removed the turf of dense mountain grass, heavy rain was gradually loosening and moving tons of gravel downward, ever downward within the wide bowl of the swamp they had drained.

With praise to God rioting in his heart, Stan recognized the rain as his ally, an ally sent by God to compensate for the lack of workers.

"It's a controlled landslide," he mused. "A worker who demands no wages, a miracle disguised as a natural phenomenon! Like the poet said:

Those clouds you so much dread
Are big with mercy and will break
With blessings on your head!

"Alleluia!" he shouted, and moved rapidly back and forth across the breadth of the dig, loosening still more soil so that the water could bear it down for him.

A few days later, two other RBMU missionaries, John Dekker and Philip Masters, arrived to take Bruno's place. Less than a week later, a radio call from Karubaga advised John Dekker that his home back in the Swart Valley, together with all his belongings, had burned to the ground.

"Hurry back, John," a voice crackled over the wireless. "Helen and the children need you!"

John left at once, making record time back across Mugwi Pass.

Stan and Iowa-born Phil Masters were left alone in the Heluk.

Affable Phil, a former farmer *cum* school teacher, and his cheerful wife, Phyliss, were recent arrivals in Dutch New Guinea. Helping Stan at Ninia was one of Phil's first assignments.

In those early days, Stan impressed Phil deeply, and Phil, his nationality notwithstanding, also impressed Stan.

One day at Ninia the two men climbed above the airstrip onto a high rock near the children's hidden waterfall. Phil walked with a slight limp. Stan, springy as a mountain goat, waited for Phil and helped him up.

They sat together, looking eastward at the jumbled mountains beyond the Heluk.

"Beyond that range, another valley," Stan mused aloud.

"And beyond that valley, another range and still another valley," Phil added, sharing Stan's inward vision.

"And so it continues for a hundred miles to the Papuan border," Stan continued. "And in every valley there are people like these, somehow existing without knowing their own Creator and His Son who came to earth!"

Phil pictured them in his mind and sensed Stan's heavy burden of responsibility for them.

"Sometimes, Phil, I sit up here on this rock and look out to the east and think of the people in all those valleys. And if I listen real hard, it's almost as if I can hear their voices calling."

With intense passion, Stan began to quote from "St. Paul," a poem by F.W.H. Meyer:

Then with a rush the intolerable craving
Shivered through me like a trumpet call:
"Oh, to save these, to perish for their saving,
Die for their life, be offered for them all!"

They came down from the rock in silence. For now the voices of those eastern valleys had found another listener—Philip Masters.

That night Phil lay awake in his sleeping bag and felt that same trumpet call shiver through his own being.

"Perhaps someday, Lord," he prayed, "You will send me across those still more distant ranges in response."

Oscar entered the Queen Juliana Hospital in Hollandia. After a period of internment, he regained composure and emerged to lead a normal, productive life. Meanwhile Bruno, after a month's vacation, returned to Karubaga to ask for a new assignment.

Bill Mallon, RBMU Field Chairman, disagreed. "We have no other task worthy of your talents, Bruno—not unless you want to join John McCain in our new outreach to headhunters in the southern swamps. But my wife, Barbara, and I hope to go there after furlough. Also we expect a new couple—Don and Carol Richardson—to arrive in April, and we hope they will go to the south as well."

"I believe my calling is to these mountain tribes," Bruno said.

"Then Ninia is the place for you," Mallon rejoined. "I know you think Stan doesn't want you back—I've gotten that impression myself from things he's said—but still I think you should go back. No matter where you move among missionaries, Bruno, you'll find strong personalities. If God hadn't made us that way, we wouldn't be here in the first place, let alone accomplish anything once we're here. But every strong personality needs someone opposite to keep him balanced. Often, I believe, our opposites are the grindstones God uses to shape us after the likeness of Christ."

"I'm sure that's true," Bruno swallowed. But inwardly he was thinking, *He doesn't understand. Stan is not just another strong personality. He's a John the Baptist.*

Mallon continued, "I've just heard from Stan by radio. Ninia will be ready for its first aircraft landing on March 22. But first an RBMU missionary must escort an MAF pilot over the Mugwi Pass to check the airstrip on the ground and radio instructions to the pilot who makes the landing."

Bruno saw what was coming.

"I have no one else to send with the pilot; I'm asking you to take him in there, Bruno. You know the way. And I ask you to stay there with Stan until our annual conference in April. Then you can ask the conference for a new assignment if you want to."

Mallon waited. And in the quietness of his heart, Bruno knew again the presence of the One who said, *If any man seeks his own fulfillment, he shall lose it! But if any man surrenders his own fulfillment for My sake and the gospel's, he shall find it!*

Bruno saw his duty and chose to do it, even though he could see nothing in it for himself.

California-born Hank Worthington, the pilot, proved himself a fast trekker for a man accustomed to soaring over the ranges on a padded, airborne flight seat. Traveling light, he and Bruno crossed the Mugwi in only three days, reaching Ninia on March 21. Bruno wondered how Stan would greet him. Reluctantly? Perhaps even with disdain?

"Hello, Stan," Bruno ventured, with an open, if slightly hesitant, smile. Stan drew himself up and faced Bruno squarely. His gaze was cool, and the tufts of his brows jutted even more fiercely than Bruno remembered.

"Hello, Bruno," Stan replied evenly. Suddenly the craggy veteran's saltlick of a face cracked open in a wide grin. "Good to see you back!"

The short arm with its stubby, calloused fingers shot out. Bruno gripped it and grinned back.

The air was clear.

Anxious as bridegrooms at a triple wedding, Stan, Bruno, and Phil Masters sat watching as lanky Hank Worthington walked over the airstrip from end to end, checking its slope, its crown, its hardness.

Then he strode back to the radio transmitter and called Bob Johannson at distant Wamena. "It's okay, Bob. Come on in!"

In that moment Stan and Bruno felt ten-and-a-half months' accumulated concern easing from their shoulders. Phil, though he had labored less than two months at Ninia, could appreciate their sigh of relief. But almost as quickly a new tension moved in—concern for Bob Johannson, who in a few minutes would have to do what no one else had ever done before: bank his single-engine craft straight at this west wall of the Heluk gorge and negotiate a safe landing on what must surely be one of the world's steepest airstrips!

"If it was all the same slope, it would be easier," Hank explained, "but Bob will have to blend his approach into a fourteen-degree upslope, run level through this excavation, and then climb an eighteen-degree upslope to the turnaround at the top. With three different slopes to keep his eyes on, there's a danger that an optical illusion may trick him into coming in either too steep or too shallow."

Minutes later, Johannson circled overhead, descending into the gorge. He saw the airstrip far below—a mere Band-Aid on a knee of the mountain. Alone with God and his instruments, skittering past jungle-bearded limestone cliffs, Bob banked into his final approach. It was a "short final" approach now, but the valley floor was still a thousand feet below him! There was no sense of "level," no reference points except the three angles of the strip itself.

On the ground Stan crouched, tense, his arms spread like wings as if trying to assist Johannson by remote control. "C'mon, Bob. Easy, man! Bring her down easy!" he whispered. Suddenly the aircraft disappeared below the edge of the strip and the sound of its engine died. Stan's heart nearly stopped, until he remembered that the foot of the strip, the end of the ski jump, was out of sight below Yarino knoll, which months of labor had not fully leveled.

As suddenly as it disappeared, the aircraft bobbed into view again, surmounting Yarino knoll and rolling easily across what once had been the swamp. Johannson pulled the throttle again in order to climb the final upslope to the turnaround at the top of the airstrip.

By now pandemonium broke out as Stan, Bruno, and Phil, their faces beaming, hugged each other for sheer joy. Stan and Bruno bounded up the slope to the turnaround, with Phil trying to keep up. There Johannson's bird perched saucily on the turnaround, its nose in the air as if proud of its accomplishment. Johannson waited for them, one arm draped over a wing strut. He appeared calm, but inwardly he was rejoicing. For Bob it was a special privilege to bring fulfillment to these rugged men for their months of exhausting labor.

While Hank and Bob discussed the landing, Stan, Bruno, and Phil stood together for a few moments in silence, looking down the great sweep of the airstrip—and remembering.

Then Johannson moved over and Hank, still sore from his three-day trek across the Mugwi, climbed into the pilot's seat. He was grateful to be leaving by aircraft instead of trekking back over that pass. In fact, the Mugwi convinced him that perhaps in the future it would not be necessary for a pilot to inspect such remote strips on the ground before a first landing. Hank gunned the Cessna's engine, raced down the "ski jump," and took off to try his own first landing.

He also negotiated a safe touchdown on the odd-shaped surface. The project was now a success; the Heluk was an opened valley! Soon Hank and Bob would introduce other mission pilots to the new landing site, and frequent concourse with the outside world would begin.

One week later Stan, Bruno, and Phil Masters flew to Karubaga for the mission's second annual conference, where they reported on the opening of the Heluk Valley.

Also at that conference, both Stan and Bruno were elected to the four-man executive committee that would meet from time to time to lead the mission for another year. It was a measure of the high esteem with which they were regarded for their "courage and persevering labor."

Bruno chose not to ask the conference for a new appointment. He had poured out too many gallons of sweat upon the stones of the Heluk Valley to leave it now. Even if he had to pour out his blood as well, he would stay until the conference itself chose to move him.

Note

1. The name "Dutch New Guinea" was changed in 1964 to "Irian Jaya" and later to "Papua."

TRIALS OF A FAMILY

Chapter 13

"THE outlook is very pretty, near a waterfall," Stan had radioed to Pat soon after he reached Ninia the previous May. Of greater concern to Pat as a wife, mother, and homemaker, however, was the "inlook" of a suitable dwelling at the new location!

Then, at Karubaga on March 30, face to face with his family, Stan admitted, "It'll be a wee bit rough, darling, until we get our home built. It won't take long, I trust, to get a house up. Oscar finished the foundation before he had to leave the valley. And at least we'll be together after all these months of separation."

Bruno, by that time, was ready to move into a small house he had been constructing, leaving "the camel's hump" for the Dale family to use until their permanent dwelling was completed.

Somewhat forewarned, Pat agreed to take their four children and accompany Stan back to Ninia following the conference. Bruno would fly back some weeks later.

After a heart-stopping landing, Pat emerged, slightly shaken, from the aircraft. As her little ones crowded around her, she felt her fortitude slipping.

Such a wild, remote landscape! Chilly, high altitude, naked Yali men, cold and sinister in their black cosmetic—*Why don't they smile like our Dani friends in the Swart Valley? Where are the women? There's not a woman in sight!*

"Mommy, I'm afraid!" one of the older children piped as a curious Yali pinched the child's white cheeks.

Seeing Pat's dismay, Stan tried to comfort her. He pointed toward the hidden waterfall beyond the airstrip, with its ideal picnic site. He drew her attention to the majestic mountains, then indicated the friendly young Yali boys, including Yekwara and Bengwok, who had been such faithful helpers in constructing the airstrip. They would probably be willing to help Pat with the housework also!

"Where is the house?" Pat asked. She craved a secure, pleasant dwelling as refuge against this strange, cold, predominantly male world.

"It's behind those trees. Come and see!"

Pat followed Stan to a shelf of land adjoining the airstrip. Her heart sank further upon seeing the "house," a grass-roofed, dirt-floored hut, far too tiny for a family. Pat had visions of her four children crawling over each other getting in and out of bed.

Just about that time, the little airplane that brought them to Ninia took off on its return flight. Pat barely managed to hide her feelings from Stan and the children. Now they were alone. With these tribesmen. In this place. Pat breathed an urgent prayer: *Dear heavenly Father, my husband is certain that this is Your will for him, and therefore it must be Your will for me also. I hope it is, Lord, because if it isn't, I won't be able to take it. And even if it is, I'm still going to need an awful lot of Your grace.*

The hut had two windows. Both were covered with an opaque plastic sheeting intended more for use on storehouses than on dwellings. The sheeting kept out flies, wind, and driving rain, and its opaqueness made it difficult for Yalis to peek inside. But it allowed no view out of the cabin and, on a dull day, would seem to increase rather than lighten the gloom. In its diffused light, one could lay on a bunk made of rough poles, listen to the dripping rain, and imagine one were dreaming while still awake.

As Stan rigged more extensive clotheslines, Pat helped the children unpack their bags, searching for places to stow things on the hut's limited shelves. Ninia fog eased down over the station and seeped in through chinks in the walls of the hut. Pat saw fingers of it drift past her, spreading dankness. She shivered and cried within herself, *Stan, when can you start on the house?*

"POLES and palm bark! Poles and palm bark!" Stan called in halting Yali. And then added under his breath, *My kingdom for some poles and palm bark!* Gradually the men of Hwim and Sivimu emerged from their *yogwas* and stared at him with kindling interest. So "Kugwarak" wanted to trade poles and palm bark for his steel tools, did he? Well that, at least, was a little more *human* than moving ridges to fill swamps. The Yali doubted strongly that the *kembu* spirits approved of changing entire landscapes, but there were no sanctions against trading!

So, by midafternoon, from Hwim and Sivimu, from Lilibal, Ombok, and Balinga, trails were threaded with shiny white poles borne on the shoulders of Yali men. With fresh materials, Stan and Bruno began laying a floor across the foundation Oscar had built.

Pat, meanwhile, was trying to reach a working agreement with a smoky little wood-stove in the grass hut. Outside her door Yekwara, Bengwok, and other Yali boys kept pinching little Rodney Dale's chubby cheeks, as if checking to see if he were ready to be eaten! And further away, near the edge of the gorge, Rodney's older brothers, Wesley and Hilary, were discussing their choice of names for individual rabbits in the new hutch Stan had built.

For Wesley and Hilary, Dutch New Guinea was paradise, and Ninia—in spite of its damp weather—was its capital city!

What more could two small boys wish for than to live in a largely unexplored land of towering mountains and immense canyons, replete with waterfalls and real live cannibals who stalked about bearing genuine bows, arrows, and spears? And who often fought real wars!

In addition to the rabbits, Dad promised they would each have their own garden and their own chickens to raise!

There was, of course, the problem of school correspondence lessons taught by Mother in the crowded hut five mornings a week. Civilization did have a way of following one, even to such remote places as Ninia. But often MAF pilots came to their rescue during school hours, zooming in with mail and packages from aunts and grandmothers. This distracted Mother for a little while at least.

"Yekwara!" Stan called, and the youth came running. "I want you to help me learn more of the Yali language."

Yekwara's bright smile beamed consent. Stan had already made good progress in Yali, considering that nearly a year had been devoured in airstrip construction.

"First of all, teach me more about your greetings."

In complete innocence, Yekwara started in with *halabok*. Equally innocent, Stan wrote it down. Then Yekwara gave him *hal bisok-sok*. Stan grinned with pleasure. At last he knew how to greet Yali in their own language. This ought to help build a relationship with them. For practice, he called out one of the greetings to a Yali passing nearby and was pleased with an immediate response.

Then he looked more closely at the phrases Yekwara had given him and discerned their true meaning. Stan turned pale. Had he, a servant of God, just said that to a fellow human being?

"Yekwara," he queried, "doesn't *halabok* mean—" and he managed to express the literal meaning in other Yali words.

"Of course!" Yekwara replied unconcernedly.

"Do you mean that your people actually greet each other—with such—sickening words?"

"What do you mean 'sickening'?" Yekwara asked in amazement. "What else would we say to each other?"

Stan's mind recoiled with revulsion. His tongue, having used the words as a greeting, felt unclean. Then his face grew serious.

"Yekwara, I shall never use these greetings again. Help me find some other way to express friendship in Yali."

"This is the best way," Yekwara insisted. "If you don't say these things, people will think you are *min* [cold-hearted]."

The look on Stan's face told Yekwara the issue was not to be decided by what the Yali might think. "Very well, you can say simply *naray* [my friend]."

Stan wrote it down.

"From now on, Yekwara, *naray* is the greeting we will use among ourselves. And we will understand it as conveying genuine love and respect, not like those other greetings, which are insulting. Pass on the word to Bengwok, Dongla, Luliap, and the others."

Amazed, Yekwara passed on the word, and as he predicted, "How can he be so cold?" they asked.

"I don't know," Yekwara answered, "but I'm sure he has his reasons."

As Stan had already used Yali stone-hewn boards to good advantage, he continued buying reasonably solid *yogwas* from anyone who was willing to sell. Dismantled, each *yogwa* yielded up to seventy boards for the walls of the fast-rising Dale residence—after a soaking in creosote killed the vermin.

One morning a man from Balinga brought palm bark to sell to Stan. Aralek, acting as Stan's assistant, counted the palm bark slabs and left to call Stan to the scene. While Aralek was away, the man moved his palm bark. Then came Hulu, a tall august priest of *Kembu*, with a face as dignified as the moon. He, too, brought palm bark, which he laid in the same spot where the Balinga man's palm bark had been.

Soon Stan arrived with the first man's pay—a valued steel adze, something the Yali very much prized for the hewing of boards for their houses. Hulu's eyes lit up when he saw it.

"Is this your palm bark?" Stan queried.

"Yes," said Hulu, and Stan offered him the adze. But before he could take it—

"Wait!" called Aralek, coming upon the scene. "A man from Balinga brought that palm bark."

Stan quickly withdrew the adze. His eyes narrowed.

"Trying to make off with another man's pay, are you?"

"Nothing of the sort!" sniffed Hulu. "This palm bark is mine!"

"But I saw a Balinga man lay it there not long ago," said Aralek, puzzled.

Hulu's jaw set with anger. His honesty had been questioned

Someone else was going to get his pay. In no uncertain terms, Hulu told Stan and Aralek what he thought of them.

Hackles rising, Stan stood up to the towering Yali, but before he knew what hit him, he took a heavy blow on his chest and was knocked flat in the dirt. At the same instant, the adze was wrenched from his hand and Hulu was gone.

With a single bound, Stan was back on his feet, burning with indignation. Many Yalis, as usual, were watching from the hillsides. They, too, were up on their feet now, straining to see what would happen to Hulu for such a bold action.

Stan realized in a flash the gravity of the situation. If Hulu got away with that adze, Stan and Bruno were in trouble. Other Yalis would aspire to the same degree of boldness, and perhaps worse. The awe which now held their violent natures in check would be neutralized.

So Stan did the thing he thought he had to do. He bounded after Hulu, just a few paces behind him, like a terrier after a greyhound.

Hulu, for his part, did not want to fight "Kugwarak." He only wanted that adze, which he knew was rightfully his. He had no doubt that he could defeat his pursuer in a hand-to-hand fight, but there were other problems. Emeroho kept warning the Yali that there were many others like Stan and Bruno beyond the mountains at Wamena. And some of them, called policemen, had been known to kill men with something called a "boom."

"Beware," Emeroho warned, "how you treat these men and their little ones. If you harm them, the policemen may come with their booms and you may not like the results."

So Hulu decided to outrun Stan. He chose an uphill trail. Running uphill was something Hulu had been doing since childhood. As Stan and Hulu wound up the switchbacks toward Hwim, watchers on a dozen ridges cheered them on. Soon Yalis by the hundreds, drawn by the shouting, emerged from their houses to enjoy the spectacle.

Pressing the pursuit with all his strength, Stan found to his amazement that he could not close the gap an inch. And when finally his lungs gave out, Hulu was still bounding uphill with impressive ease. Stan stopped, gasping for breath, and felt respect for Hulu grow within him.

"'You big black bounding beggar,'" he said admiringly, quoting another of Kipling's well-remembered lines. "I wouldna thought you could knock me down, let alone outrun me too!"

By the time Stan returned, Aralek had discovered his mistake.

"Go and apologize to Hulu," Stan said. "Tell him he's earned his adze double."

And so Stan and Hulu became friends. But it was not to be an undisturbed friendship, for Hulu was to knock Stan to the ground still another three times before the great climax that would settle Stan's disagreements with the Yali once and for all.

For two full months, as materials were available, Stan and Bruno labored together on the Dales' family home. When materials were not available, they made further improvements upon the airstrip or studied Yali language. Finally, in mid-June, they nailed on the aluminum roof and boarded in the last outside wall. Then, on June 19, 1962, Stan nailed the porch stairs in place and the family moved in.

Pat sighed with relief. The house was still just a shell, windy and cold, with no ceiling and with many inside walls still unboarded. But at least now she had space, space to move about freely, and places to put things where they wouldn't get lost or soiled or stepped on. Bit by bit they would work together to make it a pleasant home.

Many times during those harrowing two months in the little hut she wept silently in the darkness when everyone else was asleep. She wept with loneliness for family and friends in Tasmania, with concern for her children and their education in this savage, heathen environment, with the dreadful feeling that many Yali did not want them there and might eventually turn against them, and with dismay over the many inconveniences, the problems in cooking, washing, and bathing.

But still, there were compensations. The children were happier than she expected them to be and healthy thus far, in spite of the damp climate. And Stan and she were together. She had often felt so lonely for him during those long months at Karubaga.

"Stan, please don't work on the language again today," Pat pleaded one morning. "The house isn't finished. There are still no doors on the bedrooms, no cupboards, not enough shelves, no walls between some of the rooms."

Stan did not hear. Using young Bengwok as an informant, he was about to achieve a breakthrough in the conjugation of a Yali verb.

"So if it happened recently," he muttered, deep in thought, "you end the verb with -swa. If it happened long ago, with -fag. Now if I could only find the present and future tenses."

Pat repeated her pleas. This time he heard her, but it took a few seconds to disengage his mind from the verbs.

"What's that? The doors? The walls? Sorry, love, the men haven't brought enough *pandanus* bark yet."

"How long will it take?"

"I can't be sure. Most of the willing workers are away in the forest gathering a certain kind of *pandanus* fruit which is in season right now. Perhaps in a few days—"

"Stan, something will have to be done sooner than that. This lack of doors, walls, shelves and cupboards, and privacy—can't you do something?"

Stan pondered, then laid down his pen.

"I think I can. All those gunnysacks left over from the airdrops, they're washed clean and just laying in the storeroom. I'll cut them open and hang them up for temporary walls."

He lugged an armful of gunnysacks out of the storeroom, scattered them over the living room floor, and began cutting them open with his bush knife. Then, with a hammer and nails, he went from room to room, nailing sacks to the bare studs of unfinished walls.

"There, Pat—it's not much to look at, but it's functional. It'll pass for a few weeks until our workers return from food-gathering and bring us *pandanus* bark. Meanwhile these remaining bags," Stan picked up a handful of sacks he had not slit open, "will do for a time in place of shelves and cupboards." Then Stan rejoined Bengwok on the back steps.

"*Wutswa, wutswa, wutfag, wutfag,*" he practiced over and over, until the verb and its endings began to feel at home on his tongue.

It was indeed an important verb, for it enabled him to translate the verse he intended to use as one of the texts for a sermon: "Wild dogs have dens, and birds of the air build nests, but the Son of Man has no place to lay His head" (Luke 9:58).

Pat sighed and then smiled. Her husband was indeed a true follower of that Son of Man who felt no concern for His own ease and comfort. Nevertheless, for practical reasons, Pat began to await the right time and place to make Stan aware of certain other scriptures, such as, "This man began to build, and was not able to finish" (Luke 14:30)!

Stan's life revolves around verbs and verses, she sighed again, *and mine around bags and boxes.* But for the present, she simply returned to her cooking over the smoky stove.

One evening, after the children were asleep, Stan and Pat sat together in the misty living room for a time of Bible reading and prayer.

After we pray will be a good time to make a new plea about the house, Pat thought. And so they read and prayed together.

But as Stan prayed for the salvation of the Yali and other tribes beyond them, a special revelation of their spiritual need came upon him. He thought of sad-faced old Sar, who recently sold Stan an old but very well-constructed *yogwa* for the smoothly hewn boards in its walls. Sar's brother had built it years earlier, before he was killed, Stan learned.

Whatever could have happened to make that old man look so sad? Stan wondered. *No matter! Whatever it was, Christ can heal old Sar's sorrow, if only Sar could know Him!* Stan thought of tall Hulu, that splendid Yali who had done what no one else had been able to do since those early childhood days in faraway Kyogle—he had knocked Stan down and got away scot-free!

He thought of surly Libeng, who had a reputation for punishing taboo breakers, and beady-eyed Andeng, who studied everything Stan did so closely.

"Oh, God! My God! My God!" Stan groaned, as responsibility for these and thousands of others bore down heavily upon his heart. He saw—and also felt—the awesome value of each being created in the image of God, a value totally independent of skin color or culture. He burned with indignation because, for thousands of years, God's beautiful image in Yali humanity had been despoiled, subverted, smothered, denied. He thrilled with anticipation because he, God willing, would be privileged to see that image shine forth in Yali men and women, reflecting the glory of its rightful counterpart, God Himself.

Tears—something neither pain nor terror could ever have wrung from him—gushed forth under the pressure of this, the weightiest of all possible burdens.

Stan wept.

And Pat, hushed by this awesome baring of her husband's soul, deferred her complaints about the house until another day.

Chip, chip, chip. Chip, chip, chip.

Drawn by the sound, Bruno walked around to the front of the Dale house. There Stan sat, chipping away on a log.

"What are you doing, Stan?" Bruno asked.

"I'm shaping this log into a sill for a set of louver windows for our living room. That opaque plastic is alright in the other windows, but Pat and the children want a view from the living room."

The log seemed to Bruno rather large for a window sill, but of course, once finished, it could double as a shelf for knickknacks or a flowerpot or two. But in the meantime it would take an awful lot of chipping. Without a sawmill, making wooden surfaces flat was hard work, as every Yali adze-man knew all too well.

Day after day the chipping continued, punctuated now and then by the rasp of Stan's file as he ground his tools sharp for still more chipping. Stan could be so meticulous, striving for perfection no matter what the price in time.

EXPLORATIONS

Chapter 14

THUS did Christianity, after two millennia, finally achieve its initial entrance to the Heluk Valley. It was a blind intrusion at best, but unavoidably so. Still another six years would pass before an anthropologist, Klaus Friedrich Koch, would publish in 1968 the world's first description of Yali culture. And even that description would deal mainly with only one aspect of Yali life—conflict management. Eight years later Ziegfried Zollner, a German missionary to Yali clans living north of the Snow Mountains' central ridge, would earn a doctorate in anthropology by publishing the world's first description of Yali religion, the aspect of Yali culture of greatest concern to Stan and Bruno.

Obviously, Stan and Bruno could not wait for such valuable helps. Their beachhead in the Heluk, established under the still-unrealized protection of Wanla's theory, must quickly enlarge its basis of acceptance or be lost. Sensing the tenuous nature of their foothold, Stan and Bruno applied themselves diligently to learning the Yali language. They shared their discoveries with Pat, who also found time to study between sessions of teaching her children. After several months Stan and Bruno felt that the time had come to begin preaching the gospel to the Yali. The five Dani helpers who shared their initial advance into the Heluk had already returned to Karubaga for further training. Later the five would join still other expeditions, not simply as carriers and laborers, but as pastors, evangelists, teachers, and medical orderlies. But for the present, Stan and Bruno had to undertake the evangelizing of the Heluk without the help of tribal Christians from other areas. Stan took responsibility for all villages within a half-day's journey of Ninia, so that he could return to his family each evening. Bruno accepted the task of reaching all villages more than a half-day's journey away.

A seemingly insignificant two-man assault force, the men spread out across towering slopes, forded thundering rivers, scaled precipitous ridges. As Yali guides led them to hidden pockets of population, they preached, haltingly at first. But with each passing week, fluency increased.

On one of his overnight trips, Bruno ventured far to the south, through a dark and treacherous gorge, to Yalisili. It was an area in which the Wanla theory could not protect him, even if Bruno had known that such a theory existed.

"I say let's kill and eat him!" whispered one Yali man to another as Bruno began to preach.

"Do you think it would be all right?" asked a more cautious spirit. "I've heard he's some sort of odd reincarnation of a man named Marik."

"Marik is no relation to us," countered the first speaker.

"Reincarnated or not, his flesh looks real to me. And I'll wager it tastes as good as any we've ever eaten!"

"Perhaps better!" added still another member of the huddle. "A rare delicacy, for all we know."

"Stop talking that way, my brothers," urged Kwel, a Ninia man who had moved to Yalisili some time earlier. Overhearing the conversation, he had turned aside from Bruno's preaching.

"Marik is a relative of ours," he continued. "It surely would be a cause of war—a great rift in our western alliance—if you do this thing."

Bruno had requested the Yalisili people to pay close attention when he preached. Why, then, were Kwel and those others engaging in that increasingly animated discussion? Bruno had no inkling that Kwel was arguing for Bruno's life as grimly as any lawyer in a modern court.

"I don't care if the Kobak people are mocking us because they ate Selambo and we haven't eaten anyone for a long time! Marik is my friend; I'm determined to protect him while he stays here among us!"

Kwel did not tell Bruno of his danger. For as long as Bruno moved about confidently, his smile beaming and his eyes twinkling with humor, there was a chance the killer instinct of the Yalisili men might be held at bay. But if he became afraid and tried to leave the village in haste, he would fall like a suckling pig among wild dogs.

But even if my advocacy is doomed to fail and he must die, Kwel reasoned, *let his last hours be carefree!*

Throughout the night, while Bruno slept, the argument waxed on. By next morning a weary Kwel had won.

"It's a good thing for this Marik that a great arguer like you took his side!" said one of the would-be killers. "A mere youth could not have saved him."

Still blissfully ignorant of the drama surrounding him, Bruno returned the next day to Ninia. Not until years later did he learn how close he came to death.

Meanwhile, in regions immediately surrounding the station, Stan was rapidly—if unwittingly—causing the disintegration of Wanla's protective theory.

To begin with, he completely dumbfounded all the priests of *Kembu*, Wanla included, by constantly insisting that women—yes, women (not to mention uninitiated children)—must attend his meetings to hear "the message of the Great Spirit who created heaven and earth."

"How," they puzzled, "can Kugwarak, who passed all four stages of the cutting-through-of-knowledge, command this unthinkable thing? He knew the ways of the spirits better than any of us!"

As for the Yali women themselves, a mere handful of them had by this time found courage to approach Pat Dale with gifts of food on a few occasions when Stan was away. But when they learned that her husband—the great, green-eyed *duong*—now demanded their attendance at his meetings in order that they might hear the secrets of some particular *kembu*, they were horrified.

"Listen to secret words?" many retorted. "And get pig's blood rubbed in our eyes! Who does he think we are?!"

At the same time, the mere knowledge that someone genuinely wanted to tell sacred things to women kindled a new kind of wonder within certain Yali females. Once kindled, that wonder could do only one thing—grow.

The second thing Stan did, the thing that knocked the last support from under Wanla's theory, was to state openly that *"Kembu* is bad."

He said it through a hymn, perhaps the first he wrote in the Yali language, set to a tune called, in English, "I Will Make You Fishers of Men." One day he tried to teach it to a gathering of Yali men and boys.

"Repeat after me," Stan urged. *"Kembu ele nit nererim, nit nererim, nit nererim; Kembu ele nit nererim, Kembu at syak!"*

The words mean: *"Kembu's* words we reject, we reject, we reject; *Kembu's* words we reject—*Kembu,* he is bad!"

Jaws dropped open in shocked unbelief. Horror flooded every countenance.

"Ready now, sing with me—" Stan called, and began the first line again.

His voice echoed alone.

Stan looked around at their faces, momentarily taken aback by the strange way they were looking at him. One by one, Yekwara, Bengwok, Dongla, Luliap, Foliek, and others turned their gazes away. Until this moment nearly all of those present had made every concession they could possibly justify in order to satisfy the whims of this unpredictable reincarnation.

But to say that *Kembu* is bad, and to reject his words, the *wene melalek,* would require first a complete rewriting of the constitution of the heavens and the earth! Confirmed by at least a three-quarter majority of all the priests *of Kembu!*

Who could possibly bring himself to say such a thing? Only someone who wanted to draw a death penalty down upon himself, or who had lost his mind, like Bukni.

After two or three attempts to teach his song in the face of strained silence, Stan laid it aside, pondering the significance of this "impervious layer" of resistance he had unexpectedly uncovered. *How different the Yali are from the Dani,* he reflected. Among the Dani, women flock to meetings, and both men and women sing with great exuberance hymns that affirm rejection of the former tyranny of demons. But not here.

The meeting broke up. As the news spread, Yalis for miles around buried the last remains of Wanla's theory.

"He is definitely *not* Kugwarak. He is some devil incarnate who is trying to bring destruction upon us all," said many.

"We have been deceived!" said others angrily. "And while we have allowed this deception to bind us, lo, this devil and his friends have destroyed our *kembu-vam* and the *osuwa* surrounding it. Not satisfied with that, he has been teaching our young men that our greetings are 'filthy' and that we should cut our hair and stop blackening our skin with pig grease and ashes! Now he wants to teach origin secrets to women and children, while telling us that *Kembu* is bad! What next?"

And so the backlash began.

"Who showed them the way to our valley?" many asked rhetorically. "None other than Emeroho and that loudmouth Suwi! They deserve to die!"

Threats against Emeroho and Suwi, however, were only a prelude to a still more drastic obligation now taking ominous shape in the back of Yali minds, the obligation to drive all *duongs* from the Heluk Valley.

And if they wouldn't go, to kill them!

"Kembu is bad!" Stan bluntly told the Yali. Was Stan bigoted? Or was he right?

On a wider scale, was Yali religion in its entirety nothing more than a depraved system founded upon totally wrong and even harmful premises?

Not all of Christendom would have agreed that it was.

Seven hundred years ago, Pope Gregory III tried to resolve all problems of cross-cultural communication for Catholic missionaries by a single sweeping pronouncement that "People of other religions are, after all, seeking after God in their own way. Let us therefore accommodate our message to their beliefs."

Even so, many Roman Catholic missionaries who have encountered firsthand some of the more sinister faces of paganism—such as child prostitution in the temples or the burning alive of widows with the corpses of their husbands—find the problem not so easily resolved to the satisfaction of their consciences.

In sharp contrast, some Protestant theologians view the gulf between paganism and Christianity as unbridgeable. Catholic attempts at "accommodation," they say, have at times produced hybrid creeds scarcely recognizable as continuations of historic, biblical Christianity. In the words of one spokesman: "History suggests, I believe, that when Christian proclamation does not adapt to culture but demands total change and makes the decision very hard, sometimes entailing martyrdom, the result is that belief becomes deep-rooted, and deviation is less when winds of social change come along later."[1]

Stan Dale, beyond all doubt, was a confirmed disciple of this latter view. On the basis of his own experience with other tribal cultures, perceived in the light of a strongly evangelical background, Stan fully expected Yali religion to prove itself totally incompatible with Christianity.

In fact, it would shortly do just that—in no uncertain terms and with utter vengeance! But for Stan there was no other way than to clash headlong with that religion, with no quarter asked or given.

For Yali religion, no matter how intriguing it might be as an object of study for anthropologists or other specialists, in Stan's final analysis, was nothing more than a monstrous satanic deception. Stan believed that even the most violent Yali cannibal possessed within him the same image of God that made any man's soul worth saving. Yet he was equally convinced that their own animistic religion was the Yali people's worst enemy, their heaviest shackle.

Generation after generation of Yali men and women, duped by their religion, had willingly submitted themselves and their little ones to needless terrors and torments, all for the sadistic pleasure of hidden demonic forces. And if Stan had detected the extremely high and disproportionate female suicide rate in the Heluk Valley, perhaps he would have pointed to it as objective, measurable evidence of a deadly side effect of Yali religious belief.

In any case, Stan's will was now concentrated behind a single brisk decision: all of this demonic nonsense had gone far enough! Yali fathers and mothers and their children had endured it long enough! The sooner and the more decisively it could be banished from the Heluk Valley the better. He was not interested in accommodation but in revolution!

All of Stan's RBMU colleagues stood in full agreement with him that Yali religious beliefs were at best repressive. But not all agreed with Stan's aggressive methods for replacing those beliefs with Christian faith. Many, though willing to grant that *"Kembu* is bad," would have preferred to see the Yali led step by step to see that badness for themselves.

Stan did, however, speak to the Yali in terms of their own culture. He wrote, "I constantly sought for illustrations from the culture of the Yalis to make the way of salvation plain, and for [Yali] words to express the foundation truths of the Christian faith."

Discovering the Yali version of the race between the bird of death and the lizard of life, for example, Stan extrapolated from it to the biblical doctrine of the Fall of Man. But whereas many missionaries would have credited the legend as a stone-age *allegory* of the truth, Stan plainly told the Yalis it was a "distortion."[2]

Perhaps as a result, Yali minds did not identify the gospel as fulfillment of the hope expressed by the legend, as had tens of thousands of their Dani neighbors a few years earlier.

Stan wrote further, "On another occasion I was preaching on the Flood and on the appearance of the rainbow as a sign of God's mercy and His covenant with mankind. The Yali responded that they used to look up at a rainbow and, seeing the red band, would say, 'See! There is blood! Who has died?'

"This gave me opportunity to tell them of God's own Son who came down from heaven and shed His blood for sinful men, and of God Who 'put His bow in the sky'—a bow with no string—as a sign of His mercy to those Who trusted Him."[3]

Another facet of Yali culture Stan and Bruno could have appropriated with telling effect—had they discovered it—was the Yali place of refuge, a concept hauntingly reminiscent of the Old Testament six cities of refuge (see Josh. 20-21) and of the description of Christ's followers as people "who have fled for refuge to lay hold upon the hope set before them" (Heb. 6:28).

Stan and Bruno often noticed the stone-wall-surrounded areas held sacred by the Yali but somehow never discovered their significance as sanctuaries. Nevertheless, the analogies Stan and Bruno used struck many Yali with telling effect. Thus, after two years in the valley and in spite of growing opposition from priests of the *kembu* spirits, Stan and Bruno made progress. But the listeners they attracted were mainly teenagers—led by Yekwara, Bengwok, Dongla, and Luliap—and a few children. Older men rarely came near when Stan or Bruno taught.

So often it happens in New Guinea and around the world that Christian missions begin by working among the young, sometimes with the result that almost the entire older generation remains untouched. Don Gibbons, one of the pioneers who broke through with *Widi-ai-bui* among the Damal, was one missionary who chose not to allow young men to "grab the gospel and run with it before older men knew what it was all about."

As a result, Don and his colleagues later succeeded in winning Damal men and women of *all* ages to Christian faith. Stan and Bruno, however, held no reserve about beginning their work almost exclusively among the young, though their end goal, like Gibbons's, was to win the older generation as well.

Whereas adult men reacted strongly against Stan's teaching in particular, the young were shocked into listening by the sheer audacity of his pronouncements. They were fascinated by the very possibility of rejecting concepts that had been held without question for thousands of years, even more so because Stan did not merely reject the old ways, as Bukni had done, but was making a determined attempt to articulate a viable alternative. It was an idea which, once planted, could do only one thing.

Grow.

With his entire being, Stan radiated confidence that his alternative could and would work for Yalis. And so, with the passing of time, young men around Ninia felt themselves drawn to Stan's teaching sessions like moths to a lamp flame. Not that they all liked Stan. But, alternately cowed by his sharpness and fascinated by his concepts, they could not ignore him.

The priests of *Kembu*, meanwhile, kept their desire to kill Emeroho a secret from both the boy and his immediate relatives. But relatives in more distant areas caught the news and warned him, "Come and live with us! Your life is in danger there!"

But Emeroho declined their invitation. Even if his life was in danger, he couldn't bear to miss the *duong*'s teaching sessions. They were growing still more interesting as the *duong* steadily increased his powers in Yali. Emeroho couldn't bear to miss whatever Stan might say next.

But as the fascination of the young men around Ninia increased, so also did the indignation of the shamans burn the more fiercely toward Stan himself. As a result the priests gradually forgot their grudge against young Emeroho and Suwi. They were focusing now upon bigger game.

Libeng, who had risen in esteem because, long years earlier, he had shot that first arrow into Kiloho, was a particular threat to Stan, for Libeng now conceived a new ambition—he wanted to be first to strike against the *duongs*. One day Libeng sat down and began trimming a new large, bamboo-tipped arrow. Something in the way he trimmed it caught the attention of warriors passing by. And when friends, sensing trouble, asked whose death the arrow was designed to effect, Libeng replied openly, "The death of the *duong* who looks like Kugwarak."

Stan's young friends relayed the news to him. Not the least intimidated, Stan nevertheless kept a sharp eye out for Libeng. And in one letter written during those days, he referred casually to "nasty types like Libeng."

Yali resistance even took on overtones of psychological warfare. Often, when Stan was away on his one-day trips to nearby villages, rumors would reach Pat's ears to the effect that "We are going to kill you all," or "Men are on their way now to destroy the station."

It would have been a harrowing test for any woman, let alone a mother of four small children, but Pat did not crumble as some Yalis apparently intended. In spite of isolation, loneliness, inconveniences, and intimidation, she stood firmly by her husband. But with the passing of time, the strain would take its toll.

Bruno, with a "parish" scattered over much greater distances than Stan's, found it difficult to visit any one village frequently enough to achieve accumulating impact, as Stan was doing. His work was more a "sowing of seed" that, hopefully, would bear fruit and come to harvest at a later time.

It seemed that he was constantly climbing mountains and descending bone-jarring trails into deep gorges, and often fatigue brought also mental discouragement, requiring longer periods of rest at Ninia between journeys. To encourage Bruno, Stan would often trek with him as far as a one-day journey would allow, and then return lest Pat and the children be left alone too long.

On a few occasions when Bruno did not return from a long journey when Stan expected him, Stan became very concerned. Once he set out to search for Bruno, taking medical gear and fresh supplies, in case Bruno was wounded or sick.

Stan is very loyal, Bruno realized. *If ever I get in trouble out in these wild gorges, I know Stan will do his best to help.*

Beyond all doubt, fellowship between Stan and Bruno was sweetest when they were together on the trail. And it probably reached its finest expression during a ten-day trek they made together into wild, unexplored valleys east of Ninia.

Bruno wrote, "That trip really showed me what kind of man Stan was. If he set his mind to do something, then he would do it. For ten days, every day, we trekked at a hard pace over long distances into unknown territory. . . . We did not have a radio with us [to guide a pilot in for airdrops], and so had only the food we could carry. It was hard to buy enough sweet potatoes for our carriers." But Stan developed an effective method of appealing for food: "He would put his hands to his stomach like a starving man and shout *supuru! supuru!* [sweet potatoes]."

Inquisitive tribesmen, though awed by the strange appearance of the travelers, considered Stan's demonstration hilarious and usually responded by offering food in exchange for the whitest, tastiest salt they had ever put to their tongues.

During this trip Stan and Bruno achieved their first entrance into a valley called the Seng, a valley which later would play a momentous role in determining the destiny of the Yali people. Climbing beyond the Seng, Stan and Bruno camped one afternoon just below timberline in a deserted Yali village. As Bruno made preparations for an evening meal, Stan looked up at the pass into the next valley, looming high and mysterious, above their camp. The thought of still another unknown valley hidden beyond it drew Stan so strongly that he excused himself from camp and set out toward the pass, even though it was already late afternoon and the rains of night would soon begin to fall.

Higher and higher, faster and faster, Stan climbed toward the skyline, with that other poem of Kipling's echoing through his mind as if in some vast chamber:

Till a voice as bad as conscience rang interminable changes,
On one everlasting whisper, day and night repeated so,
Something hidden, go and find it;
Go and look behind the ranges,
Something lost behind the ranges,
Lost and waiting for you. Go!

Incredibly, he reached the pass while there was still enough daylight to allow him a glimpse into that next hidden valley. For long moments he stood there gazing down into the shadows, a lone mystic drinking his fill of the spirit of the unknown and renewing his vision.

Bruno wrote, "He was gone for a long time, and I really wondered if something had happened. When it was almost completely dark, he returned and told me he had gone right up to the top of the mountain and looked into the next valley. I was amazed at his eager spirit."

And so they trekked on, taking notes on the geography of the land, confluences of rivers, locations of villages, and changes in dialects, and searching in vain for future airstrip sites in that incredibly uptilted world.

At times they walked along knife-edge ridges, where they could see valleys on one side boiling with clouds while valleys on the other side basked in sunshine. And always, high above them to the north, loomed the jagged peaks of the Snow Mountains' central ridge—like the molars, cuspids, and fangs of some horrendous limestone jaw.

Five Danis and one Yali served as carriers on that difficult journey. Other Yalis had set out with them from Ninia but later deserted, being afraid of the cannibals living in the unknown world. The one Yali who remained to the end of the journey was the handsome youth whom Bruno described as a "very fine and faithful person, on whom you could totally depend," Yekwara.

Yekwara volunteered again for an even deeper probe into the eastern wilderness in June 1963.

Philip Jesse Masters, who shared with Stan those final two months of labor on the Ninia airstrip, at last returned.

Phil could not forget the haunting call of the valleys beyond Ninia. Labors among the Danis at Karubaga had been very rewarding. He and his wife, Phyliss, had grown very close to the Dani people and had added much strength to the Dani church through their teaching and example. But someone had to take God's word beyond Ninia, and Phil believed God had called him to the task.

For Phyliss it was a hard choice to accept. Karubaga, with its friendly people, fertile soil, and pleasant "north-of-the ranges" climate, was not an easy place to say goodbye to. But by the time RBMU's third annual conference convened, Phyliss was ready to say, through tears of joy, "I'm willing!"

Phil landed at Ninia with a Cessna-load of burly, cheerful Dani escorts—the biggest, strongest, and most faithful he could find. Among them Yekwara appeared a mere stripling. With Bruno they set out from Ninia on June 20. Two other Yali boys also followed them but, again, deserted the party after a day or so. Ten days later the explorers reached the furthest point Stan and Bruno had traveled earlier and went on past it. By this time they had left the Yali tribe far behind, discovering a population of pygmy-like people who later became known as the Kimyal. In each new valley they searched for a possible airstrip site but, like Stan and Bruno, failed to find one.

Finally, on the sixth of July, in a valley the pygmies called Indol, they found a suitable strip site, and a new name was written on missionary maps—Korupoon.

Notes

1. Arthur Johnston, *Christianity Today* (January 7, 1977), p. 11.
2. Stan Dale, *The Valley and the Vision* (London: RBMU, 1978), p. 18.
3. Ibid., p. 19.

THE YOUNG REPLACEMENTS

WHILE Phil, Bruno, and the Danis labored with surprisingly friendly pygmies to open an airstrip at Korupoon, the Dales were experiencing further progress at Ninia.

On January 1, 1963, Pat Dale received a delightful New Year's gift—the first visit of a Yali woman to her kitchen! Pat had waited eight months for that moment! The next day two more women came, wide-eyed and cautious. But nearly two months later an even more significant milestone was planted: forty Yali women came to the first-ever women's meeting in the Heluk Valley!

Pat was delighted. The women and their children politely called her *nisinga* (our mother), a Yali term of respect. Still another beachhead had widened under the very noses of the hostile "lords of the earth."

Three things especially impressed the Yali women who sat under Pat's teaching. First, Pat herself! She could smile and even be vivacious, qualities of personality Yali women thought could belong in such quantity only to small girls who still knew not the grim realities of female life. And she lived in the same house with her husband, not in a separate *homia!* Also, she assumed responsibility for the instruction of her sons instead of consigning them over to male lords. Most amazing of all, she talked freely and enthusiastically about obviously sacred things, without fear of punishment!

Second, Pat told them that one day the Son of the greatest Spirit of all visited a *homia* in a village called Bethany. One of the two sisters who lived in that *homia*—her name was Mary—actually came and sat at the Son's feet and questioned Him about His sacred words. Pat's Yali listeners were horrified. Pat continued, "Then Mary's sister—Martha—rebuked Mary for leaving a woman's work to do such a thing!"

Of course! the Yali women thought to themselves. *She needed to be rebuked before she got herself in deep trouble!* But Pat continued, "The Son, however, defended Mary, saying, 'Mary has chosen the best thing, and it shall not be taken away from her!' "

Wonder left its footprints all the way down into the hearts of her listeners. To cap it all, Pat concluded, "Likewise the Son expects you—women of this Heluk Valley—to choose to hear His words. The privilege is yours, and it cannot be taken away from you!"

Third, another day Pat told them that when the Son, Jesus, was teaching in a certain place, mothers tried to bring their little children to Him so that He could lay His hands upon them and bless them.

But Jesus' disciples sternly rebuked the mothers and said, "Take these children away from the Master!"

Pat's listeners thought, *The disciples were "men-of-knowledge" and they knew that uninitiated children can have no part in sacred things!*

But Pat continued, "The Son rebuked His disciples and said, 'Allow the little children to come to Me!' They came to Him, and He laid His hands upon them and blessed them!"

By this time wonder had built itself a permanent home in the hearts of Pat's listeners.

"So likewise," Pat concluded, "we women must not only come to Jesus ourselves, but also bring our children to Him as well!"

Among the listeners sat Latowen, cousin to little Nindik, who had been thrown into the Heluk for intruding upon a sacred place. Tears trickled down inside Latowen's heart as she thought, *If these words had come to us earlier, perhaps my cousin need not have died!*

Latowen later believed. And partly through her influence as well as Pat's, Yali women and girls began attending the preaching services held almost daily by Stan. They sat apart from the male listeners, with their eyes to the ground but listening all the same—at least whenever their babies were not crying. Still more people were drawn—however sporadically—until on some days peak attendances of two hundred to four hundred were recorded.

This did not mean that the enmity of the priests of *Kembu* was declining. On the contrary, it was increasing as they saw visible evidence that this new and unexpectedly virile religion was steadily gaining ground in their valley.

What restrained them from descending *en masse* upon Ninia and slaying all proponents of this "enemy" faith? Mainly the fear that militaristic government officers (whatever "government" meant), who lived just over the horizon beyond the Mugwi, would retaliate if the Yali killed a *duong*. Also, even the priests were still cowed by Stan's boldness. Had it not been for that boldness, perhaps Ninia would have been destroyed before the end of 1963.

A man who can be so bold against impossible odds, the priests reasoned, *must have tricks up his sleeve that we are unaware of. We had better be careful and let the spirits show us the right time and way to deal with him.*

Thus it happened that the Dales' and Bruno's lonely outpost survived until 1964. During that year Bruno returned to Canada for his first furlough, during which time he renewed an old acquaintance with flaxen-haired Marlys Neilsen, a trainee nurse from Calgary, Alberta.

Six days after they met, Bruno proposed to Marlys, and she accepted! Hearing the good news, Stan wrote to Bruno on September 14, 1964: "First of all, let me say how pleased I am that you have found a lovely Christian girl. Only six days! . . . You are certainly a fast worker! I trust that everything works out well for you both . . ." And then Stan indulged in a mild dig against what he considered an overemphasis on higher education for missionaries in these modern days. "I intend recommending to the Advisory Committee that Marlys—before the wedding—take Bible school college and seminary training after she has finished nursing. Missionaries have to be well-educated these days—and it will take only ten years!"

By July 1964 the Dales had completed four years' service and were due for furlough in Australia. Stan, true to character, did not think a furlough necessary for his own health but recognized Pat's dire need for a rest.

"Pat really needs a break," he wrote to Bruno. "She's just tired out . . .
I tried to persuade the Australian Council to let me stay on here while Pat
goes home."

His request was denied, and so on November 28, 1964, the Dale family flew out of Ninia for a year's furlough in their homeland.

Upon their arrival in Sydney and later Melbourne, the Dales were
welcomed jubilantly by relatives and friends, who were considerably relieved. The reports Stan and Pat had been sending home in letters con-
veyed something of the tension and danger under which the Dale family
lived during their nearly four years among the Yali.

Meanwhile, in the distant Heluk Valley, another drama was unfolding.

For some two months after Stan, Pat, and the children left Ninia station vacant, the Heluk Valley often was very quiet. As Bruno once wrote,
"Sometimes it was so quiet I used to wonder if all the people had left for
some other valley." But it was even quieter now because the priests were
sitting alone wondering about all that had happened. And would the
green-eyed *duong* return and resume it all again, or would all these strange
events soon fade into the mist and become just another half-remembered,
poorly understood legend?

It was quiet because the relative handful of men, women, and children who had begun to understand Stan and Pat and Bruno were lonely—
not just for the missionaries themselves but for their *teaching*. All those
new concepts, that amazingly different way of looking at things; would
they ever be happy again without it? Indeed, had they ever been truly
happy before they heard such words?

Also, it was quiet because, with the turning of the monsoon, still another *o-sanim* cloaked the ranges and the valley in gloom.

It was then that he came: an exuberant young Greek named Costas
Macris, missionary son of an enterprising businessman in Athens.

"We request you and Alky to replace Stan and Pat at Ninia for the remainder of their furlough," the field secretary's letter had said. But Costas
came alone first, to check things out.

As he stepped out of the Cessna onto Ninia's muddy airstrip, Costas
was not impressed. Earlier he had enjoyed the two years' ministry in the
sunny Swart Valley among the cheerful Dani people—"the tribe that makes

visitors feel like kings and queens, since the gospel changed their hearts!"

But here at Ninia the people stood back in the shadows, glowering. Only a handful came out to greet him, and even they seemed uncertain, except for Yekwara. The uncertainty was mutual as Costas swung his sleeping bag over his shoulder and waved good-bye to the MAF pilot.

The aircraft roared down the airstrip and took off for sunnier climes, leaving Costas alone in that tomb-like valley. He walked down to the Dale residence and opened the door with a key that had been given to him. No fires had warmed the house for several weeks, and its dark interior seemed even colder and danker than the weather outside.

Costas shivered.

The house, he saw at once, was still uncompleted. In the kitchen and a number of other rooms, ceilings had not yet been filled in. *Heat from the kitchen stove will quickly escape among the rafters and out through the thin metal roof, leaving the greater part of the house unwarmed,* he reasoned. *I must put a ceiling over these rooms before I bring Alky and the children here.* Then Costas saw the gunnysacks, still hanging in some of the doors and lining many of the walls. (Stan had replaced a number of them with brown waterproof paper.) As Costas watched, cold mist blew in through cracks in the walls.

This will all have to be lined with pandanus *bark,* he mused. Costas wanted to take care of these things so that Stan could give his full time to language study and helping the Yali when he returned. The split palm-bark floor was not yet nailed down in a couple of rooms and was springy underfoot, and the wind and mist seeped in through occasional gaps.

I will nail this down and cover the entire floor with a second layer of palm-bark—to cover the gaps, he decided.

Costas walked to the door and looked outside for workers he could hire, but found only faithful Yekwara. Stan and Pat had sent their Dani helpers home to the Swart Valley before leaving for Australia. In vain Costas walked the muddy trails to nearby Hwim and Sivimu, searching for workers. It was *o-sanim* weather, and even the few Yalis who remained friendly to outsiders were indisposed. So Costas returned to the mission radio transmitter. "Ple-e-e-se!" he pleaded with his most appealing Greek accent. "I need workers! Strong, w-e-e-lling Dani workers! Send me a planeload as soon as possible!"

"I'll see what I can do," replied a colleague.

All that night Costas shivered in an inadequate sleeping bag. Next morning he could have filled a cup with the condensed mist he wrung out of it!

Soon an aircraft brought six stalwart Dani men to his rescue. Shortly afterward, Costas dispatched them—with Yekwara as guide—to the surrounding jungle. And before long they began to bring down from the high forests the palm bark and split bamboo Costas needed.

Day after day Costas and his hearty crew worked—trimming, sawing, and hammering. Pat Dale would scarcely recognize her home, which her husband, in his eagerness for language study and preaching, had never completed. Gone were the drab sackcloth walls and doors. Snug, windproof walls, floors, and ceilings made the rooms seem cozy and comfortable. But exuberant Costas was still not satisfied. The house was still cold because the heat that the wood-burning stove gave was trapped in the kitchen and could not circulate throughout the house.

Resourceful, he found a way to correct the problem. He cut long rectangular slots in the walls, just below the ceiling line throughout the house, allowing warm air from the kitchen to circulate to every corner of the house. The effect was amazing. Central heating had come to the remote Heluk Valley!

Likewise Costas installed a flush toilet, along with a shower, washbasin, sink, and wall mirror in a room Pat planned to use as a pantry. No more trekking out on rainy nights to that drafty outhouse teetering on the edge of a nearby cliff!

Still not satisfied, Costas extended the flower beds Stan planted and landscaped the surrounding yard with flat-rock pathways and picturesque retaining walls.

Gradually, Ninia station began to resemble an English country garden!

I hope the Dales will be pleased with all this! Costas mused.

In any case, Ninia would at least be a pleasant place for Costas's own beloved Alky and his two fast-growing sons, Jonathan and Haris. Amazingly, the work took only six weeks out of the year that Costas was to spend as replacement for the Dales.

Having warmed the interior of his dwelling at Ninia, Costas next turned his attention to the coldness on the outside—the enmity of the great majority of Heluk Valley people.

He first experienced the hard reality of that enmity a few days after Alky and the children joined him at Ninia.

"Duong! I have a gift for you!"

But the voice sounded nervous and strained.

Costas opened the door and looked into the haunted eyes of a gaunt old priest of *Kembu.* In the next moment, the priest dropped something from his shoulder onto the pathway in front of Costas's threshold—a dead pig. The priest began backing away, as if fearing re-taliation, "I am giving you this pig to eat!"

"Thank you!" Costas replied, confused by the gift-giver's nervous manner. "Please allow me to pay you for it. What would you like?"

But the old man would not wait for payment. Slinking furtively away from Costas, he turned suddenly and fled. Later Yekwara explained the old man's sinister purpose: wild dogs, according to Yali belief, were actually incarnations of evil spirits. And whenever a wild dog, descend-ing from the high forests, succeeded in killing or even wounding a pig from Yali herds, that pig was regarded as dedicated to the spirits for their own food. If a human being were to eat the flesh of such a pig, he or she would quickly die under a curse.

The "gift pig" laid at Costas's feet was one that had been wounded by a wild dog. And so the priests conspired to trick Costas and his fam-ily into eating the flesh of that pig, to find out whether the spirits could exercise life-and-death power over the *duongs,* as they could over Yalis.

If now the spirits slew the *duong* and his family, the Yali people's *duong* problem would be solved. On the other hand, if the *duongs* proved to be invulnerable to the vengeance of the spirits, then the Yali themselves might well think twice before attempting vengeance on their own.

So they want to see if their spirits are strong enough to kill us, Costas thought. *It's a good question and deserves a decisive answer.*

"Butcher this pig for us!" Costas said to his helpers, and then called to Alky, "Tonight we're going to eat pork!"

He stepped inside the house and explained the situation to her. "We'll pray first to show the people that our trust is in God, who will protect us! These people need to see a demonstration of His power!"

Some of the friendly Yali expressed concern. "Friend, are you sure you know what you're doing?" they asked.

Costas knew. He and his family ate the pig and emerged from their home the next day hale and hearty as ever!

The Yali were amazed. The first two *duongs* had destroyed a *kembu-vam* and dug up the sacred ground surrounding it—and escaped with impunity. Now a third *duong,* and his wife and children, no less, dared to eat a pig claimed by the spirits and showed no ill effects whatever.

For those who had eyes to see, evidence destructive to the presuppositions of Yali religion was beginning to accumulate. However, the majority chose to disregard any evidence that did not confirm their ancient beliefs.

Enmity continued.

Costas ran into it again the first time he attempted a visit to Balinga, the first village Stan and Bruno had contacted.

The people of Balinga were upset. Not long before Stan and Pat left for Australia, a man from Balinga had stolen a rabbit skin from Stan. Stan went to Balinga to reclaim the skin, and a scuffle occurred, during which a Yali smashed Stan's little .22 caliber noisemaker over a rock. Ever since, the people of Balinga had maintained an angry posture, and they sent warning to Costas not to visit their village.

The warning, of course, was the same as an invitation to Costas, for he was determined if possible to heal all misunderstandings in the valley. One day he set out for Balinga with Yekwara, Dongla, a Dani, and Costas's German shepherd dog as escorts.

On the way, Yekwara and the Dani saw fresh ashes among the bushes and tensed. "See!" Yekwara said. "Lookouts were sitting there warming themselves by a fire."

"Just ahead of us there's a perfect spot for an ambush," added Dongla ominously. Costas looked up at a cliff towering above them and saw three feathered heads duck back out of sight.

"Let's wait here for a few minutes," Costas advised, and sent his German shepherd ahead to sniff out the bushes. The dog raised no alarm, and Costas gave the word to proceed.

Minutes later they surmounted a ridge and looked out across the village of Balinga. In the entire village only one man was visible—Suwi, Stan and Bruno's helper. In spite of threats against his life, Suwi still called himself a friend of the *duongs.*

"The people here say they will kill you if you enter the village," he warned. Costas shivered right down to his toes but still held his ground, praying fervently.

"Wait here," said Yekwara. "I have relatives in this village. Let me go in and talk with them."

While Costas watched in suspense, Yekwara went from one house to another, poking his head into doorways and speaking reassuringly to the warriors lurking within. Before long he persuaded first one, then another and another to come out and shake hands with Costas, who gave out gifts of razor blades and salt to each one who came.

"Soon they were coming down to us from every direction," Costas wrote later. "The trickle grew to a stream. The presence of the Lord was very precious to me as He gave us deliverance through Yekwara. I knew they could have killed me, but instead many gathered around us in a hut and listened for long hours into the night. 'Tell us more,' they said every time I stopped."

And so Costas began to hold regular meetings at Balinga, as Stan had before the rabbit-skin controversy. Soon Costas ventured on to Yabi, a village in the eastern alliance, and found a welcome there also. Costas could breathe easier now. But not for long.

Around that time Costas built a little thatch-roofed school and invited Yali youths and children to be taught.

Day after day beady-eyed Andeng watched with chagrin as an increasing number of young men and boys from Hwim and Sivimu flocked down to Costas's school. Andeng's chagrin was especially intense because his own two sons, Dongla and Bengwok, were leaders of the movement! Andeng could not understand what it was about the *duongs'* teaching that fascinated his sons so totally. He only knew that he wanted Dongla and Bengwok to follow the ways of the spirits, as he and his fathers before him had done from the beginning of the world.

Andeng had hoped that the spirits themselves would destroy the white intruders. Now it was clear that the spirits were either unable or unwilling to deal with them. Apparently a confrontation on the human level was necessary. The longer he waited, Andeng decided, the harder it would be to undermine the *duongs'* growing power. He must act now.

"The word has gone out," Dongla informed his Greek friend sadly. "The children are not to come to school anymore!"

Dongla did not mention that his own father was behind the command.

"Tell them," Costas replied evenly, "that those who don't want to come are free to stay away. But if anyone chooses to come to school, no one should prevent him! Whoever prevents them will have to deal with me!" Costas was not at all sure what he would do to anyone who accepted his challenge, but he knew he had to do *something*.

And so Costas's answer found its way back to Andeng. The challenge was accepted. The lines were drawn.

Next morning, "Why are you crying?" Costas said to little Deli, who huddled cowering in a corner of the school.

"My fathers said they will kill me if I come to school today!"

"But you chose to come anyway," Costas said softly.

"Yes," Deli sniffled, trembling.

"Don't be afraid, Deli," Costas said, putting his arm around the boy's shoulders. "I won't let them kill you. Look! I've brought a ball with me! Let's play!"

The ball flashed back and forth between them, and soon a smile brightened Deli's face. Dongla called Costas outside into the schoolyard. Grimly he pointed to the ridgeline where angry men from Sivimu were milling about, shouting.

Luliap joined Dongla and Costas as they studied the scene.

"Let's go up and talk to them," Luliap advised optimistically. Costas's brow furrowed. *Me?* he asked himself. *Go up there and face those angry men? A few days ago I risked my life at Balinga. Must I risk it again today?* Then came the subtle temptation. *I am only a replacement here. In a few months' time, the man who began this work will return and I will leave. The honor for whatever is accomplished here will accrue to him, not to me. So why should I put myself in danger? My own work awaits me in some other valley, among a people of a different language. Should I not save myself for that work and be content with a mere holding action in this troublesome Ninia?*

Then, like a buzz saw cutting through veneer, the words of Christ came to Costas as to Bruno before him: *If any man gives priority to his own fulfillment, he shall lose it.*

His dark eyes flashing, Costas set his jaw. *I am no mere bystander in this drama,* he determined. *While I am here, I am just as responsible to do my best as Stan would be if he were present!*

Then a further thought troubled him. *What about my dear Alky? What torment may she endure if she sees me going up to face those men? Surely I must ask her opinion before taking my life in my hands!*

And he did. For a few moments, deep concern clouded Alky's face. Then she replied with conviction, "Costas, I believe you should go to them. I sense within my heart that God will protect you."

Thus encouraged, Costas set out toward Sivimu. Dongla, Luliap, Yekwara, and others followed closely behind him. Andeng was ready; as Costas approached, Andeng leaped atop the stone wall surrounding Sivimu and drew bow at him. Costas saw the razor-sharp bamboo arrow aimed straight at his chest.

"Stop, *duong!*" Andeng raged. Costas's heart nearly stopped, and he turned pale. Yet somehow he kept walking closer and closer to Andeng. Looking over Costas's shoulder, Dongla saw deadly intent in his father's eyes. With all his strength, Dongla hurled Costas to one side and pushed his way in front of the startled missionary.

Alky, watching through binoculars from the edge of the airstrip, saw her husband lurch to one side.

"Dear God!" she cried aloud in anguished prayer. "Give victory to Costas in this hour!"

At that moment, Dongla was shielding Costas with his own body.

"My father!" he pleaded with Andeng. "If you want to kill this my teacher, first kill me! I live or die with this man!"

"Is he your father?" Andeng bellowed in retort. "No! I am your father! Stand aside! The spirits require the death of this man!"

Buying time with argument, Dongla moved forward, saying, "He serves a Spirit far greater than any we have ever known! He shall live!"

Dongla lunged and grabbed his father's bow. Consumed with towering rage, Andeng wrenched the weapon violently. In an instant the sharp tip of the bow sliced through the lobe of Dongla's ear. Blood gushed, yet the wounded Dongla disarmed Andeng.

Costas, Luliap, and other Christian Yalis rushed over the wall into the village—only to face a wall of drawn bows borne by Andeng's friends.

This is it! Costas gulped. *We're only a bunch of unarmed children before them. They'll kill us all!*

He shouted aloud, "We have not come to fight! We have come here unarmed to reason with you!" And then he added emphatically, "*Hit ninendao!*" (It is because we love you!)

In response the warriors advanced closer, their right elbows hitched high in the manner of Yalis who are ready to kill.

Luliap, Yekwara, and Bengwok walked confidently forward and grabbed the drawn bows of the nearest assailants. At any moment, Costas expected to see those horrendous bamboo arrowheads slice through the flesh of his friends. Half-expecting the same for himself, he joined the Christians in disarming the warriors. Amazingly, not an arrow was released. The men of Sivimu seemed suddenly confused—perhaps awed—by the composure of the Christians. They barely resisted as their bows were taken from them and laid in a pile outside the village wall. Costas himself disarmed a number of warriors. At one point he looked over his shoulder just in time to see a Yali rushing at him with a large rock upraised. Costas stepped aside, and the force of the man's lunge and the weight of the rock carried the attacker to the ground. Costas picked him up by his shoulders, sat him down on his bottom, and said firmly, "Now you just stay sitting there!"

The man obeyed Costas's command.

"You others come also!" Costas called to the other assailants, as well as to bystanders observing the struggle from the outskirts of the village. They came as if they had no choice.

His eyes filling with tears, Costas pleaded with his unexpected "captive" audience. "We came to you unarmed, in love, and you tried to kill us! You have shed the blood of Dongla—your own relative and my friend—upon this ground. All we ask is that you do not threaten or harm these little ones who want to hear the words of God."

Deeply moved, Costas wept before them.

Stunned by their apparent inability to carry out their original intent, the Yalis listened in amazement. What strange power was it that seemed to render these *duongs* and their Yali friends invulnerable?

Costas scanned their faces, searching for the slightest sign of visible sympathy for his cause. He could detect none. He noticed that Andeng had fled the scene. Had he gone to rally help from other villages?

Sadly he turned from the village and headed home. From her vantage point by the side of the airstrip, Alky ran to meet him. They stood for a while in each other's arms, trembling with relief. It was now nearly dark. Gray mist spread across the station and the airstrip. They walked together to the house. Entering, Costas turned aside into the radio room. He lifted the microphone to his lips and called Karubaga, just in case a colleague there might still be standing by at that late hour.

To Costas's relief—"Costas! This is David Martin at Karubaga. I can read you. What is your message?"

Costas began, "Call us in the morning, Dave. If we don't reply, send in an aircraft to see if we are all right. We—"

At that moment, the transmitter's carrier signal died. "Oh no!" Costas gasped. "The battery's gone dead!"

Martin kept calling, "Costas! What happened? Are you in danger? You faded out; we cannot hear you."

In desperation Costas disconnected the dead battery from the transmitter and carried it out to a small twelve-volt generator in his workshop. Quickly he filled the generator's fuel tank, primed the carburetor, and pulled the starter cord. It wouldn't start.

Costas was a man of many talents, but fixing motors was not one of them. However, he kept pulling the starter cord for twenty minutes, until finally, by some fluke of the carburetor, fuel line, or spark plug, the engine started. Sighing with relief, he charged the battery for several minutes, then carried it back to the transmitter. This time his transmission cut through the increasing static of late afternoon. Martin, his voice edged with concern, responded.

"We are in no immediate danger as far as we know," Costas assured him, "but we do not know what tomorrow may hold for us. If we do not answer in the morning—"

"I understand," Martin replied.

Next morning Costas and Alky waited in suspense to see if Yali children would come to school. To their utter delight, not only the children but all the men and women of Sivimu, including Andeng, reported for school by ten o'clock!

Not that Andeng was persuaded to become a Christian. Far from it! He remained proud and aloof while Costas and Dongla taught from the Bible. *At least the gospel is entering his mind,* Costas reasoned. *Perhaps there is hope.*

From that time forward, Yali men ceased to scoff at the gospel as a message for children. The sight of grim old Andeng sitting there listening proved otherwise. Soon Foliek was delighted to see his father Liakoho join Andeng in faithful attendance. Then came Andeng's brother-in-law, Dukuloho, and sad-faced old Sar, Nindik's ever-sorrowing father.

Some of the ice at least was melting.

During those happy days, Dongla, Luliap, Yekwara, Bengwok, Foliek, and others came to Costas and said, "Dear teacher, until now we have believed the gospel, but in the corners of our hearts there was still some doubt whether it is really meant for people like us. Now we know that it is really meant for us. We believe that Jesus Christ is the Son of God and that He died for *our* sins, not just yours."

Costas glowed with joy. The great work Stan, Pat, and Bruno had begun was growing in strength. He considered himself privileged to share in what they had begun. Nor was he finished yet.

Before coming to the Heluk Valley, Costas had taught hundreds of Danis in the Swart Valley to read and write. Now also in the Heluk he expanded a literacy program Stan and Pat had initiated. He purchased a mimeograph machine, authored a dozen or so Yali primers, and began to teach. The believers quickly became infected with Costas's enthusiasm. Their minds, moreover, proved generally sharp and receptive. Soon the syllables began to merge into words—Yali words that made sense to the readers.

"Andeng is sick!"

"Has he asked me to bring medicine?" Costas asked.

"No," replied the news-bringer. "On the contrary, he has asked his fellow priests to sacrifice a pig to the spirits on his behalf. But could we not give him your medicine as well?"

"Let him choose one or the other," Costas countered. "If we give both and he recovers, the people will credit his recovery to the pig sacrifice. The power of modern medicine will in that case only reinforce the fallacies of spirit appeasement."

High on Sivimu ridge, Andeng's fellow priests sacrificed a pig. A *hwalong*, or healer, muttered incantations. Andeng's sickness worsened. On the second day, a weakened Andeng requested the sacrifice of a second pig, followed by further incantations. The illness tightened its grip still further upon his already-stricken body.

On the third day, Andeng petitioned the spirits with the blood of still another pig, accompanied by still more fervent incantations. By now it was evident to everyone—including Andeng—that the spirits could not or would not help him. Terror gripped Andeng's heart. He could feel the shadow of death falling over him, chilling him to the bone.

His son Dongla pleaded with him, "O my father! The spirits have failed you. Let me call Costas. Perhaps it is not too late for him to help you!"

Andeng would not answer. Dongla hung his head in sorrow.

"Let's go up and give him medicine, Costas!" Luliap suggested.

"You know the rule I established," Costas responded. "Are you asking me to break it?"

"If now you give him medicine and he recovers, both Andeng and the people will know it was not the pig sacrifices and the incantations that helped him," Luliap explained. "There will be no confusion."

So Costas climbed the ridge to Sivimu again.

"There Andeng lay, breathing his last," Costas later recounted. "I called his name, but he didn't respond for several minutes. Then he recognized me and whispered my name. Leaning over him, I said gently, 'Andeng, do you want us to give you medicine and pray for you?' "

"Yes," came the feeble reply. Dongla and Bengwok looked up with renewed hope, as Costas quickly administered terramycin and penicillin and then prayed audibly that God, who alone knew the exact nature of Andeng's illness, would heal him either through the medicine or apart from it.

Twice every day for several days, Costas returned to the side of the man who had tried to kill him, administering drugs, praying, and uplifting Andeng's spirit with encouraging words. And as he labored, hundreds of Yali eyes watched.

"Throughout my year at Ninia," Costas later recalled, "I often felt like a gladiator standing alone in the center of an immense colosseum. I kept inviting my audience to jump into the center with me and share my unenviable lot, but the vast majority preferred the role of audience. A few, however, responded and leaped into the center with me. It was such a lonely place, but they endured with me. And the fellowship we shared was exciting!"

The tiny band at the center of the arena received an unexpected addition—Andeng. For he recovered his health under Costas's care and decided to join the Christians. It was a long leap down for a man of his stature, but he survived the jump, injuring only his pride.

No longer aloof, Andeng listened with close interest to the gospel from that time forward. "Andeng never missed a meeting," Costas recalled.

At the same time, however, Andeng's *yogwa* was still full of fetishes as a link to his old way of life. Costas recognized the contradiction inherent in Andeng's attempt to combine faith in Christ with dependence upon the spirits, but he bided his time. Yali comprehension of the gospel could advance only one step at a time. Costas waited patiently for the Holy Spirit's opportunity.

Before that opportunity came, Stan and Pat returned from Australia.

CONFLICT

PAT, for her part, did not want to return to Irian Jaya, as Dutch New Guinea was now called under the new Indonesian administration. She sensed with foreboding that martyrdom awaited at least her husband if he returned to the Yali people. And her five growing children desperately needed the educational benefits available in Australia.

Stan, however, persuaded her to return. The possibility of martyrdom did not deter him in the least. Indeed, in the eyes of some observers, Stan seemed almost to court martyrdom. He knew only that he must finish the mission he had initiated in the Heluk Valley, at any cost.

Before the family left Australia, Stan arranged for his two oldest sons, Wesley and Hilary, to reside at a pleasant home for missionary children in Melbourne, Australia. Here they could attend a public school within the cultural context of their own homeland. Pat would be free to teach their younger school-age children, Rodney and Joy, in Ninia through correspondence courses provided by the Australian government.

In March 1965, Stan and Pat, with Rodney, Joy, and baby Janet, returned to Irian Jaya. As they stepped out of the MAF plane onto the Ninia airstrip, they noticed some remarkable changes brought about by Costas and Alky Maoris during their one year as replacements. The Ninia airstrip was much improved; Costas had spent a thousand dollars upgrading it. Many Yalis, who earlier remained aloof from the mission, now greeted Stan and Pat cheerfully and helped to carry their suitcases to—what was that? A special elevated platform at one side of the airstrip! It was no longer necessary to set suitcases on grass muddied by hundreds of feet passing by. Rows of white stones marked the sides of the airstrip.

Costas and Alky lovingly escorted Stan, Pat, and their children along a pathway beautifully landscaped with rock retaining walls and profuse flower beds. The wall and flowers extended beyond the mission home toward the point where Bruno's house overlooked the Heluk gorge.

They entered the mission home. The double-layered palm-bark floor felt solid under their feet. Attractive sheets of beaten *pandanus* bark replaced the burlap on the walls. Ceiling rafters were covered. Cupboards lined one wall in the kitchen, and there was one sturdy wardrobe in the bedroom.

Pat looked into the small room she had planned one day to use as a pantry. It now contained an indoor toilet, washbasin, and shower. Bouquets of flowers brightened the dining room and their bedroom.

Leading Stan across to the new school building, Costas showed him several dozen Yalis avidly studying their primers.

"Costas, you didn't have to do all this," Stan said. "And I don't have money to repay you for all your expenses."

"Stan," Costas replied, "if these things will make you and your family more comfortable and free you to spend more time helping the Yali people, that is all I want."

Royally welcomed, Stan and Pat resumed their labors among the Yali people. After a few days, Costas and Alky and their two sons flew to a second assignment as volunteer replacements. Some one hundred miles from Ninia, in the sweltering southern lowlands, my wife, Carol, and I were preparing to leave for furlough after our first four years among a headhunter tribe known as the Sawi. Many Sawi had turned from headhunting and cannibalism to faith in Jesus Christ, but they still needed much counseling, teaching, and medical help.

With remarkable selflessness, Costas and Alky volunteered to delay the beginning of their own pioneer ministry for still another year, in order that young Sawi "babes in Christ" might have constant spiritual nurture during the crucial early years of their Christian experience.

One year later Carol and I returned from furlough to find, as Stan and Pat had found at Ninia, that more tribesmen knew Christ as Savior. Three new schools overflowed with hundreds of eager literates. The sick had been faithfully treated. Our own house and yard were greatly improved. And bouquets of flowers welcomed us in every room!

We looked around us in awe. Never had we seen the Spirit of Christ more exuberantly displayed than we saw it in dear Costas and Alky! Though they had greatly improved our home, they themselves had lived the year in an even smaller and less convenient structure.

Stan, though he loved beauty and appreciated the intense goodwill behind the changes Costas introduced into the mission residence at Ninia, decided not to enjoy all of them. The rock retaining walls, for example, did not suit his lifestyle. One of Stan's goals was to maintain an example for other missionaries who, in his opinion, spent far too much time and money making their surroundings beautiful and comfortable. If Stan himself lived in a beautifully landscaped setting, his example would be discredited. So he dismantled the walls and used the hundreds of rocks they contained to improve the airstrip still further.

Likewise, he filled in the warm-air slots Costas had cut just below ceiling level. And he refused to use the indoor toilet that Costas had installed. No matter how bitter the weather, he would stride outdoors to that awkward little house teetering on the edge of a steep slope behind the station.

His family, however, used the indoor facility.

When Costas later learned of these things, he smiled good-naturedly. "Let Stan live as he must live; we are not all the same!"

Two months after returning from Australia, Stan came to a crucial decision: now was the time to tackle the touchy problem of Yali dependence upon charms, fetishes, and witchcraft paraphernalia. He knew that hundreds of such objects lay hoarded within dusty *kembu-vams, dokwi-vams,* and *yogwas.* Just as political revolutionaries, in overthrowing a system they consider corrupt, will destroy not only the system itself but all the symbols associated with it, so also Stan, no less determined, committed himself to destroy the symbols of *Kembu*'s ancient sway.

Mao Tse-tung made no apology for the forceful destruction of thousands of priceless works of art in his "cultural revolution," nor did Paul the apostle—two thousand years earlier—apologize when his preaching inspired the voluntary burning of fifty thousand silver pieces' worth of sorcery manuals at Ephesus (see Acts 19:18-19). Neither would Stanley Albert Dale apologize for encouraging Yali Christians to renounce and destroy their fetishes once and for all.

Stan described his approach to this new threshold: "My wife and I went on furlough in late 1964, and on our return we found that those who professed conversion before we went home were still following the Lord. More people were learning to read and hundreds were receiving regular Christian instruction in four centers and occasional instruction at others.

"We discovered, though, that none of them had parted with his fetishes, and it has been abundantly proven in this land that a complete break with the past in this matter is necessary as a safeguard against sliding back into the old pagan ways."

Then Stan stated what he believed was the crux of the matter: "No one can wholly follow the Lord while he still has fetishes, just as he cannot be really the Lord's while he still has idols."[1]

In Stan Dale's view, as in the view of most evangelicals, Christian faith could not exist as a mere supplement to other sources of spiritual help. Christian faith could be real only when it replaced all other sources of spiritual help. Stan did not presume to improve upon the wisdom of Paul the apostle who praised young converts at Thessalonica for "turning to God from idols" (1 Thess. 1:9) and who urged pagans at Lystra to forsake "vanities [pagan rites] and turn to the living God" (Acts 14:15).

Stan concluded, "We felt the time had come when the Heluk Valley should become 'the valley of decision.' "[2]

It was soon to become the valley of much more than "decision."

"For weeks," Stan continued, "we gave additional instruction to the little company of believers regarding the need for Christians to separate themselves from evil. Then on Sunday night, the 22nd of May, 1966 . . . I challenged those present with the fact that they had not yet renounced their fetishes."

Directly in front of Stan crouched Dongla, who had become the *de facto* leader of the small Christian community. Stan's challenge pierced Dongla like a bamboo arrowhead. *Renounce my fetishes?* he thought. *Then I will not have power to avenge my forefathers who died in battle!* But suddenly Dongla realized that he no longer cared to avenge the past. His aspirations had been gradually directed toward a new and better future.

Nor will I have any further contact with the kembu *spirits,* he mused.

Dongla could never forget the day one of the *kembu* spirits had invaded his body years earlier, causing him to lose his sanity for several days. But now the Spirit of God, Creator of heaven and earth, was drawing him into a gentle fellowship of love that made his mind feel whole and pure in a way he had never experienced before. *There is a difference between the* kembu *spirits and God,* Dongla reasoned. *Stan is right when he says we cannot follow both. And since I cannot follow both, I know which One I choose!*

Dongla rose to his feet, took a deep breath, and said, "I'll burn my charms and fetishes tomorrow!" And inside he was thinking, *This, of course, will mean war!*

Yekwara, Bengwok, Luliap, and about fifteen other young Yali Christians spent a nearly sleepless night. *Will Dongla actually burn them?* they kept asking themselves. An even more disturbing question was, *Can we who are also Christians bear to watch him do it alone?*

By morning Yekwara and Bengwok decided they couldn't stand by and allow Dongla to take this dangerous step alone. Both boys, recalling how Nindik, Kiloho, and Bukni were executed for various violations of Yali law, knew that Dongla would surely suffer a similar fate, for although Nindik, Kiloho, and Bukni had broken various taboos, they had not gone so far as to desecrate the actual focal centers of Yali religion— the fetishes.

Dongla's proposed action was a violation of Yali law so undreamed of that no prohibition against it had ever been formulated! And yet Yekwara and Bengwok agreed that it was a necessary step in order to complete their transition into the new world of Christian faith.

"Let us die with Dongla!" Yekwara said. "We have experienced the reality of Christ in our hearts; we can never again return to dependence upon mere inanimate objects."

As soon as Yekwara and Bengwok announced their decision, the idea spread like a flame to other believers. Stan described what happened: "Yodeling and whooping, believers raced up the mountain to their respective villages, dove into the men's clubhouses, and started dragging bags of fetishes out of their dark corners."

There was, however, a problem of which Stan apparently was not aware—the Yali Christians themselves were not the sole owners of the objects they seized. A dozen or more men might consider themselves the guardians of any one sacred object. Thus, although Stan advised the Christians to bring only their own fetishes, it was not possible for them to do this, with the exception of minor charms. Ownership of such things was always a community affair, not a private one.

So when Dongla, burning with zeal, approached the *yogwa* he shared with his father, Andeng threatened him: "These *Kembu* objects are not yours to destroy. They belong to all of us. If you try to take them, I will kill you, even though you are my own son."

Dongla had already counted on that. "Believe me, father! These objects are actually snares keeping our lives in bondage! I will not tolerate that bondage any longer! I want to be free! You can be free also! Let me burn them!"

Momentarily awed by his son's fiery spirit, Andeng hesitated. In that moment of hesitation, Dongla ducked past him into the *yogwa* and promptly reappeared, his arms filled with net bags full of charms. Andeng screamed with horror, like a man who sees the very fabric of his universe beginning to disintegrate. But his limbs seemed paralyzed—he did not try to kill Dongla.

"NO! NO!" he roared. "STOP!"

But Dongla was gone, whooping with excitement, bearing the objects down to the airstrip—the place most central to all the local villages. *He'll come back for more,* Andeng reasoned. *I'll hide them first!* And he did.

Elsewhere also, pagan Yalis seemed paralyzed as the small band of Christians, filled with incredible zeal, took command. Stan stood calmly by the airstrip, watching proudly as his spiritual commandos executed their mission with perfect precision.

And while he stood waiting, the pile of fetishes grew at his feet.

It's exactly as it should be, he reveled. *The Acts of the Apostles is being rewritten in Yali!*

Stan described the fetishes: "There were long, oval-shaped flat stones, small round stones, molded balls of fire-baked clay, lumps of desiccated fat from pigs that had been sacrificed to the spirits, arrows that had killed or wounded people, and so on. It was as if all the hoarded fears of generations evaporated like morning mist once these evil objects were dragged out into daylight.

"At about 11:00 A.M. we gathered around the pile of fetishes, sang some hymns, and thanked God for giving the Christians courage to destroy them."

Then Stan, as commando-in-chief, threw gasoline upon the pile and resolutely added a match.

"The Christians sang again for joy," he wrote later, "as the flames leaped upwards."

"What will happen to us now?" The question was on every pagan Yali's lips.

"Surely an *o-sanim* will begin at once!" offered others.

"Our gardens will go bad now! Our pigs will sicken and die!"

"We'll all starve!"

"We won't have time to starve!" others countered. "The *kulamong* will return; we'll die like our forefathers in a plague of darkness!"

Then came the anguished cry, "Why have we not destroyed this evil influence in our midst? Why have our hands become so weak? If we kill them all now, perhaps it will not be too late to avoid destruction!"

But to the consternation of the pagans, the Christians followed up one decisive action with another. For example, Dongla—seeking to demonstrate conclusively to his people that they were in no danger from the spirits—announced that he would eat some of the sacred food growing within the sacred *osuwa* called Ninia, where little Nindik had accidentally incurred the wrath of the spirit world.

"My fathers!" Dongla shouted to hundreds of onlookers. "The priests of *kembu* have warned us for centuries that anyone who eats food from the sacred gardens will swell up and die. Protected by the power of God, I will eat that food and not die! Watch!"

Dongla executed this bold maneuver on his own initiative, without telling Stan—evidence that this sudden upwelling of resolve was anchored in the will of the Yali Christians themselves.

Dongla took a sweet potato from the Ninia *osuwa*, cooked it, and in full view of witnesses, ate it. As he predicted, he did not swell up and die. This demonstration served to further weaken the resistance of local pagans.

It now appeared certain that a death-dealing counterblow would not arise from the Hwim-Sivimu area. Meanwhile news of what the Christians had done on that first day was spreading rapidly to other areas.

During the days immediately following the first fetish burning, Stan held meeting after meeting to reassure the Christians that what they had done was right in the sight of God, if not in the sight of all men. Stan assured Yali believers their action was parallel to Moses' destruction of the golden calf the Israelites had made in the wilderness, or to Gideon's overthrowing his own father's idols in the days of the Hebrew judges.

Before long still more fetish-burnings occurred. The Christians reported one day that people living to the south at Liligan now decided to follow the example of the Christians at Ninia. Stan trekked to Liligan with a few of the young men, and a second burning took place.

While Stan was away, Erariek came running to Pat with a warning, "Men from Balinga are coming to make war against us!"

Pat gathered her children into the house while Dongla sent word to Stan. Meanwhile Pat saw warriors from Balinga massing along the Sivimu ridge. "Are the leaders of Ninia only children?" they taunted. "Why do you allow mere youths to do these things under your very noses?" But when Stan returned, the warriors soon dispersed. A strange uncertainty still kept even committed pagans from mounting a concerted counteroffensive.

Rising to the challenge from Balinga, Stan gathered the Christians around him and trekked there the following day! A few committed pagans came out with bows and arrows to resist his advance. But Stan and his "commandos" marched boldly right down into the center of Balinga!

"You have heard of the burning of spirit-objects at Ninia and Liligan," he called. "We have come here to explain the reasons behind it and to assure you that you, too, can be free from the power of such things if you want to!"

After listening to Stan's justification for the burnings, four Balinga people who had been impressed by the gospel made their decision: "We, too, will burn our spirit-objects today!"

And it was done.

As the smoke ascended, warriors from Yabi's fortresslike position descended to the Heluk River, shouting across to the Balinga men:

"STOP! You are making a terrible mistake!"

Stan turned and with eagle-sharp eyes sized up this new challenge.

The Christians already knew how he would respond, and they were ready to join him. Stan waved a signal, and down they rushed, a miniature task force armed only with faith. The Yabi warriors, meanwhile, had worked themselves into a fury. Some of them waved banana leaves, shouting, "Come over here and we'll cook your flesh in these very leaves!" As Stan approached the river, Yabi men fired a volley of arrows at him. Most of the arrows fell short. A few struck the grass near Stan, but he was not in the least deterred. Nor were his Yali companions. While Stan held the attention of the Yabi bowmen, Luliap, Dongla, and the others forded the Heluk. Then they in turn diverted attention from Stan so that he also could cross. Emerging from the bushes on the far bank, Stan saw to his relief that the Yabi warriors, though armed to the teeth, were retreating uphill as unarmed Christians advanced toward them!

Stan joined the advance, pleading at the top of his voice for the Yabi men to lay down their weapons and allow the Christians to present their case. In defiance the Yabi men fired a volley of about fifty arrows. The Christians dodged them easily and kept advancing. Stan wrote: "Three men were waiting for me as I climbed a steep rise. They began shooting at me. I shouted that I was their friend and held up my hands to show that I was unarmed. By this time, though, they were probably so worked up that they couldn't hear. The first arrow went just over my head. The second, caught by an updraught of air, went wide. The third man waited with grim determination until I was quite close, then took aim and fired, but his arrow missed me by several feet."

Discouraged by their inability to intimidate Stan and his followers, the Yabi warriors dispersed. The Christians advanced right into the center of Yabi and there, once again, found a few people who, having been under Christian instruction for a long time, expressed willingness to part with their spirit-objects. While hostiles watched in frustration from nearby forests and ridges, a fourth fetish-burning took place at Yabi.

Stan and his Yali task force returned to Ninia.

"We were all enormously encouraged," he wrote, "by the Lord's protection."

The weather continued as warm and sunny as could be expected between monsoon changes in the Heluk. Sweet potatoes continued to grow. Litters of pigs were born as usual. Sickness did not increase beyond its normal incidence. Pagan Yali were amazed. The Christians were right! The universe had not fallen apart because sacred objects had been put to fire!

"Perhaps our forefathers didn't understand the nature of things as well as we thought!" said many.

This was what Stan had been counting on. If a wholesale burning of fetishes could be achieved in one bold initiative, preferably without loss of human life, then the Yali would discern something they had never put to the test before—that fetishes were in no way indispensable to universal order.

Mankind could exist perfectly well without them.

Once this fact was demonstrated convincingly to the whole population, a major blockage in Yali minds would have been shattered. The way would be open for a new order free from war, superstition, and witchcraft in perhaps one-tenth the time less-decisive approaches would take.

Preferably without loss of human life, Stan hoped.

But it would not be that easy.

Throughout the following week, large crowds gathered at Ninia and Liligan to receive further teaching from Stan, Luliap, Dongla, and other Christians. Nor were there any more reports of hostility from Balinga and Yabi. To all appearances, the tension between pagans and Christians was subsiding. Stan looked forward to a steady increase in the acceptance of the gospel among the Yali. He did not plan to precipitate any further crises, at least not for several months.

One day at Liligan, someone told Stan that people in the lower Heluk had heard of the amazing things happening in the upper part of the valley and had sent word that they, too, were ready to follow the ways of God. Stan had visited the area a few weeks earlier and found a good reception.

He believed the report.

"Who will go to them?" he asked his "commandos" in a special night meeting. Silence hung heavy in the spacious schoolroom Costas had built, for the Christians themselves had not heard the report of interest in the lower Heluk. Instead they had heard that the people were furious over recent events in the upper Heluk.

"The paths of their stomachs are all tied in knots. Be careful!" someone warned.

"Who will go?" Stan repeated. When no one replied, Stan said, "I see you are afraid. Very well, I'll go myself!"

Yekwara winced. The premonition of danger hung heavy upon him. Somehow he had to stop Stan from traveling down-valley. There was only one way to stop him. "Very well, teacher. I'll go down and preach to them!" Yekwara said, swallowing his apprehension.

"You shouldn't go alone," Stan responded.

"I'll go with him!" Bengwok, Yekwara's faithful companion, volunteered. The two youths were almost inseparable.

"Then it's settled," Stan concluded. "The rest of us will cover all the main villages in the upper part of the valley."

Next morning Yekwara and Bengwok, who worked as launderers for the Dales, completed the morning wash in record time, picked up a picture roll and some trading salt from Stan, and set out briskly on their down-valley journey. To reach the lower Heluk, they had first to pass through a deep gorge several miles in length. Picking their way from rock to rock around foaming pools of the Heluk River, they soon broke through to Miakma, the first village of the down-valley people. There they taught the people and spent the night. Next morning the two companions forded a further small tributary of the Heluk and ascended to a village called Ilia. Stan had cautioned them not to venture beyond Miakma, but they proceeded in any case, perhaps desiring to sample the mood of still another village before returning to Ninia.

There on Ilia's narrow ridgeline, Yekwara and Bengwok gathered people around them and began to teach. The entrance to the gorge through which they would have to flee, if they were threatened, was now several hundred yards below them. On a loftier ridge, men of other southern villages were massing. Through a cover of thick jungle, they looked down at the meeting now underway in the center of Ilia village. They began their descent, dividing into two groups.

A sharp-eyed man in Ilia saw one of the groups descending rapidly toward the village. Casually, he interrupted Yekwara's sermon. "Are you aware, young preachers, that men are coming down that mountain to kill you?"

Yekwara and Bengwok looked up. They could see no one. In any case, perhaps the man was mistaken. If anyone was up there, might they not simply be coming to join the meeting?

"Let them come," Yekwara replied calmly. "Perhaps when they get here, they also will decide to listen to the good words we bring."

But then he saw the warriors emerging from the forest, and he could tell by the speed with which they were coming that there would be no opportunity to reason with them. They would kill without asking questions.

"Bengwok! Hurry!"

The two leaped over the low stone wall surrounding Ilia and raced toward the mouth of the great gorge far below. Once into its narrow confines, they could easily keep ahead of their pursuers, who would be reduced to walking single file along the slippery sides of chasms, with few vantage points for aiming arrows. But the pursuers had anticipated the way the two Christians would take—the second group was already approaching a midpoint of the trail, determined that Yekwara and Bengwok should not pass that point alive.

But the two Ninia youths moved so quickly that they passed the interception point about ten strides ahead of the interceptors. With arrows whirring past their heads, they floundered into the tributary they had crossed earlier. As they struggled up its far bank, a chance arrow struck Bengwok behind the shoulder blade.

"Friend! I'm hit!" he gasped. "Keep going, Yekwara! Don't wait for me!"

Perhaps fearing further ambushes along the main trail, Yekwara veered to the left, climbing a steep grassy slope. Bengwok followed, lagging gradually behind. The hill crested into a knife-edged ridge. The far slope was even steeper, almost a cliff. They plunged downward, grabbing at bushes to keep from plunging headlong. At the foot of the cliff, a second small tributary emerged from the mouth of a narrow canyon.

Yekwara headed into the chaotic canyon, hoping to elude his pursuers in rough terrain. At the entrance to the canyon, at the foot of a small land-slide of sparkling white limestone, Bengwok was overtaken.

He turned to face his pursuers, gasping for breath, grimacing with pain from the wound in his back. Slim and black, Bengwok stood etched in perfect outline against the pure white limestone. While some adversaries rushed past him in pursuit of Yekwara, others stopped and formed a semicircle around Bengwok. Coldly and systematically, they fitted arrows to their bows, took aim, and began firing. They kept on until he fell, a lone representative of a new order that hadn't yet won its full victory.

Among the killers were two priests of *Kembu*. One was Saburu and the other Elavo, a brother of Bengwok's mother.

"My son! My son!" Elavo cried over his nephew's corpse. "Why did you compel me to kill you?"

As for Saburu, he grasped a rough-edged piece of the white limestone. Filled with glowering rage, he sank to his knees, raised Bengwok's limp, brown fingers one by one, and laid them across a rock. Then Saburu began to bludgeon Bengwok's hands until only crushed masses of blood, flesh, and bone remained.

His chest heaving with emotion, Saburu cried over and over, "With these hands you have taken objects sacred to our spirits and destroyed them!" Likewise he battered Bengwok's feet to a pulp, crying, "And with these feet, you traveled wickedly from village to village, teaching others to do the same!"

Moments later they left Bengwok lying, staked through with arrows, upon his pristine limestone shroud. From a distance Elavo looked back one last time at his dead nephew. Only four of Bengwok's many wounds were visible—two bloodied hands and two bloodied feet.

The warning of *Kembu*'s thunder was fulfilled.

Up-valley, Stan had just finished coaching the other young preachers in the sermons they would deliver the following day at Liligan, Balinga, and Yabi. They hugged him good-bye and set out toward their respective destinations, beaming with confidence.

Stan turned and looked down-valley at the forbidding gorge through which Bengwok and Yekwara had gone. For a moment his heart filled with admiration for them. Misty-eyed at the thought of their willingness to embark upon this mission, Stan whispered, "Bengwok and Yekwara, you are like two of my own sons. With men like you, we'll win this valley yet!"

Still fleeing for his life, Yekwara leaped from rock to rock in the steep-walled canyon. Glancing back, he saw his pursuers gradually falling behind. Gasping for breath, he rounded another bend of the narrowing defile and stopped short. The canyon ended in sheer walls! In grim desperation he scanned the walls for some way to climb up. There was none. He looked behind him. It was too late to backtrack and climb out of the canyon at some lower point. The pursuers were already too close. Yekwara saw only one chance—hide under a waterfall streaming down one of the sheer walls.

Moments later the defenders of *Kembu* arrived, streaming with sweat, nearly faint with exhaustion, but still determined to find their prey. Grimly they scanned the sheer walls.

"Could he have climbed up *there*?" someone gasped incredulously.

"Perhaps he climbed out of the canyon farther down!"

"No, my brothers," said a priest of *Kembu*, "he is here somewhere. Let us look behind these rocks."

From behind the waterfall, Yekwara saw them searching among the *yogwa*-sized boulders on the canyon floor. Then two of them approached the waterfall.

There is no chance, Yekwara sighed. *They'll find me here!* Then he asked himself, *Why should I wait until they find me hiding like a man who is afraid to die? I'll step out and show them I'm ready to die for my faith!*

Unarmed and smiling, Yekwara stepped out through the glistening falls—

Wailing, barely audible, drifted down from Lilia's lofty ridgetop position. Stan paid little attention. Wailing was a familiar sound in the Heluk. Then the people of Hwim, listening from a lower ridge closer to the station,

relayed the message. Latowen heard it and ran to tell Pat. "*Nisinga!*" Latowen wept, "Yekwara and Bengwok are dead!"

Pat steeled herself to keep from showing alarm. The Yali were always
coming with reports that later proved untrue. A person who believed every
Yali report at its first telling would soon be a nervous wreck! Then Pat
turned and saw that little Rodney had overheard Latowen's announce-
ment. Stricken with shock, he looked up searchingly at his mother. For
almost as long as Rodney could remember, Yekwara and Bengwok had
been his special playmates and bodyguards. They had protected him from
centipedes and scorpions, from falling over cliffs, and from pig bites, and
had taught him to speak the Yali tongue.

"It's all right, dear," Pat said. Tears had begun to well in Rodney's
eyes. "We must not allow everything we hear to alarm us."

Yalis were gathering now outside Pat's kitchen window. They pointed
across the Heluk Valley toward an eastern village called Iptahaik. Pat and
Rodney hurried outside to see what they were pointing at.

"See that smoke rising from a ridge near Iptahaik!" an older Yali
called thoughtlessly. "That's where the southern people are eating Yekwara! If we were closer, we could see them waving banana leaves."

Rodney fainted.

While Pat attended to Rodney, Stan ran to the village of Hwim to
cross-examine those who had brought the news to the upper Heluk.
There he found an elderly Yali who claimed he was related to Bengwok.

"After the killers left, I gathered firewood and cremated Bengwok,"
the man explained. "I did not find Yekwara's body because it lay far up
in the mountains."

"How can you be sure Yekwara is dead?" Stan asked.

"I met the men who killed him; I saw blood on their arrows."

Stan returned to the station.

"We spent an almost sleepless night numbed with shock and grief," Stan
wrote. "The two young men were so close to us, it was as if our own children had been killed."

Early the next morning, Stan radioed the missionary pilot stationed
at Wamena, the main government outpost, and requested that a de-

tachment of police be flown in to investigate the reported killings. An hour later the chief-of-police, a Eurasian named Van Leeuwen, arrived at Ninia with four patrolmen. Stan was ready with supplies for the journey down-valley. Luliap and several other Christians volunteered to accompany the patrol.

As the small band climbed past Liligan before descending into the gorge, friendly Yalis rushed out to warn them, "There are not enough in your party. You will all be killed! The southern people are waiting in ambush!"

Undeterred, the patrol descended into the gorge, while Yali women on ridges behind them raised their death wails in grim foreboding.

For fifteen hundred feet they descended from Liligan and then cautiously followed the raging Heluk into a thunder-filled canyon several miles in length. At one point Van Leeuwen, the chief-of-police, fell and grazed his knee. However, the party continued until they faced a flimsy bridge of cut poles spanning the turbulent Heluk River. Van Leeuwen sat down, complaining that his injured knee was bothering him—he could go no further. The patrol would have to be canceled until some other time. The four constables likewise were quick to agree that the patrol ought to return to Ninia.

Stan heaved a sigh. It was easy for them not to care, but his own heart grieved like that of a man who had lost part of his own body. *I sent Yekwara and Bengwok on that mission,* Stan said to himself. *I cannot face the other Christians again until I have done all in my power to recover the bodies of their friends and mine.* In that crucial moment, Stan came to another incredibly fearless decision.

"Return to Ninia if you must," he replied to the policemen, "but I myself must go on. I have an obligation to fulfill." Van Leeuwen and his armed escorts urged him not to go, but Stan was determined. Amazed at Stan's decision, Van Leeuwen and his men set out on the return journey. Luliap and the other Yali Christians stood with Stan.

"You return also!" he commanded.

"My father!" Luliap protested. "We cannot let you go alone!"

Stan insisted. "Until this crisis I really did not believe they would actually kill any of us. But now that it has come to murder, I know they will not hesitate to kill any of you who go with me. There is a chance, however, that they will not kill me, because I am of a different race. That is why I must go alone. Stay with the policemen. Wait for me at Ninia."

Luliap protested again, but Stan stopped him with a look of irresistible authority, turned on his heel, and marched downstream around a bend of the gorge. Luliap and his friends gazed after him, awestruck. *How great must be the One who commands such loyalty!* Luliap mused. Even Yali commitment to the *kembu* spirits could not compare with *this!* The lesson struck home, and Luliap would not forget it—a Christian does his duty *no matter what!*

Luliap looked upstream. The police patrol was now nearly out of sight. He waved to his companions. Together they hurried after Van Leeuwen and his men.

Burdened and heartbroken, Stan pressed on through the gorge. Memories of Yekwara and Bengwok filled him with anguish as every step brought him closer to the site of their martyrdom. Coolly, he paused at each vantage point along the trail, scanning the forest ahead for any sign of ambush. Later a sense of God's presence encouraged him in that dark and lonely gorge, and he stepped out more briskly.

He had almost reached the first village below the gorge when he heard voices behind him. It was Luliap leading two of the four policemen and three Yali Christians.

Catching up to Stan, Luliap explained, "You told us to stay with the policemen, so we persuaded two of the policemen to follow you and then stayed with them as you commanded!"

Stan gripped each of the four smiling Yali by the shoulders.

"With men like you," he grinned, "this valley can be won! Come on!"

Together they entered Miakma, the first village below the narrows of the Heluk. It was deserted. They passed through the village and followed a trail that led up to the high ridge toward Ilia, now obscured by mist. Suddenly Luliap pointed to a pile of fresh ashes beside the trail.

"That man who found Bengwok," he said, "told us he carried the body close to Miakma and cremated it beside the trail. This must be it."

Stan removed his bush hat and stood at attention in honor of Bengwok, while the four Yali youths crouched beside Bengwok's ashes and wept for him. The two native policemen stood on either side, their guns ready. It was already clear that they would have to spend the night in this god-forsaken place, and the thought did not appeal to them at all!

They continued up the trail toward Ilia, scanning every slope and gully for some sign of Yekwara's body. Twilight thickened around them. They were unaware that Yekwara had turned aside from the trail they were following and led his pursuers far upstream in an adjacent canyon. Presently they forded the stream where Yekwara and Bengwok barely eluded that first ambush. Just beyond it they found a small Yali *yogwa* standing dark and deserted among low bushes. They decided to spend the night there and continue their search next morning.

Just before entering the *yogwa*, Stan scanned the surrounding hills again. *With all this fog and mist,* he said to himself, *the killers may not have noticed our approach.* Stan sent the four Ninia youths and one policeman to search the nearby hills for Yekwara's body, while he and the second constable lit a fire and boiled a pot of rice for their evening meal.

Shortly after Luliap, his three friends, and the other policeman disappeared into the mist, the remaining policeman settled down opposite the small fire, stretched his weary legs, and laid his rifle across his lap. It had been a hard trek through the narrows of the Heluk Valley. Stan was engrossed in adding salt and more water to the pot of rice when the warriors came.

Out of the same bushes from which they had tried to ambush Yekwara and Bengwok the previous day, the first of the armed horde crept. He moved closer to the door of the little *yogwa* and hid behind a large rock partially blocking the entrance. Looking over the rock, he could see Stan illuminated beside the bright little fire. Holding his breath, he eased his arrow over the rock and aimed at Stan's side. For a moment firelight gleamed on his shiny bamboo blade, especially chosen for killing. Then he drew his bow to full strength as other warriors behind him waited their turn.

As if to oblige the warrior, Stan moved across the doorway for something in his pack. In the next instant he recoiled, grasping and pulling a five-foot arrow out of his right side.

Chortling over his success, the first warrior leaped from behind the rock blind and promptly shot another arrow into Stan's right thigh. He then gave place to a second, who then gave place to another—

His eyes bulging with surprise and terror, the constable fumbled with his gun, trying to cock it. Stan could hear sounds all around the *yogwa*. There were too many attackers—arrows flew through gaps in the old *yogwa's* drafty walls.

"We're in a death trap," Stan gasped. "They can shoot at us from every direction! The fire! I've got to put it out!"

Stan lunged at the fire, trying to scatter its burning brands. As he did so another arrow struck his left thigh, burying itself deeply into his muscle. He flung himself to the far side of the hut, seeking shelter, but there was none—two more arrows struck him. One pierced through his right forearm and another penetrated his diaphragm and intestines. Stan yanked each arrow out in turn and then laughed at his tormentors in Yali, "Run away home, all of you! You've done enough!"

It was a timely warning, for the policeman by this time had cocked his gun and began shooting warning shots out through the walls of the *yogwa*. The attackers, however, paid no attention but erupted with an eerie shout of triumph, announcing to surrounding fog-wrapped villages that they had accomplished their purpose: the *duong* was dying!

Perhaps they're right! Stan thought, as pain from his five wounds stabbed through him. The floor of the *yogwa* was now criss-crossed with many arrows, five of them reddened with blood. Stan pressed against the wall of the *yogwa,* waiting for the next arrow. He saw it coming—

Outside the *yogwa* a warrior named Naliok crept up behind the rock the warriors were using for cover as they shot arrows in through the door. Just to make *sure* Stan would die, Naliok wanted to drive one more arrow to its mark. But the policeman saw him raise his head and shoulders above the rock, aiming at Stan. The gun barrel was already aimed at the door. The constable shifted it a few inches and fired. The bullet struck Naliok in the forehead. Without a cry, Naliok toppled back from the rock. His companions stared down in horror. There was no sign of an arrow in Naliok's body, but Naliok was dead!

In the next moment, the second policeman and the four Christian Yalis returned through the mist. The second policeman opened fire on the attackers, scattering them into the dusk.

Luliap entered the *yogwa* and found Stan sitting among the mass of spent arrows, his five wounds glaring red in the fire's flickering light

"O my father!" Luliap wailed.

"It's all right, Luliap," Stan whispered. "They've shot me for Yekwara and Bengwok's sake. We must move to a safer place."

To everyone's amazement, Stan struggled to his feet and helped the others stow his gear into his pack. Then he set out down the trail as if immune to pain. In fact, however, every movement, every breath shot needles of pain through his legs, his right arm, diaphragm, and abdomen. But he kept walking. The four Yali stayed close by, ready to help him if he stumbled. Once again they forded the tributary and descended to dark and deserted Miakma.

"We'll camp here," Stan said, eager to lay down and ease the pain of walking.

But Luliap interrupted, "No, my father! We must keep on walking through the night. Tomorrow you will be too stiff to move."

He's right, Stan thought. *And I'll need shots of penicillin as soon as possible; the longer I stay here, the more infection will spread through my wounds.*

Grimly Stan walked on through Miakma, staggering slightly. It was dark now, but a lighted lantern would make them easy targets for Yali archers lying in wait. They felt their way along the trail until the gorge became so narrow they knew the enemy would not be able to position themselves away from the trail itself. Then they lit a lantern. The dim light only faintly illuminated their way, and the track was rough. At times the trail descended into the river, forcing them to wade along the edge of boiling rapids. One slip in the wrong direction—

Occasionally the trail led across slippery rocks overhanging the torrent. There Luliap and the other Yalis kept their arms around Stan, steadying him on the nearly invisible trail. Gasping for breath, Stan slipped often into potholes hidden between roots of trees. Each time he slipped, excruciating pain swept over him in waves, nearly blotting out consciousness. He gasped, "Luliap, leave me alone. My insides are cut to shreds. I'm dying."

"No, my father," Luliap replied. "Come! Keep walking! God will help you!"

And Stan could hear them praying for him, barely audible above the torrent's booming thunder. Their voices seemed to merge with an old memory—a voice from the past. What was that voice saying? Gradually the words filtered back, forming sentences, daring him to believe he could survive:

If you can force your heart and nerve and sinew
To serve your turn long after they are gone,
And so hold on, when there is nothing in you,
Except the will that says to them, "Hold on!"

Rallying tattered shreds of his spirit, Stan fought off unconsciousness and forced himself to walk. Holding his hands, his Yali friends guided him, descending—wading—climbing . . . for two hours, three . . . four. Then Stan sank to his knees, his body trembling with pain and exhaustion.

"Leave me . . . Luliap . . . leave me . . . I'm dying!"

It seemed to Stan that the dark gorge had become a tunnel and he was falling into it. Despair enclosed his spirit like tightening steel bands.

"Lord, where are You?" he prayed. "Will I live, or die?"

The answer came from within his heart, an answer charged with authority far stronger than Kipling's: *You shall not die, but live, and declare the works of the Lord!*

Like a drowning man, Stan gripped that promise with the fingers of his soul and took another step. Quoting it again, he took another step. And another. And another.

After what seemed another hour, Luliap said to him, "We are coming out of the narrows now."

Stan knew what that meant. The trail at this point turned straight up the wall of the gorge, climbing fifteen hundred feet to Liligan, the first village north of the narrows. *Fifteen hundred feet uphill!* Stan gasped. But still God's promise encouraged him. Gritting his teeth, he leaned into the climb. He was fifty years old, weakened from loss of blood, and had trekked for twelve hours without food. Yet he climbed now with an energy that amazed his followers.

One of the Yalis, meanwhile, hurried ahead to alert Pat.

Nearly eight hours after his wounding, Stan reached the village of Liligan. It was still two hours before dawn. He crawled into a *yogwa* to rest while Luliap borrowed a machete, and with help from friendly folk in Liligan, made a stretcher to carry Stan down to Ninia. Minutes later they carried him out of the *yogwa*, placed him tenderly on the stretcher, and raised it to their shoulders.

The sun was rising. It was Monday, June 13, 1966.

Warned by the forerunner, Pat turned on the radio transmitter at day-break. At 5:45 the MAF base at Wamena answered her call for help. Shortly after 7:00, an aircraft landed, awaiting Stan's arrival by stretcher. Pat dressed the children for the planned flight to Karubaga, where Scottish missionary Dr. Jack Leng was already preparing to operate at RBMU's Vine Memorial Hospital.

Moments later a messenger brought word. "They've brought him to the top of the airstrip. He's still alive."

Pat hurried to meet Stan, pale and weak in his stretcher.

"Perhaps now they'll believe I love these people," he said to her as she leaned over him and kissed him. "And that I won't send them anywhere I'm not willing to go myself."

Tears welled in Pat's eyes. She turned and faced a Dani helper named Pakangen and said, "You see now, my friend, how dangerous it is to serve Christ in this valley. If you are afraid and want to leave, I will arrange a flight for you to your own valley."

"No," he replied with tears streaming down his cheeks. "I choose to stay here at Ninia."

Pat turned to the small band of Yali Christians gathered around Stan's stretcher and said, "You see how much trouble we have caused you by asking you to leave your fetishes and trust in Christ alone. After all this, do you still believe? Do you still want us here?"

"*Nisinga!*" they replied, weeping. "We choose to follow God! We no longer believe *Kembu*!"

"We'll come back to you," Pat promised as Luliap and others lifted Stan gently into the aircraft. "We won't leave you alone to face the anger of those who hate our Christ."

Nurse Jessie Williamson, newly arrived from Australia, donned her white gown and face mask and entered the operating theater. Other nurses on the Karubaga missionary staff assisted. Dr. Jack Leng and Dr. Kenneth Dresser, from another mission's hospital far to the south, leaned over Stan, examining his wounds as he lay asleep under ether, supervised by Jack's wife, Fiona, an anesthetist. At 4:00 they began repairing the dam-age to Stan's diaphragm. At 8:30 that evening they commenced the most critical part of the operation, a bowel resection. At 1:00 the following morning, the team had done all they could do. If they had succeeded in removing all of the infected bowel, Stan might live. If any infection remained, he would die. Pat, as a trained nurse, understood the implications.

That night she and many others at Karubaga and surrounding mission outposts spent many hours in prayer. Next morning, as Pat approached Dr. Leng's office to ask his opinion on Stan's condition, she saw him reading a small book. The doctor did not see her until she spoke to him. Quickly he closed the little book and laid it aside. But Pat had already noticed the title on the page he was reading: "How to Conduct a Burial Service."

"Obviously my husband is in critical condition, doctor," she said, looking down at the book.

"Yes, Pat, I have to admit that he is."

Fearing further hostility against the small community of Christians in the Heluk Valley, Bruno and his Canadian bride, Marlys, volunteered to leave their mission at Kangime and replace Stan and Pat at Ninia until the danger was past. Only a few hours after the Dales left, Bruno and Marlys landed on the Ninia airstrip and stepped out of the same small MAF plane that had taken the Dales to Karubaga. While jubilant Yali thronged to welcome them, Bruno looked thoughtfully into the faces of many he had known in earlier days, before they turned to Christ. There was such a difference now—such a radiant welcome in place of the former aloofness!

All that agony building the airstrip, Bruno decided, *was worth it!*

For the next six days, Pat remained by Stan's bedside, sponging him when he burned with fever, feeding him whenever he regained consciousness, and checking flasks of intravenous fluid during the long hours he lay unconscious.

By the end of June, it was clear that Stan would recover. Doctors recommended that Stan and Pat take a two-month rest across the border in Papua New Guinea.

First, however, they returned to Ninia so that the Yali—both Christian and pagan—could see for themselves that Stan, by the grace of God, had won at least a physical triumph over the savagery of his enemies.

"Our spiritual victory is yet to come," he assured the Christians. "Before two moons have passed, we shall return to stand by you in this battle for the freedom of your people."

As he talked with the Yali, Stan moved about freely, exhibiting almost his normal vitality. The word spread. People of the southern Heluk, still exulting in the supposed certainty of Stan's demise, listened awestruck to eyewitness reports that he was still alive and well.

"We used our sharpest broad-bladed arrows," they said. "And we scored five hard hits at close range, two of them into the very vitals of his body! No ordinary man could have survived such wounds. This man's *Kembu* must be very powerful!"

The Yali respected physical strength and worshiped courage. A man who would preach a new God to such men must demonstrate his God's ability to provide unusual courage and strength. Stanley Albert Dale, through the incident at Miakma, demonstrated courage and strength beyond all previous limits of Yali imagination, and he would demonstrate that courage in still greater measure. Yali of the southern Heluk, like most of their counterparts around Ninia, remained committed to the religion of the *kembu* spirits. But Stan's demonstration of courage could not go unheeded. The Yali of the southern Heluk were *thinking*.

During his period of rest in Papua New Guinea, Stan began a daily regime of running up hills, determined to regain his strength.

He and Pat visited their former colleagues working under CMML along the Sepik River. One evening Stan recounted the story of his wounding to a group of missionary friends. Midway through the account, one missionary fainted.

Notes
1. Stan Dale, *The Valley and the Vision* (London: RBMU, 1978), p. 23.
2. Ibid.

INTO THE WIKBOON BOWL

<table><tr><td>Chapter 17</td></tr></table>

IN 1967, in a report to his RBMU colleagues, Stan wrote: "The martyrdom of Yekwara and Bengwok has laid upon Pat and me a sorrow and
strain we have scarcely been able to endure. On the other hand, the estab-
lishing of the church of Christ among the Yali has given us some of the
deepest joy we have ever known."

Bruno and Marlys deLeeuw, during the weeks they spent at Ninia while
the Dales were away, confirmed that the church of Christ was indeed taking
firm root in Yali soil. After observing the faith and fortitude of Yali Christians at close range, Marlys wrote, "My heart went out to that small band of
Yali Christians who were carrying on so faithfully, and for whose encouragement we had come. I remember especially Dongla, as he often preached
at Ninia during those troubled days. He, though recently bereaved of his
beloved brother Bengwok, was all ardent fire, speaking fervently to his own
people of the love of Christ. I myself could not understand Yali at that time.
But Dongla's demeanor and the response of his listeners made me keenly
aware that the Presence of the Almighty was in their midst.

"Yali Christians possess certain qualities that impressed me deeply, no-
tably their strength of character as they face persecution and even death."

Convinced now that the faith of Yali believers was genuine, Stan resolved, after his return from Papua New Guinea, to prepare them as quickly
as possible for Christian baptism. As Pat wrote in her diary:

August 26, 1966: Warmly welcomed by the people at Ninia, who had our fire going, the house swept clean, and fresh flowers in our vase. Stan had a brief meeting in the schoolhouse, which was crowded.

August 27: I treated a man with an arrow wound in his chest. Gave gifts of appreciation to Luliap and Pakangen for carrying Stan over the mountain, and (of condolence) to Yekwara's and Bengwok's wives.

Sunday, August 28: Stan and Dongla preached to 130 Yali on "God, the Source of Life" . . . And so it continued.

"Aralek! Do you believe in Jesus Christ, the Son of God?"

It was December 6. Stan and Aralek stood together, waist-deep in a special pool dug out of the mountainside near Yarino knoll. With them stood Philip Masters and Costas Macris. Stan, remembering the immense contributions both men had made to the work at Ninia and the Snow Mountains people in general, invited them to share in baptizing the first Yali Christians.

Aralek looked steadily into Stan's eyes and said, "I do!"

Memories welled up within Stan, memories of long treks he had made with Aralek into distant valleys and of the time he had saved Aralek's life after the latter slipped while fording a wild river. Aralek said he traced the beginning of his Christian faith back to that day.

"I baptize you in the name of God the Father, God the Son, and God the Holy Spirit!"

Stan and Phil plunged Aralek briefly below the surface of the pool and raised him again—a symbol of Aralek's personal identification with Christ in death and resurrection.

After Aralek, Luliap descended into the water, his shoulders squared with resolve. Stan took Luliap's hand and led him to the center of the pool. Once again Stan's mind wandered, remembering: *The bright scene before me faded—it was getting dark in a dusty little hut, dark with the approaching shadow of death as arrows pierced my body or rattled against walls around me. Then—staggering through a gorge—cold black river swirling against my ankles, trying to drag me down. Luliap was holding my hand, drawing me up from some deep pit. "Come on, my father! Come on!" he was saying as I struggled to retain consciousness—*

Stan's thoughts returned to the scene before him. "Luliap," he asked, "do you believe in Jesus Christ, the Son of God?"

As each candidate climbed out of the pool, Yali Christians sang hymns of praise to God in their own language. Dongla followed Luliap into the water. Before he stepped into the pool, he proclaimed his intention to follow Christ at any cost. The death of his brother Bengwok and his friend Yekwara had not weakened his resolve but strengthened it. Dongla plunged into the pool with the same resolve he had when he led the fetish burning six months earlier. As Dongla went under the water, his father Andeng watched intently from a nearby hillside.

Still others were baptized by Stan, Phil, and Costas: Liakoho, Latowen's father, whose hot temper was now made gentle by the influence of the gospel; Engehap, once a thief but now a trustworthy helper in Christ; Yemu, who would soon share the greatest trial of all; Foliek, who nearly lost his life under the old order for eating a mushroom; Erariek, who would later translate parts of the New Testament into Yali; Emeroho, who led Stan and Bruno into the Heluk and then listened to their *words,* even under threats against his life.

A number of Yali women followed their husbands, fathers, or brothers into the pool: Latowen, Aralek's wife, who, even in the darkest hour, affirmed that "God's words would not be banished from the Heluk Valley"; after her came Balil, Yekwara's widow, who had held her strong young husband for such a short time but still clung to the faith for which he died.

Confined to the upper Heluk by continuing threats against his life from surrounding valleys, Stan devoted his days to two main tasks: translating parts of the New Testament into Yali and training Yali believers to assume full responsibility for the life and growth of their church. While some have referred to Stan as an "old school" missionary because of his emphasis on discipline, he was decidedly "new school" in his determination to vest full responsibility for the shepherding of the Yali church upon the Yali themselves, as soon as the New Testament standard for that church was firmly established in the minds of the Christian community.

"I believe strongly in the priesthood of all believers," he wrote on one occasion.

Luliap and other trained believers, well-armed with translated portions of the New Testament, continued their preaching journeys throughout the northern Heluk and across the western rim of the Heluk to other valleys. In nearly every village, they faced the dark scowls of priests of *Kembu*. In some places, shamans expressed their hatred for the gospel by erasing the footprints of its messengers from the ground around their villages. They even urged their followers not to accept "foreign" salt, knives, or other goods in trade from Stan and his helpers. "If you accept the *duongs'* hardware, you will also accept their ideas," they warned.

Some of the priests at one point sent word to Stan that if he would express regret for the burning of the fetishes and tell the Christians not to destroy any more, they would allow him to travel freely through all their valleys.

Stan's response: "Though the followers of *Kembu* may kill us, they must be shown that they cannot cow us or cause us to budge one inch from our stand for truth and righteousness, or make us cease for one moment from denouncing the evil of their fetish system. Let them do what they will. I shall not purchase immunity for myself at the cost of expressing regret for initiating the fetish burning. I have no regret at all. It was one of the best things I ever did in my life."[1]

Later, shamans from the southern Heluk sent word. "There must be no more baptisms; if more Yalis are baptized, we'll attack!" A number of believers at Liligan—the village closest to the narrows through which an attack from the south would come—withdrew their request for baptism, fearing for their lives. Five others, however, committed their lives into God's hands and accepted baptism in spite of threats. The attack did not come. But Yali shamans in the southern Heluk, recalling that Stan had twice trekked eastward into the Seng Valley and beyond, sent word to fellow shamans in that area: "The green-eyed *duong* must die! He has stopped coming to our villages since we wounded him. We are hesitant to attack him in his own area, for the number of his friends there increases steadily and may be greater than we think. Perhaps later he will trek into your valley. If he does, do not fail to kill him. But remember this: he has an uncanny ability to recover from even the deadliest wounds! Do not think that just a few arrows will kill him. You will have to use as many arrows as there are 'reeds in a swamp,' or he will get up and walk away!"

Shamans in the Seng understood the message clearly.

And they began to watch the trails, waiting for the day Stan might return.

While warriors in the Seng waited, Aralek and other Christians from Ninia found an unexpectedly warm response to the gospel in the opposite direction. In the Wose, Kai, and Soba valleys, as many as three hundred tribesmen at a time gathered to hear Aralek and others proclaim the gospel. Later Stan trekked into the area and witnessed for himself the ardent response of many people there. Concerning his visit, he wrote, "It is impossible to describe the thrill it brings to my heart to see men who formerly were steeped in evil now listening eagerly to the Word of God. The wild, cunning, almost animal look is disappearing from many faces, and there seems to be a beginning of a real understanding of the way of salvation."

In Soba Valley, one of the most scenic of all valleys in the Snow Mountains, Stan found a slope that could be converted into an airstrip. Alerting his supporters, Stan soon received funds and began to build an airstrip at Soba. Then, encouraged by this unexpected response in the west, Stan turned his attention again to the east. There the Seng, Solo, and other valleys waited, still unconquered by the gospel of Christ. Stan weighed the dangers. Four years earlier, he and Bruno had taken a southern route into the Seng Valley. That route, he knew, was now closed by those who wounded him in 1966. "Only a heavily armed party could pass safely through that area," Stan commented, and he had no intention of leading a heavily armed party on any mission to preach the gospel.

A second route into the Seng Valley lay through a mountain pass rising beyond the village of Yabi, near the northern end of the Heluk. Stan had never crossed that pass before. Had the population living beyond it heard of the killing of Yekwara and Bengwok and of Stan's wounding? If so, would they side with the cause of the southern Heluk people or remain neutral? Stan had no way to find out.

Finally Stan chose a third and logically safer access to eastern valleys. He would fly to Korupoon—Phil and Phyliss Masters' new station among the pygmy-like Kimyal people—and trek westward toward the Solo and Seng valleys respectively, turning back again to Korupoon if and when he encountered hostility engendered by southern Heluk influence.

In August 1968 Stan wrote to Phil Masters, mentioning his intention. Phil responded as Stan hoped he would, that he too wanted to explore the valleys between Korupoon and Ninia more thoroughly. Together the two men decided to search for new airstrip sites in the Seng and Solo valleys and to study variations in tribal languages between Ninia and Korupoon.

The date for the new venture: mid-September 1968. As the date drew near, "Yemu!" Stan called. Yemu was one of the men Stan baptized nearly two years earlier. "How would you like to join Phil Masters and me for a long journey?"

Yemu smiled. "Where do you intend to go?"

"We'll fly to Korupoon," Stan replied, "and from there trek this way to the Solo and Seng valleys. You can help us teach the gospel to people in those valleys. And we want to measure sites for new airstrips."

Yemu's smile changed to a frown. "I want to help you teach the gospel, my father, but I do not think you should go as far as the Seng Valley. The people there have close ties with those who wounded you."

Now it was Stan who frowned. The southern Heluk Valley people had restricted his movements long enough. It was time for the gospel to break forth to the east in spite of them, as it had to the west. "He who keeps too close an eye on the weather," a missionary named John Stam once wrote, "will never harvest a crop!"

"If you are afraid to go with us, Yemu," Stan replied, "I'll find someone else!" Yemu squared his shoulders, and in a spirit typical of nearly all of Stan's converts, said, "If you are determined to go, I'll go with you!"

On Tuesday, September 17, 1968, Stan and Pat, with Rodney, Joy, Janet, and Yemu, were ready to fly to Korupoon, where Pat and her three children planned to visit with Phyliss Masters and her son Robbie while Stan and Phil were away on trek. Bad weather, however, forced cancellation of the flight. The following day MAF pilot Clell Rogers tried again. This time he found an opening in clouds above the Korupoon Valley, circled down between formidable mountain walls, and landed on the sixteen-hundred-foot airstrip that Phil and Bruno, five years earlier, had carved out of a slope between two Kimyal villages.

While Pat and Phyliss renewed their aquaintance, Phil introduced Stan to two brawny Dani carriers—Nigit and Degen—whom Phil had chosen from among his helpers at Korupoon. Phil's many friends among the Kimyal people were too diminutive to carry the forty-pound packs Stan and Phil had prepared. They were also too fearful of potential enemies in unknown valleys to venture so far afield.

All that first night, heavy rain pounded the Masters' home. Even after daybreak it continued, finally easing at noon. (Phil had often measured as many as eighteen inches of rain per month in Korupoon's steep-walled valley.)

After eating a cheerful lunch together, the two families joined hands and sang "What a Friend We Have in Jesus." Kissing their wives and children, Stan and Phil shouldered their packs and prepared their carrier for the trip. They suddenly realized that they needed another carrier to bear last-minute additions to their equipment. A fourth carrier, Dengan, volunteered to help.

Phyliss and Pat watched from a kitchen window as Phil, Stan, and their four helpers climbed a ridge and disappeared beyond the horizon. Ever since Stan was wounded two years earlier, Pat felt a certain uneasiness every time Stan set out on a journey in the mountains. Phyliss, however, felt little concern. Never, in any of his numerous journeys in the Korupoon area, had tribesmen seriously threatened Phil. In any case, she had learned to commit her family's safety to God with a quiet spirit of trust. Whatever happened, Phil would be in God's hands.

Phillip Jesse Masters, born April 9, 1932, in Sioux City, Iowa, was sixteen years Stan's junior. Phil's parents, like Stan's grandparents on his father's side, were devout Methodists. And like Stan, Phil spent most of his boyhood on a small farm. Beyond these similarities, their backgrounds could hardly have differed more widely.

Whereas Stan, very early in life, was exposed to atheism, drunken-ness, neglect, violence, and fear, Phil grew up in such sheltered familiarity with the Christian ethic that following it became almost as natural as breathing. Yet Phil, no less than Stan, needed conversion to enable him to experience the full dynamic of Christ's teachings.

For Stan the life-changing event took place in a tent on Mount Gibraltar. Phil found Christ in the center of a high-school gymnasium. Often during his arduous journeys in the wilds of Irian Jaya, Phil reflected back upon the series of events that had launched him toward a career most men would consider highly unenviable.

It all began one day when Phil attended a service in the Billy Sunday Tabernacle in Sioux City. Pastor Glee Lockwood was showing a film about missionary work in some faraway corner of the earth. Young farmer Phil was shocked as the film portrayed scenes of his counterparts in certain foreign countries using ox-drawn wooden plows or mere digging sticks to prepare land for crops so scanty that, in spite of all their labors, their children still remained half-starved.

With my knowledge of farming, Phil thought, *I can help those people!* After the meeting Phil approached Pastor Lockwood, announcing, "I want to be an agricultural missionary."

Pastor Lockwood smiled. "Phil, before you become an agricultural missionary, let's first make sure you are a Christian!" Phil was startled. He had never thought of himself as anything other than a Christian. But as Pastor Lockwood opened his Bible and counseled further, Phil began to see that merely growing up in a Christian home was not enough. He had to make his *own* personal commitment to Christ as Savior and Lord. Right then, standing in the center of the gym floor, Phil bowed his head and asked Christ to come into his heart. He left the gym a member of a new team, engaged in a very different kind of contest.

With good weather holding, Stan and Phil forded the turbulent Erok River and climbed more than a thousand feet to a Kimyal village called Durum. Unlike Stan, Phil did not enjoy trekking. Scaling horrendous cliff faces among the Snow Mountains was gruelling enough even for the fittest men, but for Phil it was especially trying. A congenital defect caused his left leg to grow slightly less than his right leg, making it difficult at times to keep his balance in treacherous places. Nevertheless Phil managed an amazingly fast pace. His body was lean and wiry, and most important of all, his will was set to endure *anything* in order that the Snow Mountains tribes might share eternity in the Kingdom of God.

On the second day, they forded the Mavu River and struggled to the top of another high range. At its crest the track, worn to a deep trench by the crossing of thousands of tribesmen over centuries, tunneled under entwined roots of an evergreen forest overhead. For several miles Phil, Stan, and their carriers walked in a crouching position, until their backbones, already laden with forty-pound packs, felt ready to snap in two.

When at last they broke out of the tunnel, they rested on a point overlooking the chaotic Solo Valley. *It would be worth the effort just for the scenery alone,* Phil often reflected, *but how much more worthwhile to see the beauty of Christ blossom in the lives of men and women who never knew Him!*

Stretching their backs straight again, they resumed their journey, passing through numerous Kimyal villages on the descent to the Solo River. The people were friendly, as much as they could be at the shocking sight of white-skinned, straight-haired strangers. Kimyal in the Solo had not seen a white man since Phil and Bruno made their last trek in to build the Korupoon airstrip five years earlier.

Checking language variations in Kimyal villages, they forded thundering Solo River and began to climb again. The next valley they entered—the Seng—would be Yali country.

Whereas Stan was unable to fulfill his dreams for higher education, Phil studied three years at Westmar College in LeMars, Iowa. While there he met Phyliss Wills, a pretty, darkhaired high-school student. Phil transferred to Cornell College in Mount Vernon, where he earned a bachelor's degree in philosophy, while Phyliss went on to the University of South Dakota. Phil could have gone further in secular education. Instead he accepted a student pastorate at Monmouth, Iowa, and he and Phyliss were married. He pastored there for two years while Phyliss taught school.

Phil and Phyliss later resigned their respective positions and traveled to the wintry Canadian prairies. There they enrolled as students at a foremost missionary training center, Prairie Bible Institute. Since its inception in 1922, more than two thousand Prairie graduates have found their way to mission fields in almost every corner of the earth.

Phil and Phyliss found themselves especially moved by the plea of an elderly statesman of Christian missions, Ebenezer Vine. Representing the North American extension of the Regions Beyond Missionary Union, Vine came to the strategic Canadian campus in 1955, proclaiming RBMU's new advance into the central mountain ranges of Irian Jaya. As he pleaded for volunteers willing to endure almost unimaginable hardship and privation, Phil and Phyliss found grace and courage from God to offer themselves.

Reaching the pass into the Seng, Stan paused, remembering the day years earlier when he left Bruno in their camp far below and climbed to this lofty vantage point to catch his first glimpse of the Solo Valley. But there was little time for similar reflection now—they wanted to contact the Yali of the Seng Valley before dark, and it was a long way down to the first human habitation.

Phil differed in appearance from his rugged Australian colleague. In contrast to Stan's craggy features, Phil's face was smooth-skinned and seamless. His brown eyes were large and nearly always twinkling with spontaneous humor—so different from Stan's cool, appraising, eagle's glance. Phil was tall, almost six feet of wiry leanness beside Stan's five-foot-seven prizefighter form. Men who lived as Stan and Phil lived carry no extra flesh on their frames.

Differences in appearance, however, faded beside even greater distinctives in personality. Stan wore his principles like epaulets upon both shoulders. In Phil the same principles maneuvered behind a disarming diplomacy. Stan polarized all men around him into either critics or ardent admirers. Phil simply made friends.

Phil's calm approach to difficulties is perhaps best illustrated by his encounter with a boisterous Kimyal chief named Momas. Phil nicknamed him "Superman" because physically he towered high above the average height of the pygmy-like Kimyal people.

Once Phil and Bruno succeeded in opening the Korupoon airstrip, "Superman" decided that the airstrip was long enough and deliberately planted gardens upslope from the airstrip in order to prevent Phil from extending it further. Phil waited two years for Momas to change his mind and then lengthened the airstrip with Momas's cooperation. Other difficulties continued, however.

Phil once wrote to Bruno, " 'Superman' still makes a scene from time to time. He shot a few arrows at one of his wives near our home recently. My first impulse was to go out and have a showdown with him. But the Lord cautioned me to let Him handle the situation in His own time. It surely is easy to act on impulse in these situations and then suffer for it ever after, I'm sure."

Stan and Phil's sudden appearance at the Seng Valley's first Yali village startled its inhabitants. Shouting wildly, warriors wrapped in voluminous coils of split rattan scrambled for their weapons while women and children popped into their *homias*. Then, fully armed, the warriors formed a line and drew their bows. Hoping that the hostile manner of the warriors would change once they became accustomed to the presence of strangers, Stan and Phil continued on their way, seeking an empty *yogwa* for their four carriers and a place to pitch their own tent. But each time they approached a dwelling, a loud outcry and a threat of drawn bows forced them back. Warriors followed behind them and erased their footprints from the trail—an ominous sign.

At one point it seemed that the hostiles were at the point of releasing a volley of arrows at the travelers. Members of the famous Archbold expedition, encountering similar problems in the Balim Valley thirty years earlier, solved their problem by shooting two Dani warriors. Stan had a milder method of averting disaster, at least temporarily. He opened his pack and took out three small Chinese firecrackers. Moments later a hundred startled warriors withdrew in frantic haste as the firecrackers popped over their heads—one! two! three!

Finding an old man living alone in an isolated *yogwa*, Phil and Stan sent Yemu to negotiate the price in salt for a place for him and his three Dani friends to sleep. Reaching an agreement with the awestruck old man, Yemu waved to his fellow travelers. Stan and Phil set up the little two-man tent and spent the night.

Next morning Stan and Phil walked down to a slope that looked as if it was long enough for an airstrip. But as they measured it, angry warriors descended from several nearby villages and commanded them to stop. The site was too short in any case. Stan and Phil put their tape away and prepared to break camp.

It was from this point that they planned to return to Korupoon by the same route they had come. Yali warriors, however, were massing in large numbers along the trail leading up toward the pass into the Solo Valley. Could they get through safely? Would the warriors flee from the firecrackers a second time, since no actual physical harm resulted from those Stan exploded the previous day?

Stan looked west toward the high mountain wall hiding the southern Heluk Valley. It would be certain death to travel that way. There was, however, a third alternative: northward along a trail following the Seng River into a long, constricted gorge gashing through the foot of twelve-thousand-foot Lowa Peak. No white man had ever traveled that way before, but Stan knew that if they could fight their way through the gorge into the northern bowl of the Seng Valley, they would find another pass leading into the Heluk above Yabi and Balinga. There Stan knew he and Phil could count on a friendly welcome. Often, from his living-room window at Ninia, Stan had gazed up at that lofty pass and wondered what lay beyond it.

Together the two men came to a decision and told their carriers, "We'll trek north following the Seng River to its source near the main spine of the Snow Mountains! From there we'll turn west into the Heluk Valley."

And they set out. Perhaps they would even find a suitable airstrip site in the upper bowl of the Seng, beyond the gorge. Even better, perhaps they would find inhabitants of the northern Seng more amenable to the presence of strangers.

"So they're heading north," said Tio, chief among warriors massing on ridges above the mission party. "If only we had known they would go that way, we would have gone ahead to prepare an ambush. Now we will have to follow them into the gorge and watch for our chance."

The trail through the gorge was a backbreaker. Steep ascents and descents came in disheartening succession.

"We seem to be going up and down more than ahead!" Phil observed at one point, gasping for breath.

At times the travelers found themselves looking down unnerving cliff faces to the Seng River thousands of feet below. And always, at each bend of the trail, they looked back to see Yali warriors still following, shouting war cries, hounding them.

"Never mind," Stan said at one point. "They don't seem to be carrying food with them. They can't attack easily on these narrow ledges, and if we can only stay ahead of them for a few more hours, they'll get hungry. There are no villages in this steep gorge to give them food, so they'll have to return home. By tomorrow—if people north of this gorge are friendly—we'll be well on our way to home and safety before these fellows can catch up to us again."

Every cheerful viewpoint helps! thought Phil. But like the carriers, he could feel danger thickening as they pushed further into the unexplored upper reaches of the Seng. Only Stan seemed totally at ease. Finally an attack came.

At a place called Fumaha, the gorge widened into a small side valley. Seeing their chance, the pursuers swarmed on the uphill side and came down with arrows drawn.

"They're going to kill us!" Yemu warned.

Phil laid a hand on Yemu's shoulder and said, "Don't be afraid. God is with us!"

"You're just like Jesus in the Garden of Gethsemane, comforting His followers." Yemu smiled back at him, encouraged by Phil's composure. Stan opened his pack and produced three more firecrackers and a box of dry matches. As warriors came on shouting, Stan lit firecrackers one by one and lofted them into the air above the war party. By the time the third firecracker exploded, Tio's attack was dissolving into panicky flight.

Just how many more times will it work? Phil wondered as the party used the time thus purchased to hurry on across another cliff face where further attack would be impossible.

Demoralized and hungry, Tio's warriors fulfilled Stan's prediction and returned to their villages in the south. An hour later the mission party emerged from the gorge and looked down into an open, bowl-shaped arena called Wikboon. At least ten Yali hamlets beetled along crests of ridges above the bowl.

Yemu chewed his lip, asking himself, *Will they let us through?*

"I can't believe it!" said Nalimo, a heavy-boned Wikboon dweller. He was staring hard at the two fully clothed strangers and their black carriers as they filed down a ridge facing Nalimo's garden. Nalimo had a curious Yali way of expressing astonishment—he made a loud popping noise in the back of his throat. But the expression on his face never changed. Nor did his jaw and throat muscles move when he made the sound.

His friends on the far side of the ridge heard his exclamation and the popping noises. They came running to see what Nalimo was staring at

"*Duongs!*" they whispered. "Who else could they be but *duongs*?"

"Aren't we supposed to kill any *duongs* who come this way?" asked a younger man.

"Precisely," Nalimo replied, and ran downhill to meet the strangers in a village called Sohopma. Nalimo had a leaf of Yali tobacco rolled behind his ear. As he approached Stan and Phil, Nalimo took the folded tobacco leaf from behind his ear, lit it with a brand from a *yogwa* fireplace, and inhaled the smoke. Then, sidling close to Stan, Nalimo greeted him in Yali and blew a puff of tobacco smoke sideways.

Suddenly all the Yali gathering around grew tense and remembered the warning they got from the southern Heluk many months earlier: If *duongs* come to your valley, it will be to place a curse upon your homes and gardens and pigs and eventually to destroy the sacred objects in your *kembu-vams*. There is only one thing to do with them—shoot to kill!

To the three Dani carriers, the blowing of a puff of smoke out of the side of one's mouth meant nothing. But Yemu, a Yali himself, understood its significance.

"A sign has been given," Yemu said in the Dani language. "We are to be killed. We must try to leave this place."

As they shouldered their packs, Nalimo protested, "Please sleep here by our village! We want to trade with you before you continue your journey tomorrow!"

Disregarding Nalimo's invitation, the party moved on toward the north, angling down toward the Seng River.

"When are we going to kill them?" someone asked.

"Send word to all our Wikboon villages!" Nalimo replied. "We'll mass during the night and kill them first thing in the morning."

An old man named Mongul pointed his sharp walking stick at Nalimo, croaking, "Do you understand these strange beings, young man? No! You don't know what you are doing! Who knows what unknown troubles you may bring upon us all if you kill them. This is too mysterious for us. Let them go on their way unharmed!"

But the younger advocates of *Kembu* smiled sarcastically and turned away from Mongul.

Yali women began to whimper and cry, fearing the thing the young men were going to do. "Here we see only two of them! Perhaps they have many friends who will come to avenge them! Be careful!"

The same conflict of opinion raged in other villages of the Wikboon bowl, once Nalimo's call to arms spread by runners to every village.

At Kibi, directly across the Seng River from Nalimo's village, a venerable Yali elder named Kusaho pleaded eloquently for the travelers' lives. "When our friends from the Heluk thought they had killed one of these men, he got to his feet and walked away! He is protected by powerful spirits! Let us not tempt these beings and their spirits to anger."

"You are all talking like old women!" the young men replied. "The Heluk people failed to kill him, but we will do a thorough job. Wait and see!"

Kusaho sighed.

Stan and Phil and their carriers hurried across a pole bridge to the west side of the Seng. They passed directly below Kibi, where Kusaho tilled his sweet potato gardens. Above the small, unprotected expedition, hundreds of warriors rallied for attack, blackening the high bluffs and ridges on both sides of the Wikboon bowl. Soon an emotion-charged challenge echoed from ridge to ridge and from hamlet to hamlet: "*Wataluluk!* Let's kill!" And the counter-challenge came back: "*Bingiwariuk!* Shoot to kill!" The thunder of the river made it impossible for the mission party to hear the battle cries of the warriors, as well as the words that followed: "After we kill them, let's eat them!"

Several hundred yards below Kusaho's gardens, the trekkers again crossed the river to the east side. There a friendly old man—too senile to care about the political-religious fervor of the younger men—agreed to sell a few tiny sweet potatoes to Stan and Phil for their carriers' evening meal. It was getting dark now, and all six men were dog-tired after the long trek northward through the gorge. They pitched camp beside the old man's *yogwa*.

While Stan cooked an evening meal, Phil lifted the trail radio from Stan's pack, strung its wire aerial between two trees, and as they had done most evenings during the expedition, called Phyliss across several mountain ranges at Korupoon.

"We are at a place called Wikboon in the northern end of the Seng Valley, dear. We decided to detour this way to Ninia, rather than retrace our steps to Korupoon. We—" Phil pondered. Should he mention the threats to their lives during the past two days? Mentioning it would not help their own situation at all and would only cause Phyliss and Pat and the children to feel unnecessary anxiety. For there was little doubt in Phil's or Stan's minds that they would survive this trial and cross safely into the Heluk Valley the next day, just as they had survived threats in the southern Seng throughout the past twenty-four hours. So he told Phyliss, "We're all right, honey, and we expect to reach Ninia late tomorrow."

While the evening meal was cooking, more warriors and shamans of *Kembu* descended from Wikboon villages to reconnoiter the site of their victims' camp in preparation for tomorrow morning's attack. Stan un-rolled a gospel chart he often used on journeys such as this one and hung it from a tree branch in front of the surly-faced warriors. The chart por-trayed a trail branching in two opposite directions. One trail was straight and narrow and led to eternal glory. The entrance was guarded by a tow-ering cross of Christ. The other trail, broad and winding, led downhill to the brink of damnation. A large number of people were strolling blithely along the wide trail and toppling over the brink. But only a very few peo-ple walked along the straight trail; all these were received into glory.

With help from Yemu, Stan proclaimed the chart's message to the sneering crowd. Like the roughnecks he had preached to years earlier in slums of Sydney, Yali warriors jostled one another in sarcastic mirth,

taunting the preacher. But there was one major difference—the roughnecks in Sydney were usually drunk. These Yali were cold sober.

Heavy rain swept through the gorge from the south, scattering the
Seng men to their villages and driving Phil and Stan into their small
tent. Yemu and the three Danis took shelter in a dry cave the friendly old
man pointed out to them. All night long the rain battered the tent, until water began to flood under the tent walls. Stan and Phil crawled out
of their sleeping bags into the rain to dig a trench around the tent.

All six men prayed for a safe journey the next day, but Yemu was
thinking of practical measures also. He could flee further up-valley, under cover of rain and darkness, and cross the pass before enemies could
track him down. Or he could find refuge in a local *osuwa* and claim immunity from hostility.

Yemu's loyalty to the two missionaries, however, complicated the
matter considerably. He knew they would be unwilling to break camp at
midnight, in pounding rain, and try to follow in pitch darkness a trail
none of them had ever followed before, one that could lead across flimsy
pole bridges and treacherous cliff faces—even if it would save their lives!
Yemu's Christian convictions would not allow him to desert his friends
and flee for his own safety. Even if Stan and Phil knew that it was possible to claim the protection of a Yali place of refuge, which they didn't,
surely they would be unwilling to seek escape through the gods whom
they were seeking to supplant!

At least, Yemu decided, *next time we cross a bridge tomorrow (if they let us
get as far as the next bridge), we can try to cut it down behind us and escape while
they repair it! It will take them nearly half a day to repair a severed bridge!*

There was only one problem—would the two missionaries, overflowing
with goodwill and confidence as they were, agree to the cutting of a bridge?

Somehow I must persuade them, Yemu decided, and fell asleep.

At the first light of dawn, warriors of Kibi armed themselves and massed
for attack. Kusaho tried one more time to restrain them. "We don't know
why these strangers came among us; leave them alone!" One Yali woman
of Kibi took off her outer reed skirt and laid it across the trail leading
down to the mission camp. It was a Yali woman's way of demonstrating

extreme disapproval for something her menfolk were about to do. But the warriors simply picked up her skirt, tossed it aside, and streamed down the trails to a rendezvous with Nalimo and several hundred other armed men.

Together they advanced up-valley and surrounded Stan and Phil as they were breaking camp. Nalimo prepared a signal: "When I greet the shorter *duong* and lay my hand on his chest, you shoot arrows suddenly into his back!"

Minutes later Nalimo found Stan packing by himself. *"Naray!"* he called, drawing Stan's attention while other warriors sidled around behind him. *"Naray!"* Stan replied cheerfully, glad for a friendly word from people who had been so surly the day before. Nalimo laid his hand on Stan's chest. Stan in turn laid his hand on Nalimo's shoulder and gazed innocently into the warrior's eyes. Nalimo saw the would-be killers behind Stan flex their bows—then turn away uncertainly. Nalimo likewise turned away. Later he scolded his friends. "What was the matter with you? Why didn't you shoot as we agreed?"

"We don't know," they replied lamely. "Somehow it didn't seem to be the right moment."

Stan and Phil shouldered their packs and struck out toward the extreme northern end of the Seng Valley. Two or three hundred armed warriors fell in behind them, shouting loudly among themselves. Fifteen minutes later they came to a bridge, and Yemu sighed with relief. In his hand he held an axe ready. "Now!" he said to Phil and Stan in Dani. "After we cross this bridge, I'm going to chop it down. If they shoot arrows at me while I'm chopping, toss a 'boom' to frighten them away!"

Stan and Phil discussed the proposal in English, and then Phil relayed their decision to Yemu. "No, Yemu, we'll leave the bridge as it is. We think the people in this valley are afraid to kill us because very few of them have ever seen people like us before. But if we destroy their bridge, this will anger them, perhaps causing them to kill the next person like ourselves who comes into their valley."

Yemu's stomach was tied in a hard knot of concern. *It's only a matter of time now,* he said to himself. He heaved a heavy sigh. They crossed the bridge, leaving it intact. And the Wikboon warriors thronged across single file after them.

"It's just as well," Nalimo was saying. "If we had killed them earlier, their spirits would have been released near our homes, becoming more dangerous to us dead than they are alive. We'll wait until they are deep in the forest. Then their spirits will not find their way back to our gardens and villages." There was more truth in Nalimo's words than he guessed—some men's influence does grow stronger through death.

At one point along the trail, Stan and Phil met Kusaho—a rather diminutive, timid man, not a forceful, imposing leader like Nalimo. Trembling in the presence of the two strange-skinned aliens, Kusaho meekly offered them some of his largest sweet potatoes for their journey. It was his way of telling them that he had not given his consent to the killing that would shortly take place. Unaware of the significance of the gift, Stan and Phil—in a hurry to reach Ninia before nightfall—quickly thanked him, gave him a few spoonfuls of salt, and pressed on, sensing nothing of the agony rending Kusaho's soul.

As the killing party passed by Kusaho, he shouted again one last warning: "I've given them sweet potatoes as a token of friendship; don't you spoil it with hatred and killing! Let them go!"

"If we don't kill them," Nalimo and others retorted, "they will come back some day and destroy our sacred objects, and doom will befall us. What will you say then, Kusaho?" Nevertheless, a few less determined young men turned back because of Kusaho's repeated warnings.

One and a half hours from their last campsite, Phil and Stan passed beyond the last signs of human habitation in the northern Seng. Looking up toward the west, Stan caught sight of a ten-thousand-foot pass three thousand feet above them.

"From the top of that pass, we'll almost be able to see the airstrip at Ninia," Stan said to the Danis, to encourage them. Everyone quickened his pace, although the terrain was now very rough.

The large force of Yalis fell back out of sight. Yemu thought, *Perhaps they've given up; perhaps they've all gone home!*

But in the next moment, a great war cry resounded somewhere in the forest behind them, and Yemu's heart sank. *This is it!* he thought.

They were passing a great outcropping of rock called Yendoal. Yalis, attempting to cross the main ridge of the Snow Mountains, usually slept in dry places under Yendoal's overhang before climbing up above the treeline, where there was no wood for fires.

"Hurry, my father!" Yemu pleaded. "I fear they will kill you now!"

"No, Yemu, I'll stay behind. You go on ahead and help Phil make good time," Stan replied calmly. *He knows,* Yemu thought. *He heard that shout too; and he knows that this time they really mean to kill!* But Yemu stayed with Stan. The three Danis had gone ahead with Phil.

Beyond Yendoal the river grew shallow, flowing over a wide, stony bed. They waded through it for another three hundred yards and reached a gravel beach. Beyond the beach the trail left the river and climbed directly upward to the pass. Just another two thousand feet of climbing and they would be over and on their way down to safety. But the war cry resounded again, much closer now.

Suddenly they came floundering through the river, bows held high. Others streamed down through the forest, their floppy rattan coils rattling. Stan and Yemu stood at the lower end of the gravel beach, facing them. Phil was alone at the other end, fifty yards distant. The three Danis waited another thirty yards beyond Phil. As they all looked back in horror, they saw Stan raise his staff, grimly facing the Wikboon horde.

"Yemu! Leave me!" he shouted over his shoulder. He kept his staff raised, not to strike but to form a barrier against the advancing tide of warriors.

"All of you, turn around and go home!" he commanded.

A priest of *Kembu* named Bereway slipped around behind Stan and—at point blank range—shot an arrow in under his upraised right arm. Another priest, Bunu, shot a bamboo-bladed shaft into Stan's back, just below his right shoulder.

Yemu was crying now and shouting at them to stop. As the arrows entered his flesh, Stan pulled them out, one by one, broke them and cast them away. Dozens of them were coming at him from all directions. He kept pulling them out, breaking them and dropping them at his feet until he could not keep ahead of them. Nalimo reached the scene after some thirty arrows had found their mark in Stan's body.

How can he stand there so long? Nalimo gasped. *Why doesn't he fall? Any one of us would have fallen long ago!* A different kind of shaft pierced Nalimo's own flesh—fear! *Perhaps he is immortal!* Nalimo's normally impassive face melted with sudden emotion. Because of that emotion, Nalimo said later, he did not shoot an arrow into Stan's body.

Stan faced his enemies, steady and unwavering except for the jolt of each new strike. Yemu ran to where Phil stood alone. Together they watched in anguish at Stan's agony. As some fifty or more warriors detached from the main force and came toward them, Phil pushed Yemu behind him and gestured speechlessly—run! Phil seemed hardly to notice the warriors encircling him. His eyes were fixed upon Stan.

Fifty arrows—sixty! Red ribbons of blood trailed from the many wounds, but still Stan stood his ground. Nalimo saw that he was not alone in his fear. The attack had begun with hilarity, but now the warriors shot their arrows with desperation bordering on panic because Stan refused to fall. *Perhaps Kusaho was right!* Perhaps they were committing a monstrous crime against the supernatural world instead of defending it, as they intended.

"Fall!" they screamed at Stan. "Die!" It was almost a plea—*please* die!

Yemu did not hear Phil say anything to the warriors as they aimed their arrows at him. Phil made no attempt to flee or struggle. He had faced danger many times but never certain death. But Stan had shown him how to face it, if he needed an example. That example could hardly have been followed with greater courage.

Once again, it was Bereway who shot the first arrow. And it took almost as many arrows to down Phil as it had Stan.

Yemu and the three Danis waited until they knew Phil was too badly wounded to survive. Then they chucked their packs and bolted, certain that the killers would come after them as soon as Phil was dead.

One thought burned in Yemu's mind—*if they kill us, too, there'll be no one left to tell their widows what happened or where they fell!*

Lungs straining in the rarefied air, the four came to a branch in the uphill track. None of them had ever traveled in this part of the Seng Valley before—which branch would lead over the pass to the Heluk Valley? Heavy forest obscured mountain walls looming above them, and the four men had lost all sense of direction in their mad flight.

The trail to the right looked better traveled; the desperate men could at least make faster progress, wherever it led! They darted up the path to the right. They could no longer hear the killers shouting, but this gave the four men no assurance at all. Anyone pursuing them up this steep hill would not have breath left to shout, but if they got close enough, they would still have strength enough to kill.

Gradually Dengan, the slightly built Dani who joined the expedition at the last minute, fell behind the others, losing sight of them. Throughout the entire journey, a sore on his foot troubled him. The air grew colder as the fleeing men climbed into alpine forest dense with moss. As they climbed higher, they were soon enveloped in cloud.

Yemu also began to fall behind Degen and Nigit, the two burly, faster-paced Danis. Hours later, confident that the Yali would not pursue them such a great distance, Degen and Nigit found a cave to one side of the trail and stopped to wait for Yemu and Dengan.

At the site of the killings, after both missionaries had fallen on the stony beach, the Yali dragged their battered bodies away from the stones and placed each of them in separate forest alcoves, overhung with boughs.

Someone handed Bunu the steel axe. Raising it above his head, Bunu said to the rattan-coiled men around him, "You see, the reports we heard were true! These men have a supernatural hold on life. I suspect, brothers, that if we go away and leave them lying like this, they will rise again and continue on their journey. And if that happens—" Bunu's eyes narrowed grimly "—all our people will believe the message they bear!"

Bunu's meaning was clear. The killers felt trapped. Having embarked upon this course, they now had to make it work! Otherwise the *wene melalek*, their *kembu-vams* and *dokwi-vams*, their *osuwa*, and even the sacred feasts of *kwalu* and *morowal*—all would pass away! Men would burn charms and fetishes sacred to the spirits and cut their hair short! And wash their bodies clean! Women and uninitiated children would share equally in the new sacred things with men, as was already happening at Ninia!

No! Bunu and others cried in unspoken rage. *These things must not be!*

Although the Yali were not headhunters, Bunu, moved by fear, beheaded both Stan and Phil. Still not satisfied, the killers stripped both bodies naked and systematically cut them to pieces. Then they scattered bits of bone into the forest to make resurrection more difficult.

From the beginning Nalimo and his friends planned a cannibalistic feast after they killed Phil and Stan. Now an increasing number of participants began to express objections to this idea. Cannibals eat the flesh of their victims in order to increase their own life force, but perhaps eating the flesh of beings as strange as these might have a very different effect!

Stan in particular had manifested uncanny powers when he was first wounded and again during the final minutes of his life at Yandoal.

"What shall we do then," someone asked. "Leave them here to rot? Or build a fire and cremate them?"

"No!" someone else replied. "If we leave them here—even though we reduce them to ashes first—they may resurrect during the night and slip away from us! Let us carry them down to Kusaho's *yogwa* by the mountain wall and wait one night. If by morning they have not resurrected, I think we can be sure their flesh is just plain human and can be eaten safely."

The young men smashed the trail radio to small pieces, slashed Stan's tent to shreds and rifled the packs Yemu and the Danis left. Then several of the killers picked up segments of the two bodies and began a macabre procession down the homeward trail—one man carrying a hand, another a foot, another a knee or shoulder. A few men remained behind to complete one last chore. Nearly two hundred bloodied arrows lay broken on Yendoal beach. Most of the arrows lay scattered close to the water's edge where the next flood could float them away, wasting their potential as a memorial to the day's great event. The last Yalis to leave the scene carefully gathered all these arrows together and added them to other broken arrows lying in the wooded alcoves where the two victims had been cut to pieces.

No one bothered to pursue Yemu and the three Danis.

By mid-afternoon the killing party reached Kusaho's spare *yogwa* at the foot of the mountain wall. Solemnly they placed their mutilated trophies on a shelf that extended all the way around the outside of the *yogwa*, just below roof level.

"There!" someone said tensely. "Let them lie till morning. Then we'll see." The warriors turned away and continued down-valley to spend the night in the nearest village. Runners, meanwhile, hurried to all the villages in the Wikboon bowl, proclaiming, "The *duongs* are dead! Come early in the morning to Kusaho's *yogwa* at the foot of the mountain wall for the final procession before we feast on their flesh. The feast will be at Sengambut village!"

Most people in the Wikboon rejoiced that the dreadful deed was accomplished. Others warned that dire consequences would shortly ensue and began watching the sky and mountains for a first sign that their predictions would be fulfilled. Kusaho, now a lonely man in Kibi village (only a few women sided with him in his futile defense of the *duongs*), hung his head in sorrow when he heard the news.

"You came in peace, you strange beings from another world," he mused aloud. "And my people killed you. Now I fear we shall suffer for what we have done. O that I could have welcomed you into my main *yogwa* and fed and sheltered you and asked what strange purpose brought you to our Yali homeland! All I could do was give you my largest sweet potatoes before you died and shelter your remains under a roof I made with my own hands!"

Stunned by the force of Kusaho's eloquence, most of the men who shared his main *yogwa* fell quiet. When others mocked Kusaho, they said, "Leave him alone! This is a special thing with him—something we do not understand."

At dusk Kusaho emerged from his *yogwa* and stalked through the village. As he passed each *homia*, he called to the women and children, "Do not go down tomorrow to Sengambut. Do not look upon the flesh of the *duongs,* lest you be tempted to say in your hearts, 'Our young men have won a great victory!' They have done an evil thing. I will try to stop them from eating the flesh."

Somewhere below the twelve-thousand-foot crest of the Snow Mountains' main ridge, Nigit and Degen huddled close together in a lonely, tireless cave. Naked, exhausted, hungry, and crushed by the killing of their two friends, they faced the grim possibility that they would freeze to death before morning. If only Dengan and Yemu would catch up to them, there would be four of them to cling together to try to keep warm. But as darkness fell, Dengan and Yemu still did not appear.

Next day at sunrise, hundreds of Yali men and boys thronged in suspense to Kusaho's up-valley *yogwa* and were greatly relieved to see the flesh of the two victims still lying upon the shelf under the eaves of the circular dwelling. Exulting over their triumph, they milled about in a great circle in a nearby grassy area, chanting with deep throaty voices and vowing to render the same penalty to any other *duongs* who would dare enter their valley. Then they bore the pieces of Stan's and Phil's bodies down-valley to Sengambut, where cooking pits had been prepared. But as men began lighting fires to heat stones for the cooking—

"Wait!" Kusaho strode into the midst of the assembly. Slightly built, wiry, with finely honed, sensitive features and big expressive eyes, he was not an imposing figure among his people. Nor was he renowned as a man of valor, in the Yali way of measuring valor. Often in times of conflict he seemed more interested in opening negotiations than in exploiting military advantage. This occasioned disgust and embarrassment among even his closest friends.

"From the beginning of the world," he exclaimed, "we Yali have eaten human flesh—but only the flesh of people who have killed and eaten some of our own kindred. Now let me ask you—have you ever heard of a *duong* eating the flesh of a Yali?"

A murmur of negative response rippled through the assembly.

"Then what is this you are about to do?!" he asked indignantly. "Something our ancestors never taught us to do! Who do you think you are?"

The point hit hard. Even the hungriest among the cannibals could find no way to counter Kusaho's argument. Savage heads bowed in submission.

"Now you young men, bring that firewood here and build a funeral pyre!" Kusaho commanded, his normally soft eyes blazing. "We are going to give these two strangers a decent cremation."

The assembly agreed.

Weak from sleeplessness, cold, and hunger, Nigit and Degen blinked at the sunrise, let go of each other, and stood up. Staggering out of the cave, they stared numbly at a view more expansive than any they had ever seen. Clouds had cleared from all the ranges, unveiling an unsurpassable

vista of hundreds of mountain peaks; beyond them a deep blue expanse
of lowlands faded into infinity.

There was still no sign of Yemu and Dengan. "Should we backtrack
and search?" they asked each other. No, they decided. Yemu and Dengan
will know how to survive. Meanwhile they themselves must find their
way somehow to Ninia to let Pat and Phyliss know that their husbands
were dead.

Degen and Nigit had no idea they were on the wrong trail. The pass
into the Heluk Valley lay far south of their position. Blindly they set out
again following the trail that was leading them upward to the Snow
Range's main rim.

"Let's climb to the top," Degen suggested. "Perhaps we will see Ninia
from there."

Clambering across bare limestone faces, they reached the highest tur-
rets of the rim and looked down. "That must be Ninia!" Nigit exclaimed,
pointing to a distant airstrip thousands of feet below. Beside it a cluster
of shiny-roofed houses gleamed like tiny points of light. It was, in fact, an
outpost manned by Ziegfreid Zollner and a team of German missionaries who labored among Yali clans living north of the main ridge.

Degen and Nigit took heart and scrambled down the north face of
the range.

That morning at Korupoon, little Rodney Dale wanted to climb up to
the waterfalls streaming over a mountain face above the station. So Pat
packed a lunch and set out with him. Phyliss, meanwhile, arranged a picnic by Phil's fish ponds for little Joy and Janet Dale and her own son
Robbie. Pat and Rodney arrived back from the waterfalls at 1:30.

"Have you heard anything on the radio?" Pat asked.

"No news yet," Phyliss replied. Both women's faces mirrored concern. Stan and Phil had promised to call as soon as they reached Ninia,
but no call came through. Perhaps the transmitter at Ninia was out of
order or the battery was dead.

Pat returned to the task that had occupied her since Stan and Phil
set out—typing out stencils of Stan's newly completed Gospel of Mark
in Yali.

Half an hour later—"Karubaga! This is Ziegfried Zollner calling from Angeruk. I have important news for you!"

As Phyliss turned aside from her housework to listen, RBMU's David Martin replied from Karubaga, "Go ahead, Ziegfried; we're listening."

Zeigfreid's voice was tense. "David! Two nearly exhausted Danis have just arrived here at our station. I cannot understand their Dani language, but from their gestures, they seem to be saying that Stan Dale and Phil Masters have been shot somewhere south of the main ridge. They are standing here now. I will hold the microphone close while they repeat their story for you."

"Pat!" Phyliss called, and Pat left her typewriter, joining Phyliss by the radio.

For the next several minutes, Degen's guttural, rapid Dani flowed over the airwaves, broken occasionally by brief questions, also in Dani, from David Martin. Phyliss had forgotten some of her Dani since leaving Karubaga years earlier, but one word she remembered clearly kept recurring with ominous frequency in Degen's narration—*wakerak*—hit. Phyliss and Pat each prayed quietly for strength to bear the full translation of that narrative when it came. They didn't have long to wait. "Phyliss and Pat," the voice said sympathetically, "I am sorry to have to relay to you a report from two of Phil and Stan's carriers, affirming that your husbands were attacked on the trail in the Seng Valley yesterday morning about 10:00 A.M. From the account of the two carriers, I gather there is little hope that either Phil or Stan could have survived. I'm sorry. With MAF's cooperation, we will begin a search of the area immediately."

Dear Lord, Pat prayed as tears welled, *I hope You took him home quickly. I hope he didn't suffer again like he did when they wounded him.* To Phyliss she said through tears, "Oh Phyliss, I hope you won't blame me for Phil's death!"

"Pat, I wouldn't think of such a thing!" Phyliss replied, putting her arm around Pat. "Phil had a mind of his own, and I know he felt it was God's will that he go. God is in control of all things, Pat. We must not give too much credit to mere human causes. Besides, perhaps Phil and Stan were only wounded. Perhaps they're still alive somewhere, waiting for help. I haven't given up hope yet."

Phyliss turned away, remembering her final moment with Phil. *When he kissed me good-bye, there was a special sweetness that lingered with me,* she recalled. Then she prayed, *Dear God, if that was the last moment Phil and I would share on earth, thank You for making it so memorable.*

Stan's fellow-Australian, Frank Clark, was RBMU's field leader that year. Together with Dutch colleague Jac Teeuwen, Frank flew by MAF Cessna directly to Angeruk, picked up Degen and Nigit, who by this time had eaten their fill of sweet potatoes after more than twenty-four hours without food. Taking off from Angeruk, pilot Paul Pontier circled up to the crest of the rim the two Danis had crossed early that morning.

"I can't get through the clouds!" Paul said after circling for several minutes. Pontier radioed Ninia and broke the news to Luliap, who was in charge of the mission radio.

"Oh, Stan, you were like my own father!" Luliap wept after the radio conversation ended. The news of Stan's and Phil's deaths spread rapidly among the Yali of the Heluk. Hearing the report, old Andeng, Hulu, and other priests of *Kembu* who had once been Stan's avowed enemies now wept over his death.

At 6:00 P.M. that same day, a further call came from Angeruk. "Yemu has arrived. He's weary, bedraggled, and weak from hunger, but otherwise unhurt! Unfortunately, Yemu has no idea what happened to the fourth carrier, Dengan."

Next morning the word reached a small geological survey camp, 159 miles east in Papua New Guinea's Star Mountains.

"Hamilton!" the helicopter dispatcher called through a pounding rainstorm, "a couple of missionaries have been ambushed across the border in Irian Jaya. Their friends are asking for helicopter assistance. Get airborne as soon as you can."

Airborne in this rain? Bob Hamilton muttered under his breath. *My chopper doesn't fly under water!* Checking his shoes for scorpions, he put them on and trudged out into typically vile New Guinea weather.

Hamilton headed for Kawagit, where he rendezvoused with an MAF pilot who would guide him to the ambush area. By the time he was ready to take off from Kawagit, the rain eased. "Mind you," Hamilton was fond of telling friends, "the sky is a bit hard to find at times in [these] mountains." Hamilton later wrote:

The average person thinks of a missionary as something in the colonial past, or a 1920-ish character like Walter Huston in "Rain," but the fact is that they're out there right now, teaching hymns to guys with sticks through their noses, the way Stan Dale [and Phil Masters] had been doing that summer of 1968. Now . . . [I was on my] way across the jagged mountains and tangled rain forests to look for [them]—or what was left of [them] . . .

Everybody has heard of . . . smiling, handsome [South Sea] islanders with flowers in their hair . . . [but these Snow Mountains tribesmen—believe me]—were different. They're hostile— and cannibals . . . They have no conception of God as we understand the Almighty. They worship fetishes. A fetish may be almost anything from a lump of desiccated pig fat to a small stone crudely chiseled . . .

When the tribes go to war—and it's their only sport—the winners have a victory feast, with the losers as the main course. [Imagine preaching] to people like this about loving your enemies and turning the other cheek. That is why I say these missionaries have got to be nuts, and I hate to fly out into cannibal country to get them out. At the same time, they must be the most courageous men, with the strongest faith, anywhere in the world, and that is why I will [help them] every time I'm asked!

Guided by the MAF pilot, Hamilton homed in on the Heluk Valley and settled his copter beside the airstrip at Ninia. "[When I saw it], I wished [the MAF pilot] luck getting down. I mean, how do you land a Cessna 185 in 350 yards of sloping rough ground? Uphill, of course, which was the way he finally did it. We all earn our money out here."

In distant Sentani, on Irian Jaya's north coast, a friend of the Masters family broke the news that their father was "missing, believed dead" to thirteen-year-old Crissie, eleven-year-old brother Curt, and nine-year-old Rebecca. The children found it difficult to imagine anyone—even Yali cannibals—using violence against their father. As Curt expressed it through his tears, "My daddy never hurt anyone in his whole life."

With a frightened Degen pointing the way, Hamilton clattered through a pass and dropped rapidly into the Seng Valley's horrendous vortex of jumbled ridges. It took Degen a few minutes to get his bearings—everything looked so different from the sky. Finally, "There," he exclaimed, "is where we spent our last night!"

Hamilton touched down near the spot and left Degen, Frank Clarke, and a heavily armed Indonesian lieutenant alone in the hostile valley. Then he returned ten minutes later with Jac Teeuwen and two more soldiers.

For several minutes the party stood back to back, scanning hillsides around them. Even as they watched, ridge after ridge blackened with hundreds of armed men. Then they advanced up-valley, searching for signs of Phil's and Stan's last remains.

High overhead, MAF pilot Paul Pontier circled slowly in a fixed-wing aircraft flying cover. Paul kept constant radio contact with the men in the copter by way of a small line-of-sight radio transmitter.

Hamilton shuttled the search party close above the treetops as they looked for some sign of the killings—a torn piece of clothing, a bloodstain on the rocks, broken arrows. They found all three—and more—on a beach that slid suddenly into view under the copter's belly.

Degen recoiled with horror as the scenes he had witnessed on that fateful beach flooded back in memory. In the helicopter, Bob was horrified at the scene he saw. Literally hundreds of broken arrows lay crisscrossed at every possible angle in two forest alcoves just off the beach. A broken radio, shredded packs and tent, crumpled cooking utensils, a couple of shirts "polka-dotted with arrow holes," and torn pieces of note paper—poetry written in Stan's hand—were scattered about as if a tornado had ripped through in full fury. Then Hamilton saw dark brown stains of dried blood everywhere on the beach.

Soon the searchers returned to the copter bearing small fragments of human vertebrae, a jawbone, and some teeth with fillings. Any lingering hope of finding Stan or Phil alive was now totally crushed. Nor was there any sign of Dengan, the missing carrier.

In less than an hour, Hamilton returned the entire search party safely to Ninia. "Then I flew out of those ugly Snow Mountains, to the base camp. The cloud cover was denser than usual, and I kept climbing to get above it.

I began to get drowsy, and for a while I thought I might not make it. But the clouds opened up, and I got back safely. If they hadn't opened up, I would have blundered into some trees and been killed. But my death would not have meant one tenth of what the death of [Stan Dale and Phil Masters] meant. This is the whole reason why I wanted to tell this whole story . . . to have somebody know it, back there in the world."

Note

1. All quotes in this chapter by Bob Hamilton are from the article "Cannibal!" by Tom McMorrow and Jim Anderson, *Argosy*, February 1971, pp. 34-39.

Part IV

TRIUMPH BEYOND
THE RIM

GUNFIRE IN THE SENG

AS NEWS of the death of Phil and Stan spread to every corner of the Christian world by letter, telegram, newspaper, and radio, messages of condolence began to reach Pat and Phyliss in increasing volume. Tens of thousands of people in many lands began to pray for "the Yali tribe," people who would not otherwise have known of the tribe's existence.

The Seng Valley suddenly became one of the most prayed-for valleys on earth. "Now at last," many predicted, "with so much prayer concentrated upon the Yali people, surely they cannot long remain resistant to the gospel of Christ. Something will have to give."

At the same time, from the Heluk and Balim valleys, from Yali clans north of the Snow Mountains at Angeruk, and from more distant areas in lowland swamps south of the mountains came rumors that Wikboon warriors, exulting over their success in killing Phil and Stan, were now daring neighboring peoples to follow their example and kill all *duongs* within their reach—including those who called themselves the *government*.

"The two *duongs* we killed carried guns," they claimed, possibly referring to Stan's firecrackers, "but by our sorcery we made ourselves invulnerable to their bullets. We frightened away the helicopter by shooting arrows at it! You can do the same."

More detailed reports filtering through to government headquarters at Wamena in the Balim Valley took on sinister overtones: "Wikboon shamans have dried and preserved small segments of Phil's and Stan's fingers. They are sending these out as tokens to Angeruk, the southern Heluk, and to the Balim. Every clan that accepts one of these tokens thereby promises to join in a general uprising against all outsiders. These tokens will guarantee immunity from gunfire."

Over the previous ten years, both Dutch and Indonesian civil governments and police patrols used force to quell outbreaks of violence among warring Yali and Dani clans. Cowed by the appearance of police and soldiers with their guns, most Dani and Yali clans had stopped warring. But the promise of supernaturally induced invulnerability to the power of guns could easily encourage open warfare again.

Indonesian civil, military, and police officers became increasingly concerned. "If we do not send a patrol into the Seng Valley to punish instigators of this proposed uprising," said the top civil officer at Wamena, "then the uprising may indeed occur. To forestall this tragedy, I have arranged for a patrol to go in and apprehend at least some of the killers of the two missionaries and to persuade the rest not to stir up the population in surrounding valleys."

To add urgency to the matter, Ziegfreid Zollner, missionary in charge at Angeruk, called Wamena by radio early one morning, saying, "Instigators from the Seng Valley are said to be here among local villagers right now, organizing an attack against our mission and also against the new government outpost here."

Police flew into Angeruk and searched local Yali villages. But they found no one identifiable as a man from the Seng.

Was it a false report, or had Angeruk people conspired to hide the Seng tribesmen from the police?

In any case, six soldiers, seven police, one district officer, and forty carriers assembled at Ninia on October 25, 1968—exactly one month after Phil and Stan were killed—to pacify, by force if necessary, the Yali people of the Seng Valley.

Two others also joined that patrol—Frank Clarke, RBMU field leader, and me, as Frank's second-in-command.

The decision to accompany the patrol was not an easy one to make. I was at Kamur, RBMU's outpost in Sawi swamplands, one hundred miles south of the Heluk Valley, when Frank called me by radio and explained his predicament: "Don, the government has invited us to send missionary observers with this patrol. If we go along and the patrol kills Yali tribesmen, there is danger that we as missionaries will be identified with the killing. However, if a missionary is present at the critical moment of contact, I think he may be able to diplomatically restrain trigger-happy patrolmen from unnecessary violence. Also, if the opportunity comes, the missionary can assist as an arbiter in peace negotiations. For this reason I've decided to accompany the patrol. I hope my decision turns out to be the right one."

I agreed with his decision. History records many times when highly regrettable battles were fought because there was no arbiter sympathetic to both sides.

Frank went on to explain that he had worked only in the Dani language and had little experience in the Indonesian language. Someone had to be with the patrol who could communicate with the officials in their own tongue. He thought of me because I could speak the language. He commented that the mission could be very dangerous. However, since Frank had already committed himself to accompany the patrol, and since effective communication was necessary when life-or-death decisions had to be made, I agreed to go also. A few days later, I kissed my wife and sons good-bye and flew to Ninia.

Ziegfreid Zollner called Ninia with an ominous warning that large numbers of warriors were crossing the Snow Mountains to join the Wikboon people.

At noon, October 27, we reached the summit of the same pass Stan and Phil had tried to reach from the opposite direction. As we started down into the Seng Valley in blinding fog and drizzling rain at the ten thousand foot level, I thought, *Poor Dengan. Could he possibly have survived until now without clothing or shelter in this bitterly cold, damp climate?*

The chances of ever finding Dengan alive—or dead—were now very small, but still we watched for any sign he might have left.

Meantime Frank and I noticed that our present expedition might leave another Dengan lost in its wake. The seven Irianese policemen and the more experienced soldiers hurried on ahead—whether from a desire to reach warmer depths of the valley or to engage the Wikboon warriors in a fight, I could not tell, though I suspect both reasons were involved.

The remaining soldiers, chilled to the marrow, fell far to the rear. Frank and I and most of the carriers were somewhere in the middle, with little firepower to ward off an ambush. By now our carriers, naked except for their gourds, were so chilled we feared we might soon find ourselves nursing a rash of pneumonia cases, in addition to watching out for the expected ambush.

We lit a fire and huddled around it, soaking in warmth until the stragglers caught up to us. Then we descended further and soon stumbled—to our sudden horror—upon that scene of devastation surrounding the two arrow-filled alcoves by Yendoal beach. Heavy rain had long ago washed away all blood stains, but broken arrows, bits of bone, and scattered debris were enough to overwhelm us—as the killers intended they should.

I knelt first among the arrows where Phil had lain, and picked up one of his well-worn trekking boots. The Yali had not known how to untie the laces—they simply hacked his boots from his feet. I thought back to the day when Phil pleaded on our conference floor for mission approval to stake out a new claim for Christ in these wild valleys beyond Ninia. I remembered the day I saw him kiss Phyliss good-bye and leave with his hand-picked Dani team. To four hundred weeping Danis on the Karubaga airstrip, he gave a cheery wave that said, *Dry your tears, beloved— you have the gospel. They don't.*

It had been a very costly decision. Phil would say it was worth it, even if the church of Christ were never planted here. For the splendor of Christ, just to make the attempt was a privilege worth more than life itself.

I walked fifty yards further to an almost identical bower where another hundred arrows pointed with soul-wrenching emphasis to the place where Stan had died.

My mind drifted back, reliving for a moment my first conversation with Stan. We were walking together across a hillside above Karubaga, the wind in our faces. "Stan," I said, "I hear that you have a wealth of great poetry stored in your memory. Please recite for me the one poem that has molded your life more than any other." Stan paused, turned, looked at me, and recited "If" with stunning intensity.

Then he paused again, and after a moment said, "But let me add something else, Don. I've got to the place where mere words—no matter how fine—leave me cold. All I want is the *reality* of knowing Christ."

Enjoy it, Stan, I whispered over the ground where he died. *Enjoy that reality to the full. Forever.*

Frank and I and the soldiers and carriers moved on. We were all warmer now but bone-weary after climbing three thousand feet up one side of a mountain and down the other. We had no tents with us and were relieved to find, just past Yendoal beach, the massive overhang of rock normally used as an overnight shelter by Yali hunters.

Early next morning we found the main body of the patrol encamped in Kusaho's *yogwa* at the foot of the mountain wall (not that any of us had any knowledge of Kusaho's existence at that time). As yet no one had made contact with Wikboon people. Did they know we were there?

We continued down-valley. Repeatedly we passed through places where warriors with advance knowledge could have ambushed us, but no attack came. Then I saw them!

"Look," I called to those nearest me. "Up there!"

An "ant swarm," fourteen hundred feet above us. Even at that distance, we could see them leaping up and down, working themselves into a frenzy. We knew they would attack; there was no doubt about it. They would attack believing their magic would protect them from our weapons. It was just a question of when, where, and how many.

And Frank and I were praying, *Lord, somehow enable us to save the lives of many who would otherwise be killed*

We were strung out now in full view, a total of fifty-six men. We hoped it looked like more than it was. A career soldier named Fritz pushed on ahead with a machine gun. Suddenly we heard him shooting incredibly loud bursts that rumbled in echoes from mountain to mountain. Had he encountered another Yali force on the valley floor? I pushed through a bank of trees and saw Fritz pointing his weapon at a small hill across the river. Arrows were lodged in the ground around him.

"Three war-painted men" he said to me in Indonesian. "They tried to shoot me from the top of that hill." Apparently Fritz's gunfire scattered them back into the forest.

We crossed a bridge at that point—the same bridge Yemu wanted to cut in an attempt to save Phil's and Stan's lives. It took us more than half an hour because we could cross only one at a time, and some who were unsteady took longer than a minute to negotiate a safe passage.

Beyond the bridge stood a village—Sengambut—where the Yali initially planned to cannibalize the flesh of Stan and Phil. Frank bent over and picked something white out of the ashes of an old, large fire. It looked like a piece of human skull. We looked at each other grimly and followed the patrol farther down-valley.

The trail the commander chose climbed across a steep grassy hillside. At one point Degen and Nigit pointed to a place far below us, across the Seng River. "There is where we spent the last night before it happened," they said.

Without warning a number of arrows fell from above and quivered in the grass beside the trail. We flattened against the hillside. We looked up, but the attackers were well out of sight, using the advantage of height to loft their arrows down at us without exposing themselves to return fire.

Then came boulders the size of beach balls, rumbling down into our midst. We kept advancing, sidestepping arrows and boulders on the narrow trail. One of our carriers, an older Yali man from Ninia, cried out. Frank looked around and saw the man pull an arrow out of the small of his back. Right there on the trail, with the possibility of other arrows striking him, Frank took a syringe and injected penicillin into the wounded man. In New Guinea arrow wounds characteristically cause infection, which can be deadlier than the wounds themselves. Frank made sure the penicillin got a head start, and the wounded man without further assistance proved able to keep pace with the patrol.

Our trail led across the curve of a mountain, bringing us into full view of almost every village of the Wikboon area's bowl-shaped valley. And in front of every village, men were milling about or dancing, apparently in defiance. *Lord, give them the sense to stay spread out in small groups,* I prayed. *If they all join together in one mass attack, these machine guns will cut them down like grass.* Unknown to us, in every village men and women who had opposed the killing of Phil and Stan now rebuked the killers. "See what you have brought upon us! First all those sky-beings coming and going in our valley, and now this ground force coming among our villages, spewing fire and thunder!"

"Never mind!" the warriors retorted. "The thunder the Ninia *duong* threw at us didn't hurt anyone. Neither will this! Its only purpose is to make us afraid, but we are invulnerable!"

Nevertheless they were terrified—the thunder they heard from Sengambut was so much louder than the little pop they had heard from Stan.

The patrol, no longer in danger from falling rocks, now faced a steep ridge jutting out of the mountain face. Three incredibly brave Yali warriors appeared intermittently at the top of that bluff, shooting arrows down and then ducking back out of sight. We guessed that these men were testing the theory of their immunity to "thundersticks." If they died while holding that ridge, others would know to stay back out of range. If they weren't hurt, others could attack with confidence. The soldiers and policemen knew the importance of demonstrating the power of modern weapons at this point. Taking careful aim, twelve of them opened fire each time one of the three warriors looked over the bluff and released an arrow. Two of them advanced straight up the ridge, guns ready.

At the last minute, the three warriors, unnerved if not grazed by bullets, retreated to safety. Frank echoed my sigh of relief. The patrol continued on to the top of the ridge.

We were now in full view of Kibi—Kusaho's village. Kusaho, still unknown to us, had ordered the village evacuated. "You who brought this trouble upon us may flee to safety! I will face the *duongs* alone and try to save our village. Go!"

As men, women, and children streamed up a mountain face, leading or carrying babies and pigs, Kusaho, trembling down to the soles of his feet, turned and faced the patrol across a deep canyon three hundred yards wide.

"I'll stand with you!" said a voice at Kusaho's shoulder. It was Hunumu, a friend.

Holding his bow and arrows aloft, Kusaho ran back and forth on the edge of the canyon, shouting, "O people who go about in the sky! People who fill our valley with thunder! Do not destroy us! I offered a pig to your *wururu* [helicopter] when it came looking for your two friends! I will offer more pigs to you now! Please do not destroy my people!"

Likewise, Hunumu shouted, "Do not destroy us! May your bullets swerve away!"

While their words expressed desire for peace, the two elders' manner of holding their bows aloft and pacing back and forth indicated willingness to fight if necessary. For even Kusaho, while hating the thought of war, said, "The soldiers will not know who I am, and they may not hear what I shout to them nor even care to listen, so I may have to fight to protect my place."

He was right. None of the patrol could hear what Kusaho or Hunumu shouted. The lieutenant in charge—having nearly been hit by an arrow in the previous exchange—saw only that two more natives seemed to be waving their weapons in defiance. "Open fire!" he shouted, and fourteen firearms swung around and aimed at Kusaho and Hunumu, who thought, *We're six times beyond arrow range; surely we must also be beyond the range of "booms"!*

They weren't. In the next instant, it seemed to Kusaho and his friend that not only the sky but also the peaks of the Snow Mountains must be toppling upon them. Since fourteen firearms—including machine guns— were now shooting directly at them, the reports seemed to them many times louder than when the same guns were shooting in other directions. And since each of several hundred bursts of gunfire created a dozen or more equally thunderous echoes from lofty peaks surrounding the Wikboon bowl, the total impression—even to Frank and me standing *behind* the guns—was that an apocalypse was breaking loose upon the earth.

Bullets shot jets of soil into the air around Kusaho's feet and twanged against rocks. The air around him sizzled like burning fat. "What on earth is happening?" he bleated. "How are they doing this?"

Across the canyon I watched and prayed. *Whoever you are, run!* I cried within my heart, and then almost shouted the words aloud, as the two men still pranced back and forth, shouting what sounded like defiance. Clearly the soldiers and police—after firing so many shots—were embarrassed because they had not scored a single hit. Surely the tribesmen will conclude that they do indeed possess invulnerability and will attack in full force. The patrol thought, *If only we could drop at least one of those men, this would be a convincing demonstration, avoiding greater loss of life later.*

Still the hail of fire continued, and still the two men somehow survived at its very center. To be sure, it looked as if the two men were protected by some supernatural force. Frank and I, still praying, were sure that force was not mere magic.

Finally Kusaho and his friend realized the futility of their efforts and bolted, still unharmed, through the village of Kibi and over the ridge beyond.

With their ammunition now gravely depleted, the patrol proceeded around the head of the canyon and occupied the village of Kibi. Only one person remained in the village, Lumu, a senile old man.

"Did you people devour Phil and Stan?" we asked through interpreters.

"Of course we did; we *all* ate them," he lied. Seven years would pass before that lie was corrected.

Frank and I thanked God that the first day of encounter with the killers ended without loss of life.

"Tell the people up on those ridges," the government officer said to his Yali interpreter from Angeruk, "that we want them to come down from the ridges and talk with us. If they agree, then when we leave this village, we will leave the houses standing. If they refuse to talk with us, we will burn all of these houses when we leave."

It was a strong inducement. Hesitantly about fifty Yali men came down a ridge. Other Yali carriers from Ninia and Angeruk went up unarmed to escort them to the military camp. Negotiations began peacefully but ended in horror.

For the government officer, having disarmed those who came, asked Degen and Nigit to identify any of the fifty who took part in the killing of Phil and Stan. On that basis he selected eleven of the fifty negotiators and instructed them to enter a large *kembu-vam* under guard. Then he announced, "I am taking these men to Wamena as prisoners, to assure that you make no further attempts to incite surrounding tribes to violence, or shed the blood of visitors to your valley. If, after a number of months, we hear that you have remained peaceful, we will escort these men back to this valley and release them."

Frank and I were shocked. The plan was impractical for two reasons. First, the Yali had no tradition of taking prisoners and releasing them.

In Yali tradition, prisoners were taken for only one purpose—to be eaten! Thus the eleven prisoners, believing they were doomed to die, would surely break for freedom at the first opportunity, provoking the soldiers to shoot them.

Second, only if they were tied securely could the prisoners possibly be taken as far as Wamena, and the government officer had enough rope to tie only three or four men, not eleven.

Frank and I knew it was only a matter of minutes until the prisoners weighed their chances and worked up the nerve to break out of the *kembu-vam* and flee. I went to work, trying to achieve a miracle of diplomacy in Indonesian with the government officer. At my first suggestion, that we couldn't possibly take eleven prisoners to Wamena, his face clouded. He couldn't back down now without losing face.

"We'll get them there," he asserted.

If only the prisoners had given me another five minutes to reason with the officer, perhaps I could have persuaded him that losing a bit of face was the lesser of two evils. But they didn't give me another five minutes. A handsome young Yali named Kumi bolted from the door of the *kembu-vam*. Kumi was not a fast runner. Three policemen chased him to the edge of the canyon, shouting at him to stop. Kumi kept going, and one of the policemen dropped him with a bullet through the heart. Frank and I felt sick. The soldiers were tense, their guns ready. Two more prisoners were brought out of the *kembu-vam*. I caught their eye and gestured to them not to resist as the soldiers tied them up. I made a sweeping motion with my arm toward Wamena, hit myself under the armpit several times, then drew my hand back, curling it downward, stamping one foot on the ground at the same time. To my Sawi friends, in swamps far to the south, that series of gestures would mean, "You will go to Wamena for a long time and then return again right here." But would these mountain tribesmen understand? And if they understood, would they believe me? Their lives depended on it.

They seemed to understand, for they offered no resistance as their arms were tied. But they kept looking back to me for reassurance. Their names were Holonap and Sel.

There was no way that Frank or I could reassure the eight men still inside the *kembu-vam*. They began calling—then screaming—to their friends

watching from hillsides and ridges around us. The incredible nightmare
was getting worse by the second. The police tried to extract another prisoner from the *kembu-vam* in order to tie him up. He too broke free from
their grip and ran. A bullet in the head dropped him in a sweet potato
garden just ten yards from where I stood beside the two bound prisoners.
Frank was white as a sheet, and I guess I was too. We had both seen people of other tribes in their thousands peacefully accept the reality of an
encroaching civilization. We wanted every isolated minority culture to
have peaceful first encounters. It was anguish to us to see the Wikboon
people's first encounter unfolding like this one. For a moment I wished I
were a thousand miles away from the blood reddening those sweet potato
leaves and from the screams of terrified prisoners who were probably going to be killed one by one in the same way. But then I steadied myself, remembering that tribal people were massacred by Spaniards in Latin
America, by settlers in the Old West, and in Australia, Africa, the Philip-
pines, and a dozen other countries. I had often thought, *If only someone
had been there to try to change the outcome. Well, you're living through a similar
case history right now,* I rebuked myself. *Don't beg out! See what you can do!*

I headed for the commanding officer, but before I reached him, two
more prisoners bolted from the *kembu-vam* and were shot down. Five to
go! *Dear God,* I prayed, *somehow spare the lives that remain!*

The five still inside the *kembu-vam* were starting to dismantle it from
the inside, tearing at boards with their bare hands and screaming for
their fellow tribesmen to help them.

Unseen by any of us, Fritz, who had a machine gun so heavy it had
to be fired from a tripod, could stand the defiance of the Yali no longer.
He quickly mounted the gun on its tripod, aimed at the *kembu-vam* and,
without warning, crisscrossed it several times with heavy bullets.

Police and soldiers standing near the structure leaped aside to avoid
flying splinters of wood as bullets smashed through the *kembu-vam*. When
Fritz released the trigger, we all stood in shock, listening as a thousand
crashing, rumbling echoes of gunfire rebounded from the valley walls.

Then everything was deathly still. The screaming of the prisoners
had stopped; there was not even a groan from the *kembu-vam*. Fritz, still
hunched behind his gun, glared at the structure.

The government officer barked, "Let's get out of here!" Everyone began packing. I faced the lieutenant and said, "This is not what we hoped for." He sighed and walked away. Five minutes later, the patrol began pulling out of Kibi lest the Yali retaliate with a mass attack. In their haste, none of the soldiers or police went inside the *kembu-vam* to see if any of the prisoners was still alive. Their silence was sufficient proof that they were all dead.

One policeman remained behind as the patrol set out. I watched him. In violation of the government officer's earlier promise that no building in Kibi would be burned if the people negotiated, the policeman set fire to the ill-fated *kembu-vam*. Then he stood with his gun ready. An instant later, a teenage boy who must have been the youngest of the eleven prisoners, darted out of the low doorway, thinking the patrol had left the village. The policeman raised his gun and aimed.

"*Jangan!* Don't shoot!" I shouted in Indonesian. The patrolman hesitated and looked over his shoulder. Seeing that the command had come from a civilian, he raised his gun again in defiance. But the lieutenant was watching also and added his voice to my intercession. The policeman lowered his gun, and the teenager escaped.

Fritz's burst of gunfire in no way looked or sounded like an answer to prayer, but that is exactly what it was! For Fritz apparently did not know, or at least forgot, that Yali dwellings always have an upper story. He aimed all his bullets at the *kembu-vam's* walls, not at its roof. Four of the five prisoners had climbed up into the upper story in order to break out through the roof. Their companion on the ground floor was killed instantly, but the four upstairs, including the teenager, survived the blast unscathed. God alone must have given them the presence of mind to keep quiet after the shooting stopped. The teenager left the *kembu-vam* prematurely and nearly lost his life. The other men waited until the patrol left and then emerged to their loved ones waiting anxiously.

Kusaho was not one of the negotiators. He was still recovering from the shock of the previous day's experience with gunfire. But after the patrol left Kibi, Kusaho came down into the village and found Kumi, his youngest brother, lying among the five dead men. Kumi had indeed joined in the killing of the two missionaries, against Kusaho's desperate warning.

"Kumi! Kumi!" the sad-faced elder wept. "If only you had listened to me, these men would not have destroyed you."

"It is true, older brother," said another man approaching behind Kusaho. "But people from other valleys kept telling us to kill them if they came this way. We thought it must be the right thing to do. We didn't realize—"

Everyone was too shocked to gather firewood for cremation that day. So Kusaho covered the faces of the dead with leaves as a token of respect and left them overnight.

"Perhaps the soldiers will return to kill more of us!" he warned his people. "We must build extra homes high in the cold forest where they will not easily find us. We will come down to our gardens for food.

"From now on we will salt our food with tears and eat it in fear. If I could see any way to make peace, I would try to make peace. But I can see no way."

As Frank and I topped the pass leading back into the Heluk, we paused and looked back down into the Wikboon bowl far below.

"Can you think of any way, Frank," I asked pensively, "that these impossibly ruptured relations could ever be healed?"

Frank shook his head. "No, Don, I can see no way. Apart from some unexpected act of God, the door to this valley will remain closed for two or three generations."

THE UNEXPECTED

Chapter 19

TWO months later, on the last day of 1968, Kusaho and his brothers came down from their mountain hideout to break sod for a new garden. It was cold and cloudy, and there was no joy in the Seng Valley. Kibi, like all other villages in the Wikboon bowl, stood deserted, for all people were hiding in the mountains.

"The soldiers tried to take eleven prisoners, but got only one—Sel." (The second prisoner, Holonap, escaped from the patrol on the return journey to Ninia.) "So they may come back again to take more prisoners," the people said, and stayed hidden except for occasional trips to gather food from their gardens.

Poor Sel, they mourned, *what a way to end up—eaten up by the sky people!*

Kusaho and his brothers stood among the charred ashes of their *kembuvam* and of the five grim funeral pyres of the men killed by the patrol.

Poor Kumi, Kusaho wept inwardly, remembering the death of his youngest brother.

Watching carefully for any sign of danger, Kusaho and his brothers passed through Kibi village and began descending a six-hundred-foot slope toward their new garden site beside the Seng River.

"Mike Pappa Hotel calling Sentani." Menno Voth was an experienced bush pilot from western Canada, but he had served with MAF in Irian Jaya only four months, and he was still learning how to find his way back and forth across unfamiliar terrain in the interior. Normally a pilot with more experience in Irian Jaya would have taken the flight Menno was making that day, but all other MAF pilots were shuttling mourners to the funeral of a missionary who had died far to the west.

"Mike Pappa Hotel calling Sentani," he repeated, and distant Sentani airport acknowledged his call. "I've just departed from Yasakor," Menno continued. "Destination Mulia. Estimated time of arrival—11:30." Menno glanced over his shoulder at his passengers—Oregonians Gene and Lois Newman and their four children: Paul, nine; Steven, five; petite, active Joyce, three; and wide-eyed baby Jonathan, one.

"Seven souls on board," Menno added. "I'll call again before landing Mulia. Mike Pappa Hotel." He ended his transmission, looked at his compass and leaned over his controls, studying a vast expanse of almost featureless sago swamps sliding beneath. Rivers were the only landmarks visible, but they all looked the same, especially when partly obscured by low cloud. Menno knew that he would have to rely more on his compass than on visual ground contact. Unfortunately, his compass couldn't warn him that a hard westerly monsoon was steadily pushing him east, off his course.

Tall, quiet, and thoughtful, MAF accountant Gene Newman sat to Menno's right. Gene had served with MAF in Irian Jaya since 1961. His wife, Lois, was a cheerful hostess who, over the years, had served thousands of meals to passengers coming or going through MAF's main base at Sentani. The family had just completed the first half of a well-earned vacation, visiting isolated mission outposts among Sawi and Asmat headhunters south of the Snow Mountains. Now for a week's rest in Mulia's beautiful mountain-locked valley—if Menno could find it in this sea of shifting cloud.

Fifty minutes later Menno circled at ten thousand feet, looking for a window through a wall of cloud. Shrouded in that cloud loomed the Snow Mountains, with some peaks towering as high as fifteen thousand feet. Even the lowest passes—with one exception—required an elevation of ten thousand feet. That exception was the forty-mile-long Balim gorge. Senior pilots in MAF sometimes advised younger colleagues, "If you can't make it over the top, circle down and fly along the foot of the range. Some days you will find the gorge itself open at lower altitudes, and you can follow it—like flying through a tunnel under the clouds—all the way to Wamena."

It's worth a try, Menno thought, and pushed the controls forward, putting the plane in a long spiraling descent. He reported his plan to the MAF base at Wamena.

Kusaho and his brothers reached their garden and began breaking sod with their digging sticks. Cold rain drizzled upon them out of black overcast.

Which gorge is the Balim? Menno wondered as he skirted along the foot of the peaks at three thousand feet. There seemed to be a major river pouring out of the mountains every ten miles along his course. Then he spotted something.

That must be it! he thought, consulting his map. The river beneath him now was very large and turbulent, like the Balim. The configuration of its main gorge and tributary canyons seemed to match the contours on Menno's chart. *I'll fly in under the clouds and check it out,* Menno decided. *There's plenty of room for a turnaround if it proves to be a dead end.*

Minutes later, Menno radioed the nearest MAF base a second time. "I'm following the Balim gorge at three thousand feet and climbing steadily. I should be over Wamena in fifteen minutes."

Menno was mistaken. He had entered the Seng Valley. Its walls were narrowing around him far faster than he realized. Its chaotic floor, moreover, was rising to meet him sooner than the Balim gorge would have done. And only ten miles ahead, blanketed in cloud, loomed a twelve-thousand-foot escarpment of the Snow Mountains, with no passes lower than ten thousand feet—even if Menno's heavily loaded plane could have climbed that high in such a short distance.

And if the clouds could have opened to let him find a way.

Moments later Menno became uneasy. The river—half a minute earlier—churned along two thousand feet below him. Now it was so close he could almost hear its thunder above the roar of his engine. And the canyon walls suddenly narrowed to a degree that left Menno unsure he could turn safely. He should have tried. There would not be a second chance. Menno flew on hugging close to one mountain wall, looking for a wider place to turn. Beside him Gene Newman held his daughter Joyce a little tighter, sensing danger. Behind him, Lois, who disliked flying even in good weather, was already tense with fear. Five-year-old Steven, sitting beside his mother, was as unconcerned as nine-year-old Paul, sitting furthest back beside a pile of strapped-down suitcases.

Rain was sheeting against the windshield now, making it harder to judge distance—just when Menno needed clarity of vision as he had never needed it before. He pulled the throttle back to full rpm and lowered his flaps, trying to climb faster than the swift-rising floor of the canyon. His wings tilted first left, then right, avoiding buttress-like ridges jutting out from either side. But as he climbed to avoid the river, the cloud ceiling dropped to meet him, threatening to cut visibility to zero.

At that moment he broke through into the Wikboon bowl—

Kusaho and his brothers were accustomed to the sound of aircraft passing high overhead, so they were not startled when they heard an aircraft approaching—until it struck them suddenly that this time the sound originated from somewhere in the gorge *below* them!

"It must know we're here," one of the brothers gasped. "It's stalking us! In another moment it will pop up from beyond that ridge and shoot fire at us!"

The sod breakers dropped their digging sticks, snatched up weapons, and bolted uphill toward Kibi and the safety of the mountains beyond. They had not run more than a few strides when the aircraft exploded out of the narrows of the gorge, straining for altitude, its wings yawing steeply as it hugged the far wall of the gorge.

To Kusaho and his friends, the aircraft seemed to be turning straight toward them, as if it knew exactly where they were.

When he emerged from the gorge, Menno had two choices: he could try to pancake his plane on the soft, nearly flat surface of Kusaho's sweet potato garden, or he could try to turn. With only a split second left, he opted to turn.

This is my only chance, Menno gasped, *if there's any chance at all. I've got to save the Newmans somehow! Lord, I've been here in Your work only four months—*

is this the end? Where are we? Help me make it back to Priscilla and Robie—"

Menno banked his aircraft steeply into a left turn. There was nothing more he could do. Menno flicked on his transmitter and began calling. In the next instant his right wing struck a tall tree leaning out from the mountain wall.

Kusaho looked over his shoulder as he fled, then stopped abruptly. "My brothers! It's going to die!" he exclaimed. The Yali language has no word for "crash."

Even as Kusaho uttered the words, a high-pitched, eerie shriek of ripping aluminum froze the fleeing Yali in their tracks. Kusaho thought it was people screaming.

With the right wing gone, Mike Pappa Hotel whiplashed downward in a spew of high-octane gasoline. The left wing was ripped off by another tree and the tail section, just behind the cabin, was snapped off by a seventy-degree slope of flinty shale. The fuselage screeched down over the shale and slammed against a hedge of young trees, preventing it from plunging into the Seng River. The wail of shredding aluminum died under the explosive whoosh of a gasoline fire. Cracking flames jetted through the control panel and burst in through the two ruptured doors, incinerating . . . melting . . .

Nine-year-old Paul Newman, sitting far in the back of the cabin, saw the pilot and his own family engulfed. He unbuckled his seat belt as flames hissed toward him, blocking his escape through the doors. He looked behind him and saw a gaping hole where the tail section had been. Frantically he squeezed out through a tangle of broken cables. Sliding, rolling, crawling, and finally running, he escaped barely ahead of the spreading inferno.

The thunder of the river covered the crackling of the fire. The terrified boy cried for help as he struggled through dense thicket and broke out on a bank of the Seng. Directly in front of him, a flimsy looking bridge arched across the roaring torrent. *There must be people near here!* he thought as he scrambled across the bridge to clearer ground.

There he stopped and looked back at the smoke still billowing from beyond the thicket. Paul was weak with shock, but he did not let himself give way to a full measure of grief. That would come later. First he had to find someone—anyone—and tell them what happened, even if it was too late to help his family and Mr. Voth. In desperation he scanned the bleak, stony mountain walls towering above him into the overcast. Paul's vision was not clear, for he had lost his glasses in the wreckage, but a number of dark shapes on a ridge just below cloud level looked to him like Dani houses such as he expected to see at Mulia. *Perhaps that is Mulia!* Paul thought, and struck out toward the ridge.

Actually, the dark shapes were only large boulders, but Kibi village lay beyond the crest, just out of sight. Paul had no inkling that he was climbing a hill only eight hundred yards downstream from the place where Stan and Phil spent their last night. Or that hundreds of eyes watched him now from lofty mountain ridges—eyes of people who, three months earlier, hounded Stan and Phil to death. And who, two months earlier, lost five of their own number to the guns of patrolmen. In the normal course of Yali tradition, those people would relish a chance to exact vengeance for their five dead brothers, especially upon one lone unarmed figure.

Kusaho looked back and saw Paul. The elder paused. *Amazing!* he said to himself. *Whoever he is, how could he escape the destruction of that sky vehicle, let alone the fire? No doubt after the events of these past three moons, he'll expect us to try to kill him; he'll be ready to shoot us on sight!*

Vacillating between fear and curiosity, Kusaho finally hid behind one of the rocks on the crest of the ridge and studied the lone figure far below.

"Fool!" his brothers shouted in hoarse whispers. "Do you want to end up like Kumi? Come!" Kusaho waved them on and remained behind the rock, trembling with uncertainty. Moments later—"Why—it's merely a boy, a child, alone and weaponless!" he stammered.

Paul climbed steadily higher, clambering hand over foot up the steep mountain. Kusaho worked his way through descending mist, closer to the point where Paul would reach the crest. Minutes later the mist closed around Paul, too. He pressed on through it and then found to his horror that the "houses" he was seeking were only rocks. *I've climbed all this way— wasted my strength—for nothing! There's no one here!* he sobbed to himself.

Paul threw himself down into a clump of wet ferns and huddled on the ground, his head between his hands, and wept. The rain increased to a downpour, and now that he had stopped climbing, it quickly chilled him to the bone. Shivering convulsively, he looked up and saw—yes, it was a man, but the strangest looking man he had ever seen—a sprightly, agile figure leaping gingerly toward him, with hundreds of rattly rattan loops encoiling his body the way copper wires encoil a magneto!

He must not be a Dani, Paul reflected. *Danis don't wear clothing like that!*

The man also wore a pig tusk, the sharpened ends jutting fiercely from his nostrils. An equally fierce-looking necklace of dog fangs hung around his neck. His eyes, however, were anything but fierce—as they stared incredulously, as did Paul's. Then Paul saw the bow and arrows in the man's hands, and he started with fear. The killing of Mr. Dale and Mr. Masters was still fresh in his mind. Instinctively, Paul held his hand out in front of him and cringed.

"No, mister!" he pleaded. "Don't shoot me!"

Kusaho understood not a word, but the gesture was plain. He laid down his weapons and held out his hands, palms up. Paul relaxed. Kusaho looked over his shoulder, afraid that his brothers might see the boy and return to kill him for Kumi's sake. But the mist hid everyone else from view.

How very, very strange, Kusaho mused, *after my friends killed the two* duongs, *I wished I had welcomed them into my own* yogwa *and tried to protect them from the savagery of my own people. Now, so unexpectedly, I have opportunity to do what I wanted to do before—protect a* duong. *A little boy* duong *this time. It's as if someone understood my wish and arranged to fulfill it in this strange, strange manner.*

"Don't cry, little boy," he said to Paul, taking him by the hand. "Don't cry. I'm going to take care of you."

As Paul trembled with cold, Kusaho slipped an arm around his shoulder and looked straight into the small face, wet with teardrops and rain.

"Wherever have you come from?" Kusaho asked in the only language he knew besides the language of love. "I have no idea what your world is like, or where it is. If I knew where it was, I would try to take you there."

By sheer coincidence, Paul at that moment gripped Kusaho's arm and shouted, "Mulia! Mulia is where I want to go! My mother and father and my brothers and my sister and the pilot are all dead. Please take me to Mulia."

"Mulia," Kusaho repeated, catching the word by its repetition. "Where on earth could Mulia be?" Tenderly he raised Paul to his feet and led him through the mist into nearby Kibi village. "Never mind. First I've got to get you warm," he said.

Several valleys distant, MAF missionary Ruth Pontier continued calling Mike Pappa Hotel. Nearly half an hour earlier she thought she heard Menno's voice saying, "We're in a tight spot," but someone else's transmission was superimposed over the words, and it was hard to be sure. She looked at her watch. Menno should have passed over Wamena by now, but Wamena had not heard him. Ruth called MAF regional director Hank Worthington and reported her concern. Minutes later MAF search and rescue operations swung into action.

Kusaho led Paul into the new *yogwa* he built after the police patrol burned his other home. "Oh dear," he exclaimed, casting about the dark interior. "No firewood. Oh, well, no matter! I'll burn my ceiling joists. I can replace them later." While Paul watched inquisitively, Kusaho wrenched one ceiling joist after another out of the *yogwa's* upper story and split them up with a stone axe. Then he parted the ashes in the central fireplace until he found some coals still glowing faintly from an earlier fire. Kusaho blew upon them until they glimmered red. Soon he had a cheery fire crackling, and Paul warmed himself beside it.

He'll get hungry soon, Kusaho thought. *What can I offer him? For all I know, he may not be able to survive on our kinds of food. Dear—oh—dear! I can't have him starving under my care!* Fussing like a nursemaid, Kusaho rushed out into the rain and fetched sweet potatoes, taro, sugar cane, and greens from his nearer gardens. First he buried the sweet potatoes and taro among hot coals to cook, and then peeled a length of sugar cane and handed it to Paul. Paul pushed it aside. Likewise he spurned the ash-encrusted sweet potatoes and taro when they were done.

Perhaps he doesn't know how to peel them, Kusaho thought, peeling a sweet potato and offering it to Paul. Again, the boy turned his face away.

"Aha!" Kusaho exclaimed, a light of hope dawning through his desperation. "I know! You are used to eating boiled food!" He hurried outside again and found a tin can that members of the patrol discarded two months earlier. Boiling sweet potatoes in the can, Kusaho offered them. Paul took one, looked it over, and tossed it outside through the low doorway. Kusaho sighed. "I guess you don't like food cooked in an old tin can after all. Oh well, so much for that!" and he tossed the tin can outside with the boiled potato.

Kusaho heard footfalls approaching. My brothers have come back looking for me! They'll see him now! He ducked outside and faced them.

"Who have you got in there?" one of them asked.

"Just a boy," Kusaho replied.

"A boy from where?"

"From Mulia."

The brothers looked puzzled. "Hurry, Kusaho! Let's get back to our hideout before dark. That policeman we saw may be stalking around in this mist with a 'boom.'"

"Your 'policeman' is my guest," Kusaho said with a bemused smile.

"What!" They looked inside the firelit *yogwa* and saw Paul. Startled, the brothers raised their bows in self-defense. Kusaho gripped two of them by the wrists and fixed them with a cool, determined gaze: "I said he is my guest. I want you to stay with us tonight. I'm going to sleep next to him to keep him warm. You four take turns stirring the fire during the night. Now help me break up some more ceiling joists for firewood."

The brothers stared at Kusaho in shock and consternation. "Us? Take care of a *duong*'s child?"

"Why certainly. It's the least we can do to make up for what we did to those two strangers."

"Have you forgotten what that patrol did to us?"

"How could I? But we deserved it. Our brother Kumi took part in the killings."

One of the brothers shook his head in exasperation. "Only two moons ago, the *duongs* killed our brother and burned your *yogwa*, and here we find you destroying your new *yogwa* to keep one of them warm!" The speaker paused and then added, "You are a strange man, Kusaho. Who among us can understand you?"

As they were speaking, Paul picked up the first sweet potato Kusaho had offered him, peeled it, and began eating.

Hank Worthington probed in vain with MAF's twin-engine Aero Commander. "All the ranges and the Balim gorge are covered with cloud," he radioed to the full force of MAF pilots at their bases throughout Irian Jaya. "I can't see a thing. There's no possibility of starting a search this afternoon. All of you fly to Wamena and fuel up ready for a thorough air search first thing in the morning."

Later that afternoon other Yali happened by and saw Paul Newman sitting in Kusaho's *yogwa*. They spread the news to all the villages that an unarmed, harmless *duong* child was Kusaho's guest at Kibi. "We'll go down and see him tomorrow," said all the warriors of the Wikboon bowl. No one even considered going near the wreckage of the aircraft. They were all too afraid.

Next morning Kusaho saw them coming by hundreds, armed to the teeth.

What shall I do? he asked himself. *Shall I board up the door of my* yogwa *and hide the boy from their gaze? No,* he concluded finally. *If they insist on killing him, they'll get him anyway. My best chance is to set him out in the open where they can all see how innocent and harmless he is. Yes, I'll just let him win their hearts the way he won mine. Fear and suspicion will vanish when they see him as he is—human, just like us!*

"Come, boy," Kusaho said gently, taking Paul by the hand. Refreshed after a night's rest in the warm *yogwa* and a breakfast of sweet potato, greens, and sugar cane, Paul followed Kusaho outdoors. He saw armed, rattan-coiled, tusk-nosed warriors approaching from all directions. He tried to shy back into the *yogwa,* but Kusaho reassured him, "Sit here on this rock, little boy." The benign-faced elder laid a hand across his weapons. "I've got my bow and arrows ready. Don't be afraid."

Paul seated himself upon the rock and waited, squinting in the bright morning sun. At first the men kept their distance. Then gradually, as suspicion yielded to curiosity, they moved closer and formed a circle around him—a solid wall of grim-faced warriors. Some of them stepped forward inquisitively and touched Paul's white skin, his close-cropped hair, his clothing. Finally one man sighed, "Kusaho, you warned us not to kill those two *duongs,* but we did kill them and suffered for it. Now you've got this boy, and you're wondering what we intend to do. Rest easy, Kusaho, we won't harm him. You—"

"Listen!" someone shouted. "*Wururu!* [Aircraft] Lots of them! They're looking for him!"

"If they see us all standing around the boy like this, they'll think we're getting ready to kill and eat him! They'll shoot fire at us from the sky! Quick! Scatter! Hide!"

As the warriors dispersed, three aircraft appeared over the western rim. One skirted far to the south, searching the foothills. Another skimmed along the central ridge of the Snow Mountains. A third circled over the Wikboon bowl. Paul ran to the highest point of Kibi village and raised his arms toward the aircraft, waving his shirt and calling. Kusaho followed him.

"Kusaho, don't be a fool!" one of his brothers called from a far hillside. "They won't know who you are! If they see you standing beside him—"

He's right! Kusaho thought. *They'll think I mean harm to the boy; they'll shoot me!* He laid a hand on Paul's shoulder.

"Little boy, I've got to leave you! It's not safe for me to stand near you. They won't understand. But don't worry. I won't be far away. If they don't find you, I'll come back!"

Paul looked uncomprehendingly at Kusaho as the Yali elder backed away, looking from the boy to the aircraft circling high overhead, and to the safety of the mountains where the last of his people were vanishing into the forest. One of the circling aircraft dropped down into the Seng and roared past Kibi, almost on a level with Paul's position, and Kusaho fled. If the pilot, Paul Pontier, had looked out of the right window of his aircraft, he might have seen Paul waving frantically from the top of a bluff near the village. Instead Pontier was staring down in horror at the charred wreckage of Mike Pappa Hotel.

"I've found the wreckage!" he radioed, and missionaries listening by a hundred transceivers throughout Irian Jaya breathed prayers of gratitude—and tensed in horror as they heard the pilot continue. "What is left of the aircraft is badly burned—and the wreckage is located right in the center of the upper Seng Valley, only a few hundred yards down-stream from Stan and Phil's last campsite."

How incredible, we thought as we heard the news at Kamur, far to the south. Of the dozens of valleys a lost pilot could enter by mistake along the southern face of the Snow Mountains, why did God allow Menno to enter that valley? I remembered the William Cowper poem Stan used to quote so often; in fact, I could almost hear his voice repeating it: *God moves in a mysterious way, His wonders to perform, He plants His footsteps in the sea and rides upon the storm.*

I shuddered as I imagined Yali cannibals dragging Gene or Lois or Menno or those four delightful children out of that smoking wreckage and—

Just the day before the crash, the Newman family shared a meal with us at Kamur. We prayed together for safety as they continued their journey. And now this—this horrible tragedy. Unbelievers would scoff and say, "Where was your loving God? Has not the Almighty committed a heinous blunder toward people who loved and served Him?"

Lord, I prayed, struggling against unbelief, *I don't believe You make blunders. Somehow, God, confirm the reality of Your Providence in this tragedy, and encourage us who remain to carry on Your work.*

He was in fact already doing just that—and far more wonderfully than any of us could have dreamed.

By now the air over the Seng Valley was filled with MAF aircraft. One by one they dropped down into the gorge, buzzed over the wreckage at near-treetop level, and then twisted and turned through several bends of the gorge, climbing out again. On each pass pilots and spotters strained in vain to glimpse some sign of life.

"Sentani: contact that helicopter pilot standing by in Papua New Guinea." It was Hank Worthington's voice. "Tell him to try to reach Ninia this afternoon. We're all returning to Wamena. Nothing more can be learned until the copter gets here."

Paul saw the aircraft departing. Despairing, he sank down on the rock and buried his face in his hands. *They came so close, and now they're gone away again,* he sobbed.

The sight of the boy's despair was too much for Kusaho, who still hovered atop a high ridge like a guardian angel. Holding his bow and arrows high above his head, he raced down the mountain trail shouting, "Don't cry, little boy! I'm coming back! I'll stay right beside you! Let them shoot me if they want to!"

Moments later his arms were around Paul again. "Don't be sad. They'll come back again. But even if they don't, I'll take care of you. You'll learn to enjoy our food, and if your clothes wear out, I'll get you a gourd and put a hundred loops of rattan around you. Then you'll be a splendid young man indeed!"

Together they walked back to Kusaho's *yogwa*, as clouds darkened the valley, until another day.

There was no missionary resident at Ninia when the helicopter arrived. Pat Dale and her three youngest children had already returned to Melbourne, where Wesley and Hilary were still in school. Bruno and Marlys deLeeuw replaced Pat at Ninia, but at the time of the crash, they were not at Ninia. It was Luliap who met Hank Worthington and Frank Clarke when they landed to await the helicopter's arrival.

"Luliap," Hank said, "we're going into the Seng by chopper. We'll need an interpreter in case we meet some of the local people near the wreckage. Will you help us?"

"Of course," the sturdy Yali church leader replied. Moments later the copter arrived, and they were on their way.

At the first sound of the copter, Paul dashed out of the *yogwa* with Kusaho close behind. They ran to the edge of the hill and looked down as the copter settled beside Kusaho's new garden, close to the bridge Paul had crossed. Gripping Kusaho's hand, Paul tried to pull him down the hill, but Kusaho hesitated, afraid to go near the strange machine.

"Come with me! I want you to meet my friends," the boy urged. "I want them to see who it was that took care of me!"

Kusaho thought Paul wanted him to get in the helicopter and go away with him to "Mulia." Saddened because the boy he loved was about to leave him, Kusaho sighed. *If only I dared go with him!*

Paul pulled more urgently, and Kusaho followed him for a few steps, his heart torn in two directions. But his brothers came running and forcibly restrained him.

"Shoo!" they said to Paul. "Run down to your friends! We won't let you take our brother away from us!" Paul gripped Kusaho's hand one last time and ran down the hill. But one of the brothers bravely escorted Paul down the steep hillside, lest he stumble in his haste.

While a policeman stood guard beside the helicopter, Hank, a medical doctor named Jerry Powell, and Frank Clarke crossed the bridge over the Seng and pushed their way through bushes to the wreckage. One glance at the scene convinced them that no one could have survived. In their haste to get out of the valley before its inhabitants mounted an attack, they quickly pushed the victims into sacks, carried them across the bridge, and loaded them into the copter for transportation to Sentani, where burial would be arranged.

"Let's get out of here!" someone shouted. One by one, the men strapped themselves into the helicopter. The pilot turned the throttle control. The engine whine rose in pitch as the pilot prepared to lift his craft out of the valley.

"Wait!" Luliap shouted above the engine's roar. "Someone wearing clothes is running down that hillside!"

Stunned, the searchers wondered, *Who on earth could it be?* Hank stepped forward from under the swirling blades to take a clearer look at the small clothed figure racing toward them.

"Dear God! It *can't* be!" Hank shouted. "But it *is!* It's Paul Newman!" Hank bounded forward. Moments later a breathless nine-year-old threw himself into Hank's arms. "I can't believe it's really you!" Hank exclaimed, overwhelmed with joy. "Don't you have any injuries at all, son? No broken bones?"

"None!" Paul exclaimed jubilantly. "A man who lives up on that hill took good care of me!" Frank translated Paul's words into a language Luliap could understand. Luliap approached Paul's lone Yali escort, who now stood fearfully at a distance.

"Friend," Luliap said in Yali. "Tell me—please tell me—who was the man who took care of this boy?"

"Kusaho," came a fearful reply.

"Kusaho," Luliap repeated, letting the name write itself indelibly upon his mind.

Hank and Dr. Powell escorted Paul to the helicopter, but hefty Australian Frank Clarke stood rooted to the ground, gazing up in awe at a group of tiny waving figures outlined against the sky on the hillside high above him. Nearly incandescent with wonder and gratitude, Frank waved back and turned to the helicopter pilot.

"Do you think you could stay here in Irian Jaya an extra three or four hours?"

"Friend," the man replied, "the company that owns this thing charges a hundred dollars an hour for its use. I'll stay as long as you can afford it."

"Good!" Frank exclaimed. "Hank, I've just thought of a way we can show our gratitude to Paul's benefactors."

An hour later Paul was on his way from Ninia to Sentani, where he and Menno's bereaved wife, Priscilla, attended the burial of their loved ones' remains, followed by a memorial service. Frank Clarke, meanwhile, flew to Wamena and obtained permission from the chief of police to return Sel—the Yali prisoner—to his home in the Seng Valley. Later that day in the helicopter, just before clouds closed the passes, Frank tapped Sel on the shoulder and pointed down into the chaotic Seng Valley: "There's your home, my friend!"

Moments later they landed in the center of Kibi village. Frank unsnapped Sel's seat belt, helped him out of the hovering craft, and led him out from under the whirling props. Kusaho and a few others stood at a distance, leaning against the strong wind created by the fearful machine.

When the Yali saw their friend Sel running to them, their eyes opened wide in surprise. They ran forward and embraced him. Frank waved to catch their attention and then deposited a pig, a number of steel axes, and some knives on the ground as gifts for Kusaho and for any who helped him to take care of Paul. Then he climbed back into the copter and immediately the pilot lifted up and out of the Wikboon bowl, racing against fast-closing weather.

In the valley below, Kusaho watched the helicopter vanish among clouds.

"They understand now," he beamed. "At last they know who I am. They know I love them, and they have responded to me with love."

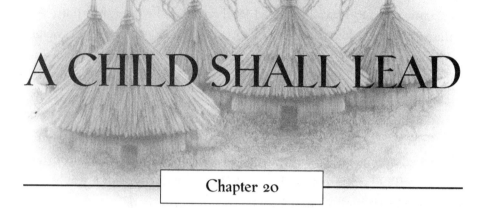

A CHILD SHALL LEAD

WHEN news of the killing of Phil and Stan reached Ninia, the priests of *Kembu* immediately renewed their threats against the small Christian community. As Costas Macris described it, "Kill! Kill! Kill!" was the slogan everywhere. Like wolves stalking their prey, savage men were closing in on the small Christian community. As a result Dongla, Luliap, and other Christians went armed to their gardens to gather food. At night some kept watch while others slept. Dongla voluntarily stood guard near the Dales' house to protect Pat and her children from attack.

Only a handful deserted the ranks of the believers under the intense intimidation. The others had become so committed to Christ as Lord that—after the example of Stan, Yekwara, Bengwok, Bruno, Costas, and Phil—even the threat of death could not deter them. This was true even of normally timid Yali women like Latowen, who affirmed staunchly, "In spite of all that has happened, I believe that the Word of God will prevail. It cannot become as nothing, no matter what its enemies may do!"

Latowen's words found startling confirmation when two leading priests of *Kembu*—in the very hour when the success of their cause seemed most assured—joined the ranks of the Christians. One was sad-faced old Sar, Nindik's father.

"Ongolek," he said to his wife one day, "if this message had come earlier, our little girl and Alisu, Lalo, Toli, and Bukni need not have died.

"Now these men are laying down their lives so that others need not die as they did. I cannot deny it any longer; this new way is better. Come, let us believe on Jesus Christ. I see now that He can change our whole world. As Stan Dale kept telling us through the years, Christ can make all things new."

Later Latowen gazed in wonder at Sar's face. The lines etched deep by years of sorrow were still there, but Sar was smiling now as he had not smiled since the day he ordered Nindik cast into the Heluk. And when Sar, Yali patriarch, trusted in Christ, so also did many of his relatives, including Deko and Selan, the two uncles who with their own hands hurled Nindik to her death in the Heluk.

The other priest who turned was none other than Hulu, the august warrior who on four occasions knocked Stan Dale to the ground. In spite of their frequent mutual disagreements, Hulu secretly admired Stan's spirit, and he sensed that Stan, beneath his surface bravado, respected him. Hulu became very pensive after Stan was killed. Luliap, noticing the change in Hulu's manner, said to him one day, "My friend, don't you realize that Jesus died for you?" Luliap quoted a key verse that Stan had translated from the Gospel of John: "For God so loved the world, that He gave His only begotten Son, that whoever believes on Him should not perish, but have everlasting life."

Hulu's eyes opened wide with awe as the full significance of the gospel bore in upon him for the first time. In that moment Hulu believed and found himself delighting in all that Stan and Bruno and Costas and his fellow Yali Christians had ever told him about the gospel.

In addition to the example and the preaching of men who loved Christ enough to die for Him, the lesson of the Seng patrol struck a death-blow to Yali confidence in the power of their sacred objects. For when the patrol returned safely from the Seng, the myth that sorcery could render warriors invulnerable to bullets was forever shattered.

The day after the Seng patrol returned to Ninia, I spent an hour with Zeigfreid Zollner, German missionary and author, at Angeruk, a mission outpost north of the Snow Mountains.

"Come with me, Don," he said. "I want you to see evidence of the transformation that has occurred here in just twenty-four hours, since news of events in the Seng came over the mountains."

Zeigfreid led me to a schoolhouse. We entered and found it packed to the windowsills with nearly five hundred mature Yali males. Each man wore heavy rattan coils, the characteristic dress of Angeruk and Seng Valley people. All waited quietly, expectantly, for Zeigfreid to teach them.

"It is clear to them now that a new era has dawned," Zeigfreid explained, "and that they need something stronger than their sacred objects to help them cope with that new era. We are giving them the gospel as that vital alternate. The death of Phil and Stan and the subsequent crises of the past few days have helped crystallize this new perception in their minds."

The same new perception was rapidly gaining ground in the Heluk Valley also, but it took time to become manifest. One of the first signs of change appeared when the men who killed Yekwara and Bengwok made restitution for their deed by sending a number of pigs as payment to relatives of the two young martyrs. Then, in March 1969, not only Bruno and Marlys deLeeuw but also—on a part-time basis—Costas and Alky Macris were assigned to continue Stan Dale's work among the Yali. Joining forces with the Yali believers, these two courageous couples gradually built new bridges of communication with thousands of Yali who knew that now they wanted to make peace with Christ and the gospel but needed help taking the right steps.

In September 1969 Bruno and Marlys deLeeuw's three-year-old daughter, Rohanni, became critically ill. The deLeeuws departed immediately for medical furlough in Canada, leaving Costas and Alky with full responsibility for RBMU's ministry to the Yali people. The responsibility was not misplaced.

Encouraged by so many signs of response among the Yali people, Costas turned his full energies loose. Within the next two years, he won Yali acceptance for the construction of seventeen strategically placed schools in all major villages. He manned those schools with seventeen Dani teachers, raised funds to pay their salaries, maintained their supply lines, and printed lesson materials in the Yali language. He built two new missionary dwellings. He encouraged the building of better quality footpaths linking Yali villages. He taught and prayed and counseled, while Alky treated the sick. Then, spontaneously, the harvest that Stan and Bruno envisioned when they first crossed the Mugwi Pass long years earlier began to ripen.

One day Costas looked across the Heluk Valley and saw a large Yali house burning in one of the villages of the eastern alliance. "How sad," he said to little Haris, his son, "someone's house is burning down."

Next day Costas learned the startling truth. The Yali people on that side of the valley had voluntarily burned their own *kembu-vam* to the ground. Along with it, they destroyed all objects associated with spirit worship. Costas could hardly contain his joy. Five years earlier men of that same village threatened to kill him when he tried to visit them.

Spontaneous destruction of *kembu-vams* in other villages followed faster than Costas could keep track of them. Soon thousands of Yalis in four valleys flocked to receive almost daily instruction in the gospel. Hundreds of men and women requested Christian baptism. But Costas deferred their baptism until Bruno and Marlys returned. Bruno had been there in the very beginning of the Yali work, and Costas believed the privilege of baptizing should be his.

When eventually Bruno returned, the hundreds of Yalis whom he and the Yali church elders baptized included Elavo and Siruruk, two of the men who killed Yekwara and Bengwok and then crushed their fingers. Elavo also shot two of the five arrows that wounded Stan Dale in 1966.

All of this in the Heluk and in the valleys to the west—but what of the Seng?

Thousands of Christians around the world were praying daily for the time when the killers of Stan Dale and Phil Masters would surrender to the love of Jesus Christ. We knew it was only a matter of time—but which time? We wanted to go in at the right moment—not too early and not too late. For although Kusaho and his brothers had shown kindness to Paul Newman, how could we be sure of a welcome from other families and clans in the Seng?

While we awaited God's timing, Luliap happened one day to meet a man from the eastern side of the Heluk, Weyo. Weyo enjoyed a special close relationship as a "trading partner" with certain men living in the Wikboon area.

"Guess where I have been, Luliap!" Weyo exclaimed. "The Seng Valley! I told the people there not to be afraid; I assured them that the government planned no further action against them. I told them also that all the villages in the Heluk Valley have welcomed teachers of the gospel. And I said, 'If you, too, want teachers, let me know, and I'll pass on the word to Luliap.'"

"What did they say?" Luliap asked eagerly.

"Kusaho said he wants you to come."

"And the others?"

"I know of no one in Kibi village who would attack you, even though they still don't understand what the gospel is all about. I can't be sure about the other villages you will have to pass on your way," Weyo said thoughtfully.

"I think the time has come," Luliap said. "Weyo, I've never been to the Seng Valley on foot. Will you show me the way?"

"Indeed I will! When do you want to make the journey?"

As soon as Luliap announced his intention to visit the Seng, his family reacted with horror. "You'll be killed for sure! We won't let you go!" And they began to monitor Luliap's movements, to make sure he did not slip away from them secretly and go to the Seng Valley. They might as well have tried to restrain a sunbeam. Early one morning, under cover of a heavy mist, not only Weyo and Luliap but also five of Stan's other young but well-trained spiritual "commandos" vanished from their *yogwas*. Everyone knew where they had gone.

"Why must our young men offer their flesh to the Wikboon cannibals?" someone grouched. But others sighed with resignation and said, "When we served the *kembu* spirits, we willingly slew even our own loved ones to fulfill their harsh demands. How much more must servants of a just and merciful God count their own lives expendable for His sake?"

When Costas learned of Luliap's intention, he said, "Luliap, I'll go with you!" But Luliap refused. "We will go unarmed and naked except for our gourds, and they will see that we are people just like them. If you go in wearing clothes, they will be wary, perhaps hostile. Let us make the first probe alone."

Crossing the Seng pass at ten thousand feet, seven potential martyrs descended quickly to rocky Yendoal beach where two piles of white cane shafts still served as tombstones for Stan and Phil. Pressing on, they passed boldly through the midst of Sengambut village, now partially rebuilt. Wikboon tribesmen burst out of their *yogwas* to stare at them uncertainly, heavy brows beading with concern. No one raised a hand against them. Walking straight and tall under a bright mountain sun, the seven climbed a steep slope beneath ponderous scrutiny from Walohovak and Bahabol villages.

Finally they walked unscathed into Kibi village, where Kusaho welcomed them. "Stay with me! Tomorrow I will kill a pig and stage a feast in your honor. You must tell me two things: first, where is that little boy who fell out of the sky right into my lap? And second, what is this message called 'the gospel'? Is it really a more authentic guide than the *wene melalek*? What is it about the gospel that made those two *duongs* determined to come here, even at the risk of their lives?"

Luliap smiled, scratched Kusaho under the chin, and began his reply.

Two days later, the feast completed, Luliap and his friends returned as they had come. Kusaho and his immediate family had learned enough about the gospel for one visit. Luliap would return again and again throughout the following year, gradually winning a wider audience for the gospel.

"Costas, my friend!" Luliap beamed. "I have just returned from the Seng. Not only Kusaho but leaders of all other villages in the Wikboon section of the valley told me yesterday that they want us to place resident Christian teachers in all their villages. And Kusaho invites you to construct an airstrip beside Kibi village! They said, 'Tell the *duongs* that if they forgive us for killing their two friends, we want them to come and visit us again, so that we can extend a very different reception!' "

"If we forgive them," Costas chuckled. "Bless their hearts!" But then his face darkened. "How sure are you, Luliap, that this is not a ruse to lure us into a trap?"

"I'm sure that they are sincere, Costas," the young evangelist replied. "But if you have any doubts—"

"No," Costas interjected. "I trust your judgment concerning your own people."

Not long after, Costas consulted with me—I happened to be field leader that year—for my opinion about an RBMU missionary's venturing again into the Seng. (After the loss of Phil and Stan, we decided as a mission that none of us would enter the valley again without colleague consultation.) The result of our consultation—made jointly with Frank Clarke—was unanimous: Costas, Frank, and I would trek again into the Seng Valley during September 1970 (exactly two years after the death of Phil and Stan). We would travel in company with two Indonesian government escorts, since the government had earlier forbidden non-Yali personnel to travel in the Seng without armed escort.

To prepare our way and to facilitate more frequent travel between the Seng and Heluk Valleys in the future, ten Yali villages in the Heluk volunteered ten men each to carve a new, more direct trail between Ninia and Kibi villages. The trail was completed in only ten days, under Costas's incomparable managerial skill. On the tenth day, Costas, Frank, and I looked down from a lofty Seng Valley ridge at the first village in our path—Bahabol. Luliap, the two government escorts, and the one hundred trail breakers were strung out beside us.

"Which way from here, Luliap?" I asked

"We descend to the bottom of this gorge and then climb up to Bahabol," he replied.

"Why do we not simply follow this ridge around and descend to Bahabol from above?" we asked naively, not relishing the more arduous down-and-up route.

Luliap grinned. "It is bad etiquette to approach a Yali village from above. That is what enemies try to do to give themselves military advantage. To show goodwill and peaceful intention, you must take the trouble to descend below the village and then climb up to it, placing yourself at a disadvantage."

We sighed simultaneously. We were all bone-weary after the long trek down from the pass. And so we began a knee-breaking, one-thousand-foot descent into a gorge. *May no one ever tell Emily Post about rules of etiquette like these!* I murmured to myself. An hour later—after our knee ligaments were jarred almost to jelly—we leaned into a near vertical six-hundred-foot climb toward Bahabol's aerie-like position. We looked up, expecting to see friendly Yali faces beaming a welcome down to us as we climbed. No one was in sight. Nor were any birds singing in tree-covered ridges overlooking our position. I began to feel uneasy. Luliap had assured us that the Wikboon Yalis wanted us to visit them. Why, then, didn't they show themselves? Had they changed their minds? Perhaps one of their seers had a vision last night telling the warriors that they must ambush and kill us.

Lord, I prayed, *should we continue or turn back?* For an answer, peace welled up within, and I began climbing at a faster rate. In case Luliap was deceived—in case there was an ambush waiting at the top of the slope—I intended to trigger it while the others were still far below, giving them time to escape. As a trained distance runner, I stood a better chance of breaking out than Costas or Frank.

I reached the top of the slope. Barricaded behind a stone wall, the *yogwas* and *homias* of Bahabol crowded together along a narrow ridge. I mounted the stone wall and scanned in all directions. Still—not a soul in sight! And no smoke sifted out through *pandanus*-leaf roofs. *The village is deserted,* I thought. I was wrong. Moments later a wiry, wide-eyed Yali elder popped from behind a *yogwa* and ran toward me, whispering in hushed tones: "Wah! Wah! Wah!"

He took me by the hand and smiled in welcome as seventy or eighty other warriors emerged from the nearby forest—all of them apparently leaving their weapons out of sight. They thronged around me, beaming smiles and shouting their friendly greeting, "Wah! Wah!"

It was hard to believe that these were the same men who rained a hail of arrows upon us and dislodged boulders into our midst just two years earlier. Soon Costas, Frank, the government escorts, and the Yali Christians reached the top and joined our hugging match in the sky! From Bahabol we descended the other side of the same ridge toward Kibi village, where Kusaho waited. Moving single-file through lush gardens, we were soon stretched out over nearly a mile of trail. Our more than one hundred escorts each carried a newly trimmed white pole for the construction of a makeshift overnight structure at Kibi. We were far too many to find lodging in Kibi's already crowded *yogwas;* we preferred to build our own "hotel."

The one hundred shiny white poles created an odd visual effect—like a hundred bold stitches of white thread holding that immense green slope together. But then my eye caught a spectacle far more interesting. I looked across the Wikboon bowl and saw three different trails filled with people streaming down to intersect the trail we were following. I glanced in another direction and saw the same phenomenon. In fact, I soon realized that people were streaming down from every village visible on high ledges of the great bowl-shaped valley.

It was like a spring thaw. The winter of fear had ended. People were flowing down like rivulets, and when they came closer, we could even hear their laughter burbling like brooks. I heaved a great sigh and laughed for gladness myself. Hundreds of smiling Yali men lined along the trail and reached out their hands to touch every one of us as we passed. Then we rounded a bend in the trail and passed through lines of shy Yali women, most of them bearing small children on their backs or on their shoulders. "Wah! Wah! Wah!" they all called softly. Even little brown children scarcely two years old reached out with tiny hands in friendship. A powerful feeling of release tingled through the very air we breathed.

Yekwara, Bengwok, Stan, Phil, Dengan, Menno, Gene, Lois, Steven, Joyce, and Jonathan—I wish you could be here to touch these uplifted hands and look into these beaming faces. Perhaps you are. Perhaps you can.

At the entrance to Kibi village, Kusaho stood, his arms outstretched in welcome. I realized when I saw him that what I had imagined was true—weighed in the light of cultural differences, Kusaho must be regarded as one of the most unique human beings on earth. In his untaught compassion toward strangers, his clear-sighted anticipation of unknown truth, and his willingness to differ from the majority, Kusaho towered above his peers higher, perhaps, than many great men in our culture have towered above us. Costas, Frank, and I thrilled as Kusaho pointed to the place where he first met Paul Newman fleeing from the burning wreckage in the valley below. The kindly faced Yali leader drew his fists against his chest with great force, describing how he first embraced Paul. It was an act that opened a door of help for thousands.

Next morning Kusaho and two other Yali leaders prepared a pig feast in our honor, while Frank and I measured a proposed airstrip site near Kibi and Costas supervised the building of a teacher's house. We found the site too short for an airstrip. Next morning hundreds of Wikboon Yali men, women, and children gathered on clear ground between our new temporary "hotel" and the new teacher's house. They sang hymn after hymn which Luliap had taught them, and then listened as Luliap and Costas taught the Word of God. While the service continued, Frank and I slipped away from the crowd and walked down to the wreckage of Mike Pappa Hotel. Buried under twisted pieces of half-melted aluminum, we found a man's and a woman's wedding bands and a woman's wristwatch. Engraved on the inside of the man's wedding band were the words, *I love you forever; Lois, 6-7-57.*

The hands of the wristwatch had stopped at six minutes and ten seconds past eleven o'clock.

We wrapped these tokens carefully and mailed them to Paul Newman at his new home in Sierra Madre, California.

Soon after the placing of the first teachers in the Seng Valley, Bruno and Marlys deLeeuw returned from furlough. Costas handed over to them a work that had advanced unbelievably under his care. That work was to achieve still greater dimensions under the deLeeuws' further guidance in years ahead. In 1972, two years after the placing of the first teachers in the Seng Valley, Bruno and Luliap, together with John Wilson, a new RBMU colleague from Scotland, baptized the first thirty-five Christians in the Seng Valley. The thirty-five included a number of men who had joined in the killing of Stan and Phil. Following the baptism, the believers shared a communion supper, using one of Mike Pappa Hotel's wings as a table for the host.

Kusaho himself was baptized with some seventy other tribesmen in April 1977, about the same month that Wesley Dale, Stan's eldest son, was accepted by RBMU Australia for service in his father's stead in Irian Jaya.

While awesome transformations were occurring among the Yali, Phyliss Masters transferred her work among the Kimyal pygmies at Korupoon to Paul and Kathryn Kline from Pennsylvania, who were joined later by Bruce and Judy McLeay from New Zealand and Bible translator Elinor Young from Spokane, Washington. Now throughout the Korupoon Valley and beyond, Kimyal congregations meet to worship God with heartfelt trust and devotion, remembering always the love of the limping stranger and his wife who first crossed the ranges to share God's love with them.

Phyliss herself returned to Karubaga and her former work among the Dani people in November 1968. Through the years her cheerful spirit has been to thousands a poignant evidence of the Holy Spirit's power to heal even the most severe wounds that may crush a human heart.

In 1974 Phyliss and three other women missionaries trekked from Ninia to Kibi village in the Seng Valley. Phyliss's purpose—to see for herself the transformation God had wrought in the hearts of those who had slain and, as we all still thought at the time, devoured her husband and Stan.

Phyliss was greeted at Kibi by a matronly Yali woman named Suwi—the woman who laid her outer skirt across the trail in front of the war party in a vain attempt to keep them from killing Phil and Stan. Phyliss thanked Suwi, and the two became immediate friends.

Then, in May 1975 and again in March 1977, I returned to Ninia to engage in research for this account of the Yali people, their beliefs, and the men who dared to challenge their beliefs and turn their allegiance away from *Kembu* and toward the Christ of God, Jesus. Scottish colleague John Wilson, newly fluent in the Yali language, assisted my research by calling together at Ninia not only leading Yali Christians like Engehap, Dongla, and Yemu (Stan's carrier at the time he was killed) but also Kusaho and Nalimo, the latter supplying eyewitness details of Stan's and Phil's final moments. It was at that time that I first met Sar and Ongolek and learned the poignant details surrounding the tragic death of their daughter Nindik. Engehap led us one sunny afternoon down the same trail Nindik followed to her rendezvous with fate at Ninia, the now-abandoned *kwalu* refuge. I lingered within that once-sacred, once-dreaded stone wall, among pine trees that whispered as if discussing my presence, and found in the grass a tiny mushroom such as Foliek (now a graduate of a Bible school at Mulia) once plucked and ate, nearly sealing his doom.

Andeng and Wanla by that time were dead, but Dongla, Andeng's son, supplied me with many details about his father, his uncle, Bukni, Bengwok, and Yekwara. Later, John Wilson and I trekked to the very place where Bengwok once lay dying on a rock-slide of white limestone, and to the spot where Stan was wounded. Yalis we met reenacted the event in detail for us. Nearby stands a small stainless steel plaque engraved with the words:

> STANLEY ALBERT DALE
> Loved husband of Patricia
> Martyred Seng Valley
> 25th September, 1968
> Revelation 2:10
> RESURGAM

Afterward we retraced the route Stan followed in his nightmare escape through that black and thundering Heluk gorge, reliving in our imagination a few mere shadows of the agony he suffered.

Then we walked up-valley to Balinga and interviewed Suwi and Sunahan, who told us of the death of Kahalek just outside the *kwalu* refuge called Mobahai.

One weekend at Ninia, I attended a communion service along with about one hundred Yali men and, yes, an equal number of devout Yali women. And it is no coincidence that in a valley where women now enjoy privileges of worship and religious instruction on an equal basis with men, the female suicide rate—once at least ten times higher than the male suicide rate—has now fallen almost to zero!

At the end of our last interview with Kusaho, John Wilson and I tested the feasibility of using the Yali "place of refuge" concept as an analogy pointing to Christ as man's *perfect* Refuge.

We said, "Kusaho, your Yali *osuwa* was limited to just one geographical location. If a beleaguered man couldn't get to it in time, he died without mercy. And it offered protection only from physical danger, not spiritual. For this reason God saw that your people needed a better kind of *osuwa*, one that could be around you in any geographical location—one that could deliver you from spiritual as well as physical danger. That is why He sent His Son.

"Christ is mankind's perfect *osuwa!* Do you understand this?"

Response was immediate. "Of course I understand it! Those words are very meaningful to me. When I return to Wikboon, I will explain the gospel to my people in this way, so that many more may believe."

Even as Kusaho was speaking, we heard a strange popping sound from Nalimo, one of the killers at Yendoal beach. He had been sitting to one side, listening. As the concept of Christ as a spiritual *osuwa* flooded his mind, he expressed his excitement by that unusual popping noise which seemed to require no movement of vocal muscles.

Before he left, Kusaho begged to ask a question. "That boy I took care of," he said wistfully. "Please tell me. What is his name?"

"Paul Newman," I replied.

"Ahaa!" Kusaho exclaimed. "As soon as I get home, I'm going to name my youngest son 'Paul Newman' so I won't forget how to say it." Kusaho and Nalimo turned and set out toward the Seng Pass.

POSTSCRIPT

THIRTY-ONE years and more than a dozen print runs after Regal Books released its first edition of *Lords of the Earth* in 1977, it is my privilege now to pen this postscript for the 2008 edition. My heart overflows with praise to God for report after report I have received over these last three decades documenting the marvelous spiritual and numerical growth of the church among the Yali people. Now readers of *Lords of the Earth* can savor for themselves the joy and the bounty of Yali devotion to Christ by viewing *The Yali Story*, a DVD featuring in person many of the remarkable personalities described in the preceding chapters (available at www.donrichardsonbooksales.com).

Under the sponsorship of World Team (formerly Regions Beyond Missionary Union) and the tutelage of my colleague John Wilson, Yali Christian leaders themselves have translated the entire Bible into their own language! Literacy is now common in all the villages. Improved health, sanitation and diet enable today's Yali to enjoy longer life. It is a different place than it was when this story was lived out and then first written. All praise goes to God for the transformation.

How surprised I was recently. An email report from my brother in Israel announced that a party of Christians from Papua (formerly Irian Jaya)—equipped with Indonesian passports and airline tickets they had purchased themselves—arrived in Jerusalem to *donate* gold from the mountains of Papua for the future construction of the temple in the Holy City! One of those intrepid emissaries was Otto Kobak, a Yali church leader.

There can be no doubt—the gospel that went out *from* Jerusalem 2,000 years ago has in striking ways come back around *to* Jerusalem!

God bless you, young Yali leaders! You may not be "lords of the earth" in the sense your fathers thought they were, but know this: as you stand in Christ—your perfect *Osuwa—"The earth is yours and everything that's in it."*

Don Richardson

BIBLIOGRAPHY

Dale, Stanley. *The Valley and the Vision*. London: RBMU, 1978.

Hitt, Russell T. *Cannibal Valley*. Chicago: Zondervan Publishing House, 1973.

Home, Shirley. *An Hour from the Stone Age*. Chicago: Moody Press, 1973.

Klaus-Kock, Friedrich. *War and Peace in Jalemo: The Management of Conflict in Highland New Guinea*. Cambridge: Harvard University Press, 1974.

Manning, Helen. *To Perish for Their Saving*. Minneapolis: Bethany Fellowship, Inc., 1971.

Mickelson, E. H. *God Can*. Harrisburg, PA: Christian Publishing, Inc.

Richardson, Don. *Peace Child*. Ventura, CA: Regal Books, 1974.